£16.50

D0554270

Robin
Best of Health

Alan Cross

# SELLING SICKNESS

### How the World's Biggest Pharmaceutical
### Companies Are Turning Us All into Patients

RAY MOYNIHAN

ALAN CASSELS

GREYSTONE BOOKS

Douglas & McIntyre Publishing Group

Vancouver/Toronto

*For Marian, Lynda, Morgan and Chase*

Copyright © 2005 by Ray Moynihan and Alan Cassels

05  06  07  08  09   5  4  3  2  1

All rights reserved. No part of this book may be reproduced,
stored in a retrieval system, or transmitted, in any form or by any means, without
the prior written consent of the publisher or a licence from The Canadian
Copyright Licensing Agency (Access Copyright). For a copyright licence, visit
www.accesscopyright.ca or call toll free to 1-800-893-5777.

Greystone Books
A division of Douglas & McIntyre Ltd.
2323 Quebec Street, Suite 201
Vancouver, British Columbia
Canada V5T 4S7
www.greystonebooks.com

Originated by Allen & Unwin, Sydney, Australia.

*Library and Archives Canada Cataloguing in Publication*
Moynihan, Ray
Selling sickness : how the world's biggest pharmeutical companies
are turning us into patients / Ray Moynihan and Alan Cassels.
Includes bibliographical references and index.
ISBN-13: 978- 1-55365-131-4.  ISBN-10: 1-55365-131-6

I. Drugs—Marketing. 2. Drugs—Advertising.
3. Pharmaceutical industry. I. Cassels, Alan, 1963– II. Title.
HD9665.5.M69 2005   381'.456151   C2005-902510-7

Jacket design by Howard Grossman
Jacket photograph by Harry Giglio/Nonstock
Printed in Canada by Friesens
Printed on acid-free paper that is forest friendly (100% post-consumer
recycled paper) and has been processed chlorine free.

We gratefully acknowledge the financial support of the
Canada Council for the Arts, the British Columbia Arts Council, and
the Government of Canada through the Book Publishing Industry
Development Program (BPIDP) for our publishing activities.

# Contents

# Introduction

It was Canadian Naomi Klein who helped us all understand the importance of branding in the modern world of mass marketing. Corporations like Nike and Starbucks no longer sell products, writes Klein in her classic book, *No Logo;* they sell brands, and brands are about lifestyles and concepts, not commodities.

Some of the most sophisticated branding comes from the global drug giants, who have brought us celebrity pills like Prozac, Viagra and Celebrex. These days, though, the drug companies are also promoting a different sort of brand—not just their drugs, but, increasingly, the diseases that go with them.

As *Selling Sickness* reveals, the pharmaceutical industry is working behind the scenes to help define and design the latest disorders and dysfunctions in order to create and expand markets for their newest medicines. Too often the aim is to turn healthy people into patients. As you will see, Canadian thinkers are playing a big role in explaining and criticising this extraordinary phenomenon before an international audience. Canadians like

Barbara Mintzes, Joel Lexchin and Ken Bassett are helping us all understand how pharmaceutical marketing strategies fundamentally shift our perceptions of illness and deeply affect the very experience of what it means to be human.

Canada's commitment to a universal public health system was recently reaffirmed by the wide-ranging Romanow Commission and subsequent boosts to federal health spending. Yet the underlying principles of our public system enshrined in the Canada Health Act could be seriously undermined by the growing corporate influence documented in *Selling Sickness*. A medical profession too inebriated by the largesse of profit-driven drug companies cannot serve the public interest. Patient groups overly dependent on funding from Big Pharma likewise fail to serve the interests of their constituents. Politicians and policymakers who fall for the PR propaganda about the wonders of the latest blockbuster drug do us all a disservice. Ultimately, as Selling Sickness makes compellingly clear, a health system that allows drug companies to play a role in defining who is sick is fundamentally unhealthy.

Fortunately for Canada, one of the worst forms of selling sickness is largely prohibited here: the direct-to-consumer advertising of prescription drugs. Citizens of the United States, however, are marinating in billions of dollars of in-your-face drug marketing. It is Canadian-led criticisms of such drug advertising that has helped many other nations maintain their prohibitions in the face of enormous pressure from the pharmaceutical and advertising industries. But although Health Canada outlaws drug advertising, there is the very real problem of border seepage, as well as the backdoor form of advertising known as "disease awareness" campaigns, which constantly urge you to see your doctor for practically everything.

Some might argue that living beside the elephant has made Canadians more prone to resisting outside cultural or corporate forces. After all, Canada is the birthplace of Greenpeace and Adbusters, the group arguing that corporate consumer culture perniciously pollutes our mental environment just as industry's heavy metals pollute our rivers.

Closer to the mainstream, Canadian medical academics have gained an international reputation for resisting the degradation of medicine by commercial forces. Canada has been largely responsible for initiating a global reform movement called Evidence-Based Medicine. The principle is simple: that professionals and patients should base their health care decisions more on good evidence and less on expert opinion or commercial hype. Canadians have also played a key role in the creation of the Cochrane Collaboration, an international network of thousands of researchers producing solid systematic reviews of the best evidence about many medical treatments, all available on the Web.

*Selling Sickness* also introduces other Canadian characters, little known by the wider public but near-celebrities in the arcane world of health research, who are actively opposing the corporate-sponsored selling of sickness. In this book, you will meet people at the University of British Columbia's Therapeutics Initiative, who, for more than a decade, have offered genuinely objective analyses of clinical studies of drugs—basically tossing a lifeline to physicians to prevent them from drowning in the sea of spin. And they have done so with great courage and sometimes under intense criticism from the pharmaceutical industry. You will also meet people like Wendy Armstrong, the quintessential Canadian consumer advocate, with the Alberta Consumers Association, who has better insights into the corrosive effects of privatization of health care in Canada than almost anyone else.

So what is the antidote to the selling of sickness? It is that quality many Canadians seem to have in abundance: skepticism. We hope *Selling Sickness* will stoke the fires of global skepticism towards the corporate-backed marketing of fear and help wind back commercially driven conceptions of disease, which threaten to bankrupt our medical system and turn more and more healthy people into patients.

The first step is simply a conversation. Perhaps Canada can help start it.

# Prologue

## Selling sickness

Thirty years ago the head of one of the world's best-known drug companies made some very candid comments. Close to retirement at the time, Merck's aggressive chief executive Henry Gadsden told *Fortune* magazine of his distress that the company's potential markets had been limited to sick people. Suggesting he'd rather Merck to be more like chewing gum maker Wrigley's, Gadsden said it had long been his dream to make drugs for healthy people. Because then, Merck would be able to 'sell to everyone.'[1] Three decades on, the late Henry Gadsden's dream has come true.

The marketing strategies of the world's biggest drug companies now aggressively target the healthy and the well. The ups and downs of daily life have become mental disorders, common complaints are transformed into frightening conditions, and more and more ordinary people are turned into patients. With promotional campaigns that exploit our deepest fears of death, decay and disease, the $500 billion dollar pharmaceutical industry is literally changing what it means to be human. Rightly rewarded for saving life and reducing suffering, the global drug giants are no longer content selling medicines only to the ill. Because as Wall Street knows well, there's a lot of money to be made telling healthy people they're sick.

At a time when many of us are leading longer, healthier and more vital lives than our ancestors, saturation advertising and slick 'awareness-raising' campaigns are turning the worried well into the worried sick.[2] Mild problems are painted as serious disease, so shyness becomes a sign of social anxiety disorder and pre-menstrual tension a mental illness called pre-menstrual dysphoric disorder. Everyday sexual difficulties are seen as sexual dysfunctions, the natural change of life is a disease of hormone deficiency called the menopause, and distracted office workers now have adult ADD. Just being 'at risk' of an illness has become a 'disease' in its own right, so healthy middle-aged women now have a silent bone disease called osteoporosis, and fit middle-aged men a lifelong condition called high cholesterol.

With many health problems, there are people at the severe end of the spectrum suffering genuine illness, or at very high risk of it, who may benefit greatly from a medical label and a powerful medication. Yet for the relatively healthy people who are spread across the rest of the spectrum, a label and a drug may bring great inconvenience, enormous costs, and the very real danger of sometimes deadly side effects. This vast terrain has become the new global marketplace of potential patients—tens of millions of people—a key target of the drug industry's multi-billion-dollar promotional budgets.

The epicentre of this selling is of course the United States, home to many of the world's largest pharmaceutical companies, and the stage on which most of the action in this book takes place. With less than 5 per cent of the world's population, the US already makes up almost 50 per cent of the global market in prescription drugs.[3] Yet spending in the US continues to rise more rapidly than anywhere else, increasing by almost 100 per cent in just six years—not only because of steep increases in the price of drugs, but because doctors are simply prescribing more and more of them.[4]

Prescriptions for the most promoted categories, like heart medicines or antidepressants, have soared astronomically in the US, with the amount spent on these drugs doubling in less than five years.[5] In many other nations the trend is also up. Young Australians took ten times more antidepressants in 2000 than they did in 1990.[6] Canadian consumption of the new cholesterol-lowering drugs jumped by a staggering 300 per cent over a similar time period.[7] Many of those prescriptions enhanced or extended life. But there is a growing sense that too many of them are driven by the unhealthy influences of misleading marketing rather than genuine need. And those marketing strategies, like the drug companies, are now well and truly global.

Working from his mid-town Manhattan office in New York City, Vince Parry represents the cutting edge of that global marketing. An expert in advertising, Parry now specialises in the most sophisticated form of selling medicines: he works with drug companies to help create new diseases. In an astonishing article titled 'The art of branding a condition', Parry recently revealed the ways in which companies are involved in 'fostering the creation' of medical disorders.[8] Sometimes a little-known condition is given renewed attention, sometimes an old disease is redefined and renamed, and sometimes a whole new dysfunction is created. Parry's personal favourites include erectile dysfunction, adult attention deficit disorder, and pre-menstrual dysphoric disorder—a disorder so controversial some researchers say it doesn't even exist.

With rare candour Parry has explained how pharmaceutical companies now take the lead, not just in branding their block-buster pills like Prozac and Viagra, but also in branding the conditions that create the markets for those pills. Working under the leadership of the drug marketers, Madison Avenue gurus like Parry get together with medical experts to 'create new ideas about illnesses and conditions'.[9] The goal, he says, is to give drug company customers around the world 'a new way to think about things'.[10] The aim, always, is to make the link between the con-dition and your medicine, in order to maximise its sales.

The idea that drug companies help to create new illnesses may sound strange to many of us, but it is all too familiar to industry insiders. A recent *Reuters Business Insight* report designed for drug company executives argued that the ability to 'create new disease markets' is bringing untold billions in soaring drug sales.[11] One of the chief selling strategies, said the report, is to change the way people think about their common ailments, to make 'natural processes' into medical conditions. People must be able to be 'convinced' that 'problems they may previously have accepted as, perhaps, merely an inconvenience'—like baldness, wrinkles and sexual difficulties—are now seen as 'worthy of medical intervention'.[12] Celebrating the development of prof-itable new disease markets like 'Female Sexual Dysfunction', the report was upbeat about the financial future for the drug industry. 'The coming years will bear greater witness to the corporate sponsored creation of disease.'[13]

The unhealthy influence of the pharmaceutical industry has become a global scandal. That influence is fundamentally distorting medical science, corrupting the way medicine is practised, and corroding the public's trust in their doctors.[14] The burying of unfavourable research studies on children and antidepressants, the dangers of the anti-arthritis drugs and the investigations into the alleged bribing of physicians in Italy and the US are just the latest in a string of embarrassments.[15] Exploding drug expenditures have helped produce double-digit increases in the costs of health insurance premiums, fuelling further widespread anger towards the industry, particularly in the US. As a result, many doctors, scientists, health advocates, politicians and medical journal editors are moving to try to wind back the industry's influence over scientific research and doctors' prescribing habits.[16] The time is ripe to understand how that influence now extends right to the very definitions of disease.

Marketing executives don't sit down and actually write the rules for how to diagnose illness, but they increasingly underwrite those who do. The industry now routinely sponsors key medical meetings where disease definitions are debated and updated. In some instances, as we will see, the medical experts writing the rules are at the same time taking money from the drug makers who stand to make billions, depending on how those rules are written. Many of the senior specialists deciding whether your sexual difficulties should be defined as sexual dysfunctions, whether your stomach complaints should be seen as serious medical conditions, and whether your everyday risks should be portrayed as deadly diseases, are on the payrolls of the companies seeking to sell you drugs. The payment of money doesn't necessarily buy influence, but in the eyes of many observers, doctors and drug companies have simply become too close.

With many medical conditions, there is great uncertainty about where to draw the line that separates the healthy from the sick. The boundaries that separate 'normal' and 'abnormal' are often highly elastic, they may differ dramatically from country to country, and they can change over time. Clearly, the wider you draw the boundaries that define a disease, the wider the pool of potential patients, and the bigger the markets for those making drugs. The experts who sit down to draw those lines today are too often doing so with drug company pens in their hands, and they are drawing the boundaries wider and wider almost every time they meet.

According to these experts, 90 per cent of the elderly in the US will have a condition called high blood pressure, almost half of all women have a sexual dysfunction called FSD, and more than 40 million Americans should be taking drugs to lower their cholesterol.[17] With a little help from a headline-hungry media, the latest condition is routinely portrayed as widespread, severe and, above all, treatable with drugs. Alternative ways of understanding or treating health problems, and lower estimates of the numbers affected, are often swept away by a frenzy of drug company promotion.

While the boundaries defining disease are pushed out as widely as they can be, by contrast, the causes of these supposed epidemics are portrayed as narrowly as possible. In the world of drug marketing, a major public health problem like heart disease can sometimes be reduced to a narrow focus on a person's cholesterol levels or blood pressure. Preventing hip fractures among the elderly becomes a narrow obsession with the bone density numbers of healthy middle-aged women. Personal distress is seen as being due largely to a chemical imbalance of serotonin in the brain, an explanation as narrow as it is outdated.

Like most everything else that happens in health care today, our ideas about sickness are being shaped in the long shadows cast by the global drug giants. Yet the narrowing of the focus is making it harder for us to see the bigger picture about health and disease, sometimes at great cost to the individual, and the community. To use a simple example, if an improvement in human health was our primary aim, some of the billions currently invested in expensive drugs to lower the cholesterol of the worried well might be far more efficiently spent on enhanced campaigns to reduce smoking, increase physical activity and improve diet.

There are many different promotional strategies used in the selling of sickness, but the common factor amongst them all is the marketing of fear. The fear of heart attacks was used to sell women the idea that the menopause is a condition requiring hormone replacement. The fear of youth suicide is used to sell parents the idea that even mild depression must be treated with powerful drugs. The fear of an early death is used to sell high cholesterol as something automatically requiring a prescription. Yet ironically, the much-hyped medicines sometimes cause the very harm they are supposed to prevent.

Long-term hormone replacement therapy increases the risk of heart attacks for women, while antidepressants appear to increase the risk of suicidal thinking among the young. At least one of the blockbuster cholesterol-lowering drugs has been withdrawn from the market because it was implicated in *causing* deaths. In one of the most horrific cases of all, a drug sold as helping with common bowel problems led to constipation so severe for some people, they simply died. Yet in this case, as in so many others, the official government regulators somehow seemed more interested in protecting drug company profits than the public's health.[18]

The pharmaceutical industry and its supporters defend their marketing campaigns as raising awareness about misunderstood diseases, and providing quality information about the latest medicines. Company executives talk of empowering consumers with advertising, and their paid celebrities are said to educate the public about health conditions via glossy magazine articles and on TV talk shows. Certainly there are some valuable examples of industry-sponsored efforts to de-stigmatise a health problem or stimulate much-needed action, as has occurred in the area of HIV-AIDS. Yet in other cases these campaigns are not education at all, but plain old promotion: skewing our understanding of the causes of human illness and distorting our knowledge of the remedies, playing up the benefits of drugs and playing down their harms and costs.

A loosening of advertising regulations in the late 1990s in the US has delivered an unprecedented onslaught of drug marketing targeted at ordinary people, who now watch an average of ten or more of these advertisements every day. Likewise, viewers in New Zealand are subject to this sort of promotion. Elsewhere in the world the industry is fighting relentlessly for similar deregulation. For the supporters, this marketing is a valuable service; for the critics, it is putting disease at the centre of human life. It is pushing the genuinely ill towards a limited range of the most expensive drug solutions, and making tens of millions of the healthy start to fear that their bodies are broken, dysfunctional, deficient, and decaying. This disease-mongering is an assault on our collective soul by those seeking to profit from our fear. It is no dark conspiracy; simply daylight robbery.

*Selling Sickness* unmasks the latest marketing techniques from the drug industry's multi-layered campaigns. Technique by technique, condition by condition, a pattern emerges, a formula for changing the way we think about illness in order to expand markets for drugs. The diseases explored here are not the only ones being oversold; they are, though, among the most dramatic, compelling and freshest examples we have. Once you become familiar with the formula, and start to recognise the tricks of the trade, you'll begin to see the black magic of disease marketing at work everywhere.

Some of the promotional strategies may already be familiar, but the dirty tricks and covert operations are likely to shock and anger many readers. The aim of *Selling Sickness* is not to further discredit a much maligned drug industry, or its many valuable products. Nor is the goal to denigrate the many fine and principled people who work inside these giant corporations and who are motivated, like many hardworking medical scientists outside, to discover and develop safe and effective new therapies. Rather, the plan is to expose the way in which the industry's promotional machinery is turning too much ordinary life into medical illness, in order to expand markets for medications.

Over three decades ago a maverick thinker called Ivan Illich raised alarms that an expanding medical establishment was 'medicalising' life itself, undermining the human capacity to cope with the reality of suffering and death, and making too many ordinary people into patients.[19] He criticised a medical system 'that claims authority over people who are not yet ill, people who cannot reasonably expect to get well, and those for whom doctors have no more effective treatment than that which could be offered by their uncles or aunts'.[20] A decade ago medical writer Lynn Payer described a process she called 'disease-mongering': doctors and drug companies unnecessarily widening the boundaries of illness in order to see more patients and sell more drugs.[21] In the years since, these writings have become ever more relevant, as the industry's marketing roar has grown louder and its grip on the health care system much stronger.

Soaring sales have made drug companies the most profitable corporations on the planet during particular years of the past decade.[22] But the flip side of healthy returns for shareholders is an unsustainable increase in costs for those funding the health system, whether they are governments or private insurers. It is no surprise that the industry's unhealthy influence has become part of the political debate in many nations, which exploded in Australia during negotiations over the recent free trade deal with the US. As the public learns more about industry's influence over the definitions of disorders and dysfunctions, and its methods for creating 'new disease markets', the selling of sickness will likely move closer to the centre of those debates.

Like the best of scientific inquiry this work of journalism is offered as part of an ongoing conversation, to be continued with friends, families, and physicians, with other health care providers, work colleagues, health officials and elected representatives: a conversation that questions the corporate-sponsored selling of sickness, and explores new ways to define and understand disease. It is a conversation that could ideally benefit from the energy and enthusiasm of a whole new global collaboration of independent researchers and health advocates, whose primary aim is to promote a more rational and informed public debate about human health, rather than simply selling fear in order to sell pharmaceuticals.

---

*Note:* Unless otherwise indicated, all $ amounts in this book refer to US$.

# Selling to everyone

## *High cholesterol*

L ittle known as a health complaint when Henry Gadsden was still managing Merck 30 years ago, the fear of a condition called 'high cholesterol' has quickly come to dominate the personal health concerns of tens of millions of people around the globe. For those selling pills, promoting that fear has paid off handsomely: nations everywhere have spent more on cholesterol-lowering drugs in recent years than any other category of prescription medicines.[1] As a group, these drugs now generate revenues of more than $25 billion a year for their manufacturers, a rollcall of the biggest names in the global industry, including Germany's Bayer, the British–Swedish company AstraZeneca and America's Pfizer.[2] In less wealthy countries, including some states of Eastern Europe, the spiralling costs of this group of drugs on their own can threaten to bankrupt entire health systems.[3]

Contrary to what many might think, cholesterol itself is not a deadly enemy, it is an essential element of the body's make-up, and is vital to life. There is scientific evidence showing that for many people, a raised level of cholesterol in the blood is associated with an increased risk of future heart attacks and strokes.

But with otherwise healthy people there's uncertainty about exactly how much that raised cholesterol will increase your risk of heart disease, and for how many people this might really be a problem.

What *is* widely accepted is that having high cholesterol is only one of many factors that affect your chances of future heart disease. Yet it attracts a huge share of attention because it can be modified with drugs—drugs that now boast promotional budgets rivalling those of some brands of beer or soda. For specialists in prevention like the British researcher Professor Shah Ebrahim, the new cholesterol-lowering drugs—called statins—are a valuable course of action for people who've already had some heart disease. Yet for most healthy people there are much cheaper, safe and effective ways to try to stay healthy than using statins. Improving diet, increasing exercise, and stopping smoking are the obvious and well-known strategies.

Ebrahim is one of many researchers who feel the narrow focus on cholesterol is a potentially dangerous distraction from the real business of prevention. Already, one of the statins, Bayer's Baycol, has been pulled from the market after being implicated in several cases of death.[4] The newest statin, AstraZeneca's Crestor, has also faced calls for its withdrawal, because of very rare but debilitating side effects of muscle wasting and kidney failure.[5]

The dawn of the new age of cholesterol came in 1987, when Merck launched the first of the statins, Mevacor, amid much excitement in the medical marketplace. Mevacor was approved to lower cholesterol levels, which meant the drug could be promoted and prescribed to otherwise healthy people—a potentially enormous market. Several competitors have been approved in the years since and the promotion of both the drugs and the condition has become frenzied. But one pill in particular has leapt ahead of the pack, and now commands almost half the total market—Lipitor. Racking up sales of more than $10 billion a year, Lipitor is the world's top-selling prescription drug, ever.[6] Its manufacturer Pfizer is the world's biggest pharmaceutical company. With head offices in Manhattan, and a market value around $200 billion, Pfizer is one of the largest corporations on earth, thanks in no small part to widespread fears of high cholesterol.

Sales of these drugs have soared in the last decade because the number of people defined as having 'high cholesterol' has grown astronomically. As with many other medical conditions, the definition of what constitutes 'high cholesterol' is regularly revised, and like other conditions the definition has been broadened in ways that redefine more and more healthy people as sick. Over time, the boundaries that define medical conditions are slowly widened and the pools of potential patients steadily expanded. Sometimes the increase is sudden and dramatic. When a panel of cholesterol experts in the US rewrote the definitions a few years ago they lowered the levels of cholesterol deemed necessary to qualify for treatment, (among other changes), essentially relabelling millions of healthy people as sick, and virtually overnight tripling the numbers who could be targeted with drug therapy.[7]

According to the official US National Institutes of Health's cholesterol guidelines from the 1990s, thirteen million Americans might have warranted treatment with statins. In 2001 a new panel of experts rewrote those guidelines, and effectively raised that number to 36 million, in a scene reminiscent of Henry Gadsden's dream of selling to everyone.[8] Yet five of the fourteen authors of this new expanded definition, including the chair of the panel, had financial ties to statin manufacturers.[9] In 2004, yet another new panel of experts updated those guidelines again, recommending that alongside the value of lifestyle changes more than 40 million Americans could benefit by taking the drugs.[10] This time, the conflicts of interest were even worse.

Eight of the nine experts who wrote the latest cholesterol guidelines also serve as paid speakers, consultants or researchers to the world's major drug companies—Pfizer, Merck, Bristol-Myers Squibb, Novartis, Bayer, Abbott, AstraZeneca and GlaxoSmithKline.[11] In most cases the individual authors had multiple ties to at least four of these companies. One 'expert' had taken money from ten of them. The links were not mentioned in the published version of the cholesterol guidelines, and the extent of the conflicts was not publicly known until media organisations uncovered them, sparking a major controversy.[12] The existence of such ties should not imply that any of these guideline writers would make recommendations in order to please their drug company sponsors. The problem is the growing perception of coziness.

The full details of all those financial ties were subsequently published on a US government website and it is worth taking a look at them for yourself.[13] Strange as they may seem to those outside, such extensive conflicts of interest have become all too familiar to those within the world of medicine. Yet here is a clear case where the doctors writing the very definitions of what constitutes high cholesterol, and recommending when drugs should be used to treat it, are at the same time paid to speak by the companies making those drugs.[14] Cholesterol, though, is no different in this regard than many other common conditions. It is estimated that almost 90 per cent of those who write guidelines for their peers have conflicts of interest because of financial ties to the pharmaceutical industry.[15]

The ties between guideline-writers and the industry are just one corner of the vast web of interrelationships between doctors and drug companies. The industry's influence over doctors' practices, medical education and scientific research is as widespread as it is controversial—not just distorting the way physicians prescribe medicines but actually affecting the way conditions like 'high cholesterol' are defined and promoted. As one researcher candidly put it, the closeness between doctors and the pharmaceutical industry has now become a 'way of life'.[16]

The entanglement starts with the free pizzas for the hard-working hospital residents and interns, and from then on it never stops.[17] As US physicians graduate from the hospital wards out into their own practices, there to greet them daily is an 80 000-strong army of drug company representatives—or detailers—always ready with a smile, some warm doughnuts, and a dose of friendly advice about the newest drugs and the latest diseases. As those who study these interactions tell us, these are the foundations of lifelong relationships between the industry and the profession.[18]

Next comes the continuing medical education, the refresher courses that physicians are strongly encouraged and sometimes formally required to attend. In the US this is now a billion-dollar enterprise, with close to half of that funding flowing directly from the pharmaceutical industry.[19] Doctors are being 'educated' about how to use drugs, and how many of us should take them, in venues sponsored by their makers.

After the education comes the scientific research. An estimated 60 per cent of biomedical research and development in the US is now funded from private sources, mainly drug companies.[20] In some areas, like the testing of drugs for depression, the figure is closer to 100 per cent. Almost all the clinical trials of the new antidepressants were funded by their manufacturers rather than public or not-for-profit sources.[21] And that research evidence is discussed and disseminated at more than 300 000 scientific meetings, events and conferences sponsored by the industry every year, and often hosted by medical societies like the American Heart Association, themselves partially underwritten by drug companies.[22]

At the top of this hierarchy are the so-called 'thought-leaders'—or key opinion leaders—the senior physicians who write the guidelines, conduct the sponsored research, educate their colleagues at sponsored conferences, and publish papers in medical journals kept afloat with drug company advertisements. Many of the thought-leaders hold positions at prestigious academic institutions, at the same time as being on drug company payrolls as advisers and paid speakers.

One of those thought-leaders in the cholesterol field is Dr Bryan Brewer, a senior official at the publicly funded National Institutes of Health (NIH) based in Bethesda, just outside Washington, DC. In the lead-up to the launch of the newest statin, AstraZeneca's Crestor, Dr Brewer delivered a presentation at an American Heart Association seminar describing the controversial drug in very positive terms, as safe and effective.[23] His talk was considered an important and influential one, and it was later published in a special supplement of the *American Journal of Cardiology*, which is read by prescribing physicians.[24] The timing could not have been better for the drug's manufacturer, as the journal article coincided with Crestor's launch into the massive US market.

The American Heart Association seminar and the special journal supplement were both sponsored by AstraZeneca. So too was Dr Brewer, though his links were not disclosed in his article in the journal supplement. At that time he was a paid adviser to the company, and a part of the company's stable of paid speakers. According to later public hearings in the US Congress, Dr Brewer received in the order of $200 000 a year from outside private interests including drug companies, while simultaneously holding down a position as branch chief at the government's NIH.[25]

The attempts to clean up these entangled relationships between doctors and drug companies have received much publicity in recent years, but they have often been little more than self-serving window-dressing. For example, under a voluntary code created by the industry, it remains acceptable for a drug company to fly 300 supposedly independent doctors to a golf resort, pay them to attend, 'educate' them about the company's latest drug, and then train them to become part of the company's stable of paid speakers.[26]

The golf resort scenario was in fact strongly endorsed by an industry spokesperson as an entirely appropriate way for a drug company to train the large numbers of speakers needed to support its 'communications effort'.[27] And therein lies the fundamental danger of such cosiness: doctors, the people we trust to give us untainted advice about powerful pills, become part of the marketing campaigns for those very same pills, no matter how independently minded they might be—not just helping to sell the medicines, but helping to sell a particular definition of disease that expands markets for those medicines. In this case, high cholesterol has been defined so as to classify more than 40 million Americans as sick and potentially in need of drugs. One of the members of the expert panel who wrote that definition was Dr Bryan Brewer, who is financially tied to eight other drug companies, on top of his ties to AstraZeneca.[28]

Among some independent health advocacy groups there is a view that the company-tied cholesterol 'experts' have gone too far this time, have pushed the boundaries of illness too wide, and caught too many healthy people in the net. The Center for Science in the Public Interest, based in Washington, DC, has become so concerned it has mounted a public campaign calling for an independent review of the official cholesterol guidelines.[29] More than three dozen physicians, health researchers and scientists have put their name to a strongly worded letter to the NIH director, arguing that the guidelines, with their expanded recommendations for drug therapy, are not supported by the scientific evidence-arguments flatly rejected by the NIH. [30]

This grassroots campaign was inspired in part by a blistering critique from Harvard University clinical instructor and author Dr John Abramson. He argues that the guideline panel painted an overly positive picture of the scientific evidence about the risks and benefits of the cholesterol-lowering drugs, and that it has ultimately misled doctors and the public.[31] 'This is a perversion of science,' he says. 'I think they've gone way too far.'[32] Abramson is a strong supporter of using these drugs for people at high risk of heart disease, particularly those who have, for example, already suffered a heart attack. Yet he is also one of the voices within the scientific world arguing that prescribing statins to healthy men and women at relatively low risk of future heart disease may offer them no meaningful benefit and even bring real dangers.[33]

While the campaign for an independent review of the cholesterol guidelines was getting under way, another very different and much better funded campaign was being launched elsewhere in the US. A new patient advocacy group called the Boomer Coalition sprang onto the world stage with an advertisement broadcast during the televised Academy Awards ceremony in 2004. The ad kicked off a campaign to make heart disease 'the most-talked-about disease' among American baby boomers.[34] It featured the famous Henry Winkler, better known to maturing generations around the world as sitcom wise guy The Fonz, who, along with Wonder Woman Lynda Carter and the estates of former heart-throbs James Coburn and Errol Flynn, has become part of this curious new celebrity coalition.[35]

Along with suggestions about stopping smoking and doing more exercise, the group urges people as a priority to see their doctors and get their cholesterol levels tested on a regular basis. Its website suggests you should 'know your numbers' at all times and carry them around routinely 'like a driver's license'.[36] The group's home page is adorned with slick images from the 1960s civil rights campaigns and peace protests, playing on themes of emancipation activism and rebellion.

While the Boomer Coalition might look to some like a hip new movement, it is little more than the latest attempt at *astro-turfing*: the creation of fake grassroots campaigns by public relations professionals in the pay of large corporations. According to the *Wall Street Journal* the concept for the coalition was reportedly dreamt up by a Dutch PR company and funded by Pfizer—the makers of the cholesterol-lowering drug Lipitor —with an initial investment estimated at less than $10 million.[37] While the messages about getting tested might on the surface seem a valuable public service, the group's materials reflect none of the uncertainty or controversy that exists in relation to the definition of this condition and who should be treated for it. In contrast to the astro-turfing of the star-studded coalition, genuine grassroots groups like the Manhattan-based Center for Medical Consumers encourage a more healthy scepticism towards the promotion of high cholesterol as a fearful condition. That group—which is not on the industry's payroll—stresses that cholesterol is only one of many risk factors, and that drug benefits are often greatly exaggerated.[38]

The pharmaceutical industry's financial entanglement with the medical profession is fast being replicated in the consumer field—through the creation of groups like the Pfizer-funded Boomer Coalition. A global survey from Britain estimated that two-thirds of all patient advocacy groups and health charities now rely on funding from drug companies or device manufacturers. The most prolific sponsor, according to the survey results, is Johnson & Johnson and number two is Pfizer.[39] While creating the appearance of corporate generosity, such sponsorship can bring many benefits to the sponsor as well as the recipient. Chief among them is that patient groups are a great way to help shape public opinion about the conditions your products are designed to treat. With high cholesterol, there are clearly differing views within the wider health community about how to define the condition, and for whom drugs might be appropriate. Sponsoring advocacy groups that tend to keep messages simple, and keep the focus on the fear of high cholesterol, will inevitably help to maximise the sales of cholesterol-lowering drugs.[40]

Up at White River Junction, set amongst the green mountains of Vermont in the north east of the US, the fear-mongering around cholesterol is starting to unsettle practising physicians like Dr Lisa Schwartz. 'Patients worry a lot about cholesterol,' she says, 'and a lot of them come in wanting their cholesterol checked.' [41] Schwartz tries to reassure her patients that cholesterol is not so much a condition as one risk factor among many that can raise your chances of heart disease or stroke in the future. Her husband, Dr Steve Woloshin, encounters similar worries from many of his patients and agrees cholesterol is not a medical condition but a risk factor. 'I try to put it in the context of other risk factors people are facing,' he says. 'If you are a smoker, for example, probably the most important thing to do is stop smoking.'

Schwartz and Woloshin, based at the Veterans Affairs Medical Center in White River Junction, support the use of cholesterol-lowering drugs for people who have already suffered some heart disease, and others at high risk of future disease, but they worry that for otherwise healthy people at low risk, long-term use of the statins may offer little benefit and unknown harms. Obsessing unnecessarily about cholesterol levels may also bring unhelpful anxiety for many.

Trained on the busy wards of New York City hospitals, the medical duo moved to Vermont to take up academic postings at the prestigious Dartmouth Medical School, where they are both now associate professors, along with their VA work. Unlike most of those who wrote the latest definitions of cholesterol, these two have no financial ties to the pharmaceutical industry. As physicians working in a federal government hospital, they never see drug company detailers, and they refuse offers of industry-sponsored speaking work. Both publish regularly in the world's top medical journals, and they can have a room full of hardened researchers in stitches with their intelligent and witty performances.

One of their most recent projects involved a critical look at the official cholesterol guidelines. While those guidelines recommend more than 40 million Americans could benefit by taking drugs to lower their cholesterol, Woloshin and Schwartz estimate there are over 10 million currently taking them.[42] Among the more than 30 million who are therefore 'untreated' there are many that this pair believe could benefit from drugs. But there are also many who could lower their risks of heart attack or stroke just as easily without drugs, by other means, such as by stopping smoking. 'While we worry about overtreatment, these figures show there is also a lot of undertreatment,' says Woloshin. 'But we need to do a better job focusing in on the people who really stand to benefit the most from drugs, rather than get distracted by having to treat so many people at low risk,' adds Schwartz.

Their examination of the cholesterol guidelines is part of a bigger look at the way definitions of many common conditions are being widened, and how as a result the pool of potential patients likely to be prescribed drugs and other therapies is being expanded. Cholesterol is for them a prime example of what they see as a growing trend. 'It's an effort to make everybody sick,' says Schwartz. 'And the trend is global,' adds Woloshin.

One of the key ways of making healthy people believe they are sick is direct-to-consumer advertising of drugs and diseases—and there is now more than $3 billion dollars' worth of it every year in the US alone; more or less ten million dollars a day. One recent TV advertisement on high rotation in the US featured stunning footage of a middle-aged female surfer riding perfectly formed waves. The mellow mood, though, is broken when the surfer runs in to the beach, and accidentally knocks over a row of surfboards that had been planted neatly in the sand. Somehow, through the magic of marketing, the accident with the surfboards is related to her cholesterol numbers being too high, and that is where the statin that's being advertised can help.

We've 'scared everyone into this state,' says Schwartz, 'and drugs offer an easy way that you can do something about it. There is a sense that the goal is to lower your cholesterol numbers. You hear this idea that "it's all about your numbers", but it's not really—it's about whether you have lowered your risk of heart disease. Because cholesterol has become a condition, you can define a treatment's success as having a lower cholesterol level, as if cholesterol is of itself the problem.'

The *problem* here is finding effective ways to reduce heart disease, stroke and premature death, *not* cholesterol levels. For some people, there is no doubt lowering cholesterol with drugs can help; for others, the drugs may be useless, wasteful and even harmful. According to rigorous and independent analysis of all the clinical trials of the statins, there is no good evidence these drugs offer benefits to healthy women who have not already had some heart disease—women like the healthy-looking surfer in the surfboard ad.[43] For women who have already experienced some form of heart disease, the drugs may offer slight reductions in the risk of future heart problems, lowering the chances over five or so years from 18 per cent to 14 per cent.[44] But there is no good evidence that the drugs can reduce the chances of a premature death for women.

For men the situation is a little different. For those who already have some heart disease, and others at high risk, the drugs can reduce the chances of further disease and premature death. The large Heart Protection Study published in the British journal *The Lancet* showed that those with heart disease taking a statin for five years reduced their chances of death from roughly 15 per cent to 13 per cent, and reduced their chances of further heart attacks and strokes from 25 per cent to 20 per cent.[45]

For most men who have not already suffered any heart disease the benefits are not so clear. There are differing views on the scientific data for this group, with some scientists claiming major benefits, and others like Harvard's Abramson arguing there is no good evidence that the drugs reduce the risk of heart disease or death in any meaningful way. One recent review of the evidence suggested that for people who have not experienced any heart disease, the drugs provided 'small and clinically hardly relevant improvement'.[46] So in summary, for many otherwise healthy men and women, there is no definitive proof that these drugs can meaningfully contribute to the prevention of an early death.

Yet the suggestion that taking cholesterol-lowering drugs lowers your chances of an early death has been one of the key messages promoted far and wide, even in countries where direct drug advertisements are still banned and mass marketing takes the form of 'disease awareness-raising'. The use of the fear of death to market the statins has provoked outrage from independent scientists, consumers and physicians around the world. The concern is twofold. First, for most of the healthy people being targeted by this mass marketing, there is no good evidence that the statins can reduce the chances of an early death. Second, and more importantly, the promotional focus on cholesterol takes attention away from other effective and efficient ways to make life longer and healthier.

In 2003, several officials from the World Health Organization became so alarmed by some of Pfizer's 'awareness-raising' activities that they wrote a statement denouncing the promotion, published as a letter in *The Lancet*.[47] The WHO experts were appalled in particular by an ad that appeared in newspapers and magazines displaying a corpse in a morgue, along with the caption: 'A simple test of blood cholesterol could have avoided this.' Like a lot of modern pharmaceutical promotion, the ads were not directly promoting a named drug—but rather they were attempting to expand the market for drugs by promoting fear—and offering misleading and distorted information about health and illness along the way. The ad was supposed to increase public awareness of heart disease—a widespread health problem related to many risk factors including smoking, a sedentary lifestyle, an unbalanced diet, obesity, high blood pressure, diabetes, and high blood cholesterol. The problem with the ad, according to the

WHO officials, was that of all the major factors accepted as risks, 'only cholesterol is addressed'.

> To us, the implication is that smokers, obese individuals, or those who live a sedentary lifestyle can safely continue to smoke, remain overweight, or take little exercise, provided they take medication to reduce their cholesterol values.

The WHO letter went on to argue that the Pfizer-funded campaign was not 'accurate, informative, or balanced'. Rather, it was misleading and likely to induce 'unjustifiable drug use'. The letter concluded by stressing the need for health authorities to be more vigorous in regulating pharmaceutical promotion, and in producing more independent and balanced health information to counter it.

The problem here, though, is not just about misleading information, and the need for people to be better informed. Promotional campaigns like this are far more pernicious. As others have observed, saturation selling campaigns promoting high cholesterol as a major health problem and cholesterol-lowering drugs as a key solution also affect those charged with protecting and improving public health.[48] The cultural obsession with 'lowering the numbers' keeps the attention of many official decision-makers narrowly focused on just one small part of the picture, restricting their ability to more creatively and effectively fight heart disease.[49]

The unhealthy obsession with cholesterol has reached the highest levels of decision-makers around the world, as we have seen with official US government-backed guidelines recommending that almost one in four adults should be taking statins. Those same guidelines recommend that the entire population over twenty years old—around 200 million people—should have their blood cholesterol levels regularly tested.[50] Other nations do not yet have such sweeping recommendations, in part because of questions about the escalating costs and unnecessary harm that can flow from the inappropriate treatment of healthy people.

For London-based Dr Iona Heath, the whole idea of prevention is being perverted by pharmaceutical promotion. A hardworking inner-city general practitioner, and a long-time official with the Royal College of General Practitioners, Heath brings a tough, ethical approach to medicine, and she has written extensively about the link between poverty and ill health. She and many of her colleagues are becoming increasingly concerned that there is far too much focus in modern health care on the 'rich well' and not enough on the 'sick poor'.[51]

Like Lisa Schwartz and Steve Woloshin across the Atlantic, British doctors such as Iona Heath are now measured on how successful they are at lowering the risks of heart disease for their patients. In the US, the government-funded Veterans Affairs system formally rates its doctors like Woloshin and Schwartz on how conscientiously they test and treat the risk factor of high cholesterol, particularly in people who have already had some heart disease. In the UK, the government's National Health Service has similar arrangements.[52] Schemes like this that measure doctors' performance do have some benefits, says Heath, in terms of making sure they take heart disease seriously. But in her view they also act as strong incentives for the doctors to prescribe the quick fix—cholesterol-lowering drugs. The concern in such a system is that with so much focus on lowering the risks of the well, 'the needs of the sick can get marginalised'. Looking more globally, Heath argues that a similar distortion of priorities is occurring, as billions are being spent to slightly reduce the risks of future heart disease among the wealthy healthy. 'It's so tied in with the greed of the rich countries and the fear of dying—people seem able to deny the reality of death, right up to the last moment. But getting cholesterol down in the west, while not treating those dying of AIDS in African nations, is just obscene.'[53]

Heath's concerns about the perversion of prevention are echoed by Bristol University's Professor Shah Ebrahim, who specialises in ageing and heart disease. A believer in prescribing statins for those who have already had a heart attack, he sees the benefits for most others as being so small that they do not warrant 'making patients out of people like me'—a generally healthy middle-aged man.[54] He says the scientific evidence suggests the health system should spend less time prescribing statins to healthy people, and more time getting strict anti-smoking policies enacted, making sure people have more opportunities for regular exercise and better access to shops selling fresh fruit and vegetables. And those sorts of broader changes, according to Ebrahim, will produce a lot more health benefits than simply reducing heart disease.

While there is no doubt statins can produce health benefits for many people, their side effects, in some very rare cases, can be deadly. All drugs carry downsides and the cholesterol-lowering medicines are no different. When a drug is being prescribed to a healthy person—as they often are when the drugs are designed to *prevent* illness—those side effects become much more important. Yet despite the fact that this category of drug is one of the biggest-selling classes ever, and people stay on them for years, their long-term side effects have been very poorly studied. A recent review of all of the clinical trials of the statins found that only a third of those trials fully reported on side effects.[55] 'It's just a scandal,' says the normally mild-mannered

Ebrahim, who is gravely concerned about such a gaping hole in the scientific evidence, 'it's quite remarkable'. From the evidence that *has* been collected on side effects, there are at least two very important ones—though they are extremely rare: a debilitating muscle-wasting condition call rhabdomyolysis, and liver damage. Yet with so many millions taking the statins worldwide, even rare side effects start to mount up.

Reports of sometimes fatal muscle-wasting linked to Bayer's statin Baycol, when taken in conjunction with a second drug, led to a voluntary withdrawal from the market several years ago, and the company and its insurers have had to put aside more than a billion dollars to fight or settle thousands of the resulting lawsuits.[56] The company's view is that it marketed the statin responsibly, and it is fighting each suit on a case-by-case basis. Without admitting any wrongdoing Bayer has so far settled 3000 cases, and has another 8000 pending.[57]

With the newest statin, Crestor, its manufacturer has had to fight off calls from the consumer watchdog Public Citizen for the drug's withdrawal, and there have been ongoing reports that a very small but increasing number of people taking the pills are experiencing muscle wastage and in some cases even kidney failure.[58] While conceding that rare cases of muscle wasting and kidney failure have been linked to Crestor, AstraZeneca maintains its drug is just as safe as the other statins and accuses Public Citizen of causing 'undue concern'. In early 2005, however, the company informed regulators that there was a report of a patient's death, possibly linked to the drug.[59]

In the United States decisions about whether or not a drug like Crestor should be withdrawn are made by the Food and Drug Administration (FDA), the government body charged with assessing the safety and effectiveness of medicines. The FDA is well known around the world, and its decisions can influence those of many nations. Yet just like the doctors, the patient groups and the professional associations, the FDA itself now relies on partial funding from the drug companies whose products it is assessing. A new system of user pays, introduced in the 1990s, has meant that more than half of the FDA's drug review work is now funded directly by the pharmaceutical industry—a situation similar to that of many nations, including Australia, Britain and Canada.[60] The call to pull Crestor from the market has been assessed by people who know that some of their salary—and the salaries of their colleagues—is funded by AstraZeneca and the other drug giants.

The campaign against Crestor has been led by Dr Sidney Wolfe, the director of Public Citizen's Health Research Group. A six foot two piano-playing intellectual who walks to his Washington, DC office every morning, Wolfe is one of the most well informed, aggressive and influential health advocates in the world. Despite decades in the business, he continues to be outraged by what he sees as the unhealthy conflicts of interest that riddle the global medical establishment, even reaching into the heart of regulatory agencies like the FDA.

It was Wolfe and his colleagues who decided to make an example of the conflicts of interest of a senior official at another public agency, the National Institutes of Health, when he discovered the extent of Dr Bryan Brewer's dual role as government employee and paid speaker for Crestor's manufacturer AstraZeneca. Wolfe wrote to the NIH director raising questions about Brewer's links with the company and noted that they were not disclosed in his influential journal article endorsing Crestor.[61] In response, the NIH director expressed regret that Dr Brewer's financial ties with the drug maker were not disclosed, but indicated that it was acceptable for senior government researchers to work for drug companies in their own time.[62]

Dr Brewer declined a request to be interviewed about the matter, though in a letter to the NIH director he defended his public presentations about Crestor as 'unbiased'.[63] And he is certainly not the only senior NIH researcher to have close financial ties to the drug industry. Revelations by investigative journalists and others in recent years have uncovered extensive conflicts of interest, and ultimately sparked congressional inquiries.[64] At one hearing on Washington's Capitol Hill, the site of Congress, committee members expressed dismay at one case where an NIH researcher had received $430 000 from industry sources, and another where stock worth almost $2 million had been held.[65] Initially defending some of the links, in late 2004 the NIH unexpectedly announced a moratorium for all scientific staff on all financial ties with private companies.[66]

Ironically, even if the industry-funded FDA decided to vigorously investigate the safety questions surrounding Crestor, and it convened a committee of its advisers to deliberate, the panel would most likely include physicians with strong financial ties to statin manufacturers—a conflict of interests endemic within many of the regulator's advisory panels, and many of the influential decision-making bodies across the health care landscape.[67] In a bizarre postscript to the controversy over the government's cholesterol guidelines, two of the guideline writers have left their former positions and gone to work for the pharmaceutical industry, one joining the late Henry Gadsden's firm, Merck.[68]

Whatever the future of Crestor and the other statins, or the prospects for more independent drug regulation and more unbiased guidelines, there is a growing scepticism about the selling of high cholesterol and the value of the drugs to treat it.

In fact, right from the beginning of the cholesterol boom in the 1980s, critical thinkers like investigative journalist and health researcher Thomas Moore have been exposing the weaknesses in the arguments of those who would seem to welcome statins in the drinking water.[69] Similarly, researchers like Lisa Schwartz and Steve Woloshin, and their colleagues from Dartmouth, have developed international standing for promoting a more informed and sceptical approach to the risks and benefits of all therapies, and for raising concerns that expanding disease definitions put us all in danger of becoming patients unnecessarily.

Perhaps the biggest obstacle to a more rational debate about cholesterol, heart disease, or any other health problem, is the simple fact that too many of the people we turn to for advice on such matters—our doctors—are tied to the makers of drugs. Sometimes those ties involve several hundred thousand dollars a year, sometimes just a few warm doughnuts.

## 2

# Doughnuts for the doctors

*Depression*

The aroma of fresh baking wafts from Michael Oldani's car as the door swings open and he jumps out to open the trunk. He lifts out a carton of free drug samples and stacks on top two other boxes, all of them festooned with stickers bearing the name of a popular antidepressant. As one of an army of 80 000 detailers working as sales representatives for drug companies in the US, Oldani had started his morning bearing the most beguiling of gifts—warm doughnuts.[1]

With his jet-black hair and dark Italian good looks, Oldani was at the time making daily forays to the front-line of physicians' offices, wielding the industry's weapons of mass seduction: food, flattery, friendship—and lots of free samples.[2] His primary goal was maximising the sales of his company's antidepressant, but a key strategy to achieve it was selling a certain

---

*Note:* The drugs discussed in this chapter have different names in some countries. For example, Paxil is Aropax in Australia and Seroxat in the UK. Zoloft is called Lustral in the UK.

view of depression. For almost two decades, Oldani and thousands like him have helped instill and reinforce the notion that depression is a widespread psychiatric disease most likely due to a chemical imbalance in the brain, best fixed with a modern group of drugs called selective serotonin reuptake inhibitors, or SSRIs, that includes Prozac, Paxil, and Zoloft.[3] Their work has paid off handsomely: in some countries prescriptions for these pills more than tripled through the 1990s, making antidepressants one of the top-selling categories of drugs, and generating combined sales of more than $20 billion for their makers.[4]

Drug company spending on sales representatives and their free samples is the biggest component of the roughly $25 billion dollars now outlaid annually in the United States for promotion, and it is the foundation of the global web of financial entanglement between the industry and the profession.[5] What starts with doughnuts for the doctors ends with lavish banquets for thought-leaders in five-star hotels. And at every opportunity, it is not just drugs being sold, but very particular views of disease.[6] As specialists in mental illness remind us, the idea that depression is caused by a deficiency of the brain chemical serotonin is in fact just one scientific view among many—and a simplistic and outdated one at that.[7] But it is a theory kept very much alive by the massive marketing machinery that starts with the morning deliveries of pharmaceutical company sales representatives.

After a major change of heart, and career, Michael Oldani is now working on his PhD in anthropology at Princeton, where he is trying to make sense of the interactions between drug detailers and doctors. The detailers who succeed in such a competitive environment are, he explains, 'masters at establishing trust, forging alliances, and acquiring commitments through the sharing of information and the giving of oneself.'[8] Human beings have a natural tendency to want to repay kindness, and the best way doctors can do that is by prescribing the products that the detailers are pushing.[9] For Oldani, these two-way relationships become highly personal, and 'business transactions per se, are never conducted . . . never witnessed'. Though these intimate dealings are largely hidden from public view, they are highly effective for those bankrolling them.

Contacts between detailers and doctors tend to lead to less rational prescribing habits, yet many physicians deny they are being influenced.[10] Research suggests doctors exposed to company reps are more likely to favour drugs over non-drug therapy, and more likely to prescribe expensive medications when equally effective but less costly ones are available.[11] Researchers have even suggested there is an association between the dose and response: that is, the more contact between doctors and detailers the more doctors latch on to the 'commercial' messages as opposed to the 'scientific' view of a product's value.[12]

In the case of the new antidepressants, the gap between the commercial messages and the scientific view has become frighteningly wide, with the benefits of these drugs far more modest, and risks far more serious, than a decade of promotion has suggested.[13] According to independent analysis of the clinical trials—almost all of which have been funded by their manufacturers—on average the advantages of these antidepressants over placebo or dummy pills are modest at best, yet their side effects can include sexual problems, severe withdrawal reactions and an apparent increase in the risk of suicidal behaviour among the young.[14] Somewhat ironically, part of the marketing of these new antidepressants has played directly on fears that suicide could result if a young person's depression was left untreated.[15] While many doctors and researchers believe the drugs do indeed prevent suicide for some people, the available evidence suggests that the children and adolescents who take these medications are likely increasing their risks of suicidal thinking and behaviour.[16] Importantly, the scientific evidence doesn't point to an increase in actual suicide, rather, suicidal thinking and behaviour.


As the clouds and mist of an early May morning swirl around the rooftops of Manhattan, thousands of psychiatrists stream into a giant mid-town convention centre to learn about the latest in scientific developments, at the annual congress of the American Psychiatric Association, the APA. On their way in they couldn't have missed the massive billboards advertising the meeting, adorned with the name of one of the congress's key sponsors, Pfizer, the maker of the world's top-selling anti-depressant, Zoloft. Inside the cathedral-like convention centre the first port of call for the swarming visitors is the gigantic exhibit hall, which offers a surreal trip inside the entangled world of drug company-funded psychiatry.

The first display inside the exhibit hall is Pfizer's. It's still early on a Sunday morning, the five-day conference has only just opened, yet already hundreds of doctors are lining up at the stalls like eager kids at a carnival, filling out forms and entering their names into competitions in the hope of winning tiny trinkets and treats. At one booth, the prize on offer is a simple laser pointer, but the excitement runs high nevertheless. It's circus time and working the crowds like well-dressed ringleaders are dozens of friendly and efficient salespeople. 'Very nice meeting you,' says one, politely.

Psychiatry's intimate relationship with the pharmaceutical industry has become notorious. When the former *New England*

*Journal of Medicine* editor Dr Marcia Angell published her famous editorial 'Is Academic Medicine for Sale?', it was this group of specialists that she chose to illustrate her point.[17] She wrote that when journal staff were searching for an experienced and independent psychiatrist to write a review article about antidepressants, they had great difficulty finding one, because only 'very few' in the entire United States were free of financial ties to the drug makers.

The psychiatrists' industry-sponsored annual congress has similarly become legendary.[18] In 2004, drug companies paid around $2000 for each tiny 10 foot × 10 foot (3 metres × 3 metres) square of real estate in the gargantuan exhibit hall.[19] But not only did companies pay for space for their stalls, they actually sponsored over 50 scientific sessions throughout the week-long congress. The APA will not confirm how much the organisation charges companies for the privilege of sponsoring a symposium, but it has been reported to be tens of thousands of dollars per session.[20]

For the psychiatrists attending, the sponsorship created an orgy of culinary indulgence, because somehow the industry-funded symposia always seemed to coincide with meal times. At the New York congress psychiatrists learnt about bipolar disorder at a breakfast session in the Marriott Marquis Hotel courtesy of Lilly, the makers of Prozac.[21] At a lunchtime session in the Grand Hyatt sponsored by Paxil manufacturer GSK, delegates were educated about maternal depression.[22] And for the dinner symposia, the conscientious doctors heard about generalised anxiety disorder in the Grand Ballroom of the Roosevelt, thanks to Pfizer.[23] Welcome to the modern world of medical science.[24]

Not all psychiatrists have stayed seated on the gravy train. The Harvard-trained psychiatrist Dr Loren Mosher caused a stir a few years ago when he quit his professional association in disgust. An APA member for nearly three decades, Mosher said at the time that in his view, 'psychiatry has been almost completely bought out by the drug companies' and that he, for one, did not want to be a 'drug company patsy'.[25] He counselled that the APA and other groups like it around the world were doing a serious disservice to human health care and urged them to 'get real about money, politics and science. Label each for what it is . . . that is, be honest.'

What irked Loren Mosher most was not the unholy alliance per se, but the corrosive effect he believed this alliance was having on the practice of psychiatry. He was horrified by what he saw as the narrowing focus on drug therapies, making physicians everywhere less able to 'understand whole persons in their social contexts'. Because he saw a more noble cause for psychiatry, beyond the mere technical role of realigning patients' neuro-transmitters—including serotonin—he said he could no longer stand by while his profession condoned the 'widespread use and misuse of toxic chemicals'.

Mosher's voice is by no means the only one critical of the close links with industry and the narrowed focus on chemical causes and chemical solutions. University of Wales psychiatrist, Dr David Healy, is a specialist in the history of psychiatric drugs, a practising clinician who prescribes antidepressants to his patients, and an occasional consultant for several drug companies. In recent years, with many articles, books and media appearances under his belt, he has emerged as a leading critic of the way pharmaceutical marketing is shaping our perceptions of illness.[26]

Healy maintains that early theories suggesting that a serotonin imbalance causes depression have not been verified by later research. While acknowledging a role for biological causes, Healy argues that the serotonin theory has been overplayed in order to help sell the selective serotonin reuptake inhibitor drugs, including Prozac, Paxil and Zoloft. It's been overplayed because companies realise it makes 'wonderful marketing copy' he says.[27] 'It's the kind of thing that a GP [family physician] can use when they're trying to persuade a person to have pills.' It's also the kind of rationale that drug reps like Michael Oldani can use to persuade physicians to use their products. 'They're trying to get us to think a particular way,' Healy says. 'They are trying to get us doctors to see the illnesses that we will then see in you, the patients, and the sales of their product will then follow . . . I consume, by putting pills in your mouth, and you're the one who's going to have to suffer the consequences of things if they go wrong.'[28]

While the industry's marketing might help to *narrow* the focus on to chemical causes and chemical solutions, it also helps to promote *wide* estimates of how many people are affected by mental disorders like depression. Over the past decade many of us have heard repeatedly that perhaps a third of the population suffers with a mental illness. A major source for that figure was a survey of Americans conducted in the early 1990s, which claimed to have found that in any given year, 30 per cent of people had a mental disorder.[29] While the figure may sound so absurdly high as to be laughable, it has been widely cited around the world, in marketing and elsewhere, and it has helped build the impression of untold millions being undiagnosed and untreated.[30]

One of those who thought the figure sounded a little on the high side was psychiatrist Dr William Narrow, at the time working for the government-funded National Institutes of Health in the US. He and his colleagues started taking a closer look at exactly how the survey results had been put together. What they found was that a lot of the people classified by the survey researchers as having a 'mental disorder' did not have a 'clinically significant' disorder. In other words, they most likely didn't have a disorder that warranted treatment.[31] When Narrow started to separate out those who had a 'clinically significant' disorder from those who didn't, a very different picture emerged.

In 2002, Narrow and his colleagues published a scientific paper called 'Revised Prevalence Estimates of Mental Disorders in the United States'.[32] Reading between the polite lines of academic language in the paper, the findings of the original survey were being well and truly questioned. The orthodoxy that one-third of people were mentally ill with depression and other psychiatric disorders was being directly challenged. The widely quoted estimates were dramatically revised downwards, slashing the total rate of those supposedly suffering a mental disorder in any given year from 30 per cent to less than 20 per cent.

In the revised estimates, the proportion of people said to be suffering major depression was virtually halved from 10 per cent to under 5 per cent. Most importantly, Narrow and his colleagues argued that because of problems and limitations with the methods of the original survey, it was likely the true rates of disorders were significantly lower still.[33] The bottom line was that a lot of people with mild problems had been included in those original estimates, which as a result were highly inflated.

'When you're trying to get visibility, one way to do that is to shock people with big numbers,' says Narrow, speculating on why the original survey researchers chose to publish such extraordinarily large figures.[34] Asked whether he thought the original figures were fundamentally misleading, he said, 'I'm going to reserve judgment on that.' A practising psychiatrist, Narrow says one of his key motivations is to make sure that people who need help get it. But there is a real danger, he says, that by including the millions of people with mild problems in your estimates of mental illness, you risk losing public support for treating those people who have real disorders.

Dr Ron Kessler, the lead researcher of the original survey, concedes that it's hard to believe 30 per cent of people suffer a mental disorder, but he sticks by his findings, and rejects William Narrow's revision as simply wrong. Kessler, a Harvard professor of health care policy, argues that even those with mild forms of mental disorders like depression have a higher risk of killing themselves than others, and should therefore be treated—however you want to label them.[35] 'If you don't want to call mild problems disorders, then don't. Let's just say mild disorders are not disorders. Let's call them risks if you want to, but whatever the case—let's treat them. We have to keep them on our radar screens because it's an area of human suffering that we should be thinking of doing something about. I like the idea of calling it a disorder because it keeps it in front of our eyes as something we need to keeping working on.'[36]

Kessler's estimates of widespread mental disorders are of course music to the ears of drug marketers and while his original survey was govenment funded, now companies regularly court him. While he does not work as a paid adviser or speaker—financial ties many other senior researchers accept with relish—he has taken funds from several companies to help support his ongoing survey work—most recently from Lilly, GSK and Pfizer—the makers of the world's three top-selling antidepressants.[37]

One of Kessler's latest studies involved surveys in fourteen nations, conducted between 2001 and 2003. The massive project was funded by many public and private organisations, including Lilly, GSK, and the Pfizer foundation, though the surveys were run at arm's length from the sponsors.[38] The findings reveal some extraordinary differences between countries. Despite the criticisms from Narrow and others, this international survey declared that in any given year 26 per cent of people in the United States still meet the criteria that defines them as having a mental disorder. In Mexico, the number was 12 per cent, in China and Japan 9 per cent, and in Italy 8 per cent. Yet, of those he classified as having a mental disorder, many were in fact 'mild' cases according to the definitions Kessler and colleagues were using. In the US, more than one-third were mild cases, meaning they may not even warrant treatment—depending, of course, whether you listen to William Narrow or Ron Kessler.

On the issue of what's commonly called 'unmet need' the latest Kessler study also offered fascinating, though somewhat contradictory, new insights. It found that around half of those classified as having a *serious* disorder were not getting the medical treatment they needed. In other words here was evidence of undertreatment. Yet the international study also found that at least half of the people who were receiving treatment may not in fact have needed it. The write-up of the study, published in the *Journal of the American Medical Association* by Kessler and colleagues, stated that 'either the majority or a near majority of people in treatment in each country are either noncases or mild cases'.[39] The global obsession with 'unmet need'—a notion that is constantly pushed by doctors and drug companies as the justification for aggressive drug marketing—may well be helping to create a strange new phenomenon: 'met un-need'.[40]

One educational program that strongly promoted the idea of 'unmet need' was run in Australia in the 1990s.[41] Groups of general practitioners attending 'continuing medical education' events were told that a third of people who walked into their surgeries were suffering a mental illness—and they were urged to be more aggressive in their detection and treatment of depression. Like a lot of medical education, the program was part sponsored by a drug company. The response to questions about the obvious conflict of interests, where a company making antidepressants was part funding doctors' educational programs about depression, was that it was in everyone's interest to increase the numbers of people being treated, whether with psychological therapies or drugs.[42]

Those educational seminars were in fact part of a much bigger project attempting to raise awareness among Australian doctors and the public about depression, funded in part by Bristol-Myers Squibb, the makers of an antidepressant called Serzone. Funding also came from state and federal governments. In turn, this project was just one of many similar programs to 'educate' doctors, funded generously by the makers of the other antidepressants throughout the 1990s. The programs reaped major benefits for their private sponsors. The volume of antidepressant prescriptions in Australia tripled between 1990 and 2000.[43] Among the young, aged 15–24, the rates increased tenfold.[44]

One of the key components of the Bristol-Myers Squibb funded educational program was a simple screening test—a checklist of questions—designed to be used by family doctors to diagnose whether their patients had a mental disorder. Yet this test was so broad, it classified 49 per cent of people as having a 'mental disorder'—roughly one-half of that 49 per cent having what was described as a 'Level 1' disorder and the other half having a less serious 'Level 2' disorder.[45] While this is clearly good news for Bristol-Myers Squibb and other drug makers, the figures may appear to dispassionate observers as absurdly inflated estimates that would immediately raise questions about a potentially flawed test.

In fact, researchers from the Monash Medical Centre in Melbourne later rigorously examined that screening test, and pointed to major problems. According to their calculations, the majority of people diagnosed in this test as having a mental disorder most likely did not have one at all.[46] There are obvious dangers when well-intentioned doctors use tests that may falsely classify many people as sick—not only is there a potential for inappropriate labelling, but also the potential to expose relatively healthy people to the side effects of potent medicines. It is a danger the Monash researchers themselves highlighted.

> Labelling a significant number of people who are not depressed as 'probably depressed' might reasonably be considered a potential harm. We do not want to replace a situation of under-recognition with one of over-recognition, neither being of benefit to the patient.

These heavily promoted antidepressants have serious side effects. As it turned out, the side effects associated with Bristol-Myers Squibb's antidepressant Serzone were considered so serious it was withdrawn from the market around the world following evidence linking it to hepatitis and even liver failure in some patients. The company however explained the withdrawal was for commercial rather than safety reasons.[47] As for Prozac, Paxil and Zoloft, it is well known they can cause serious sexual difficulties including problems achieving orgasm.[48] With Paxil, perhaps as many as 25 per cent of those prescribed the drug have problems getting off it because of worrisome withdrawal symptoms. But most serious of all have been revelations that the drugs appear to increase the risk of suicidal behaviour and thinking among children and adolescents, discovered only after health authorities—under pressure from consumer activists and others—

demanded to see the complete set of company-funded trials, some of which had been buried deep inside drug company archives.[49] These revelations came at a time when the prescriptions of these medicines to children were rising dramatically.[50] In 2002, there were more than 10 million scripts written for people under eighteen for the three top antidepressants in the US alone.[51]

So vociferous was the public outcry about the issue of suicidal behaviour that even the industry-friendly FDA was forced to convene meetings of its advisers to investigate. The first of two historic public meetings was held in February 2004, at the Holiday Inn in Bethesda on the outskirts of Washington, DC. 'Our daughter Julie had been excited about college and had scored 1300 in her SATs,' Tom Woodward told the FDA advisers soon after the hearings began. A few weeks after her final school exams, following what her parents describe as a normal bout of teenage troubles, Julie was diagnosed with depression and prescribed Zoloft. After a week on the drug she went into the family garage and hung herself.[52] 'Instead of picking out colleges for our daughter, my wife and I had to pick out a cemetery plot for her,' Woodward said, his voice full of sadness and anger. 'Instead of looking forward to visiting Julie at school, we now visit her grave.'

The causes of any individual case of suicide are almost always highly complex, and disentangling the role of any underlying disease from the effects of a drug is a difficult task. In Julie's case, while her parents have strong beliefs about the cause of their daughter's suicide, at the time of writing there has been no investigation into her state of health before death, or the potential role of the drug. Yet her story was one of many presented at the all-day hearing in Bethesda that helped focus the attention of the drug regulator on the potential harms of these widely prescribed antidepressants. Summing up a growing sense of unease among the expert advisers who had listened to Julie's parents and many others, Professor Mark Hudak from the University of Florida urged the FDA to take action to protect children with milder health problems from being treated with potent medications.

> If they are clearly very ill, anything that can be done should be done. But for a lot of the people who spoke this morning . . . the picture that was presented of their child or someone they knew, was not someone who was very, very ill, it was someone who had relatively minor type findings, put on these drugs with terrible consequences.[53]

Ultimately, the regulator's analysis of all of the company trials in children and adolescents, including the unpublished trials, would suggest that the drugs on average increased the risk of suicidal behaviour and thinking from 2 per cent to 4 per cent. In other words, according to a summary of the trial results, 2 per cent of those taking a placebo experienced suicidal thoughts or behaviours. Of those taking the antidepressants, 4 per cent did.[54] The trials showed no increase in cases of actual suicide.

What's more, for almost all the drugs, except Prozac, there was no evidence from the clinical trials in children that the antidepressants worked any better at relieving depression than a placebo or dummy pill. British authorities moved in late 2003 to try to stop the drugs being prescribed to children.[55] A year later authorities in the US demanded that companies add a 'black box' warning to antidepressant labels—more than a decade after the drugs had first appeared on the market.[56] A strongly worded 'black box' warning is one that appears on all prescribing information, and is the toughest form of safety warning available. For

Tom and Kathy Woodward, no matter how tough, the warnings were simply too late.

At the time when the middle-class couple had been considering drug therapy for their daughter's emotional difficulties, no one told them of the potential risk of suicidal behaviour.[57] For Tom Woodward, his daughter's death highlights what he sees as a gross failure of regulation, made worse by the fact that the FDA relies on industry funds for much of its drug review work. 'These drugs are being prescribed like candy,' says Woodward. 'They're being given for practically everything, it seems today, and the consequences are frightening.' A long-time Republican, Woodward has become a grassroots activist exposing what he sees as the pharmaceutical industry's unhealthy influence over the US Congress and the White House, and a campaigner for much tougher and more independent drug regulation.[58] 'We're going to try to reach out to as many people as we can, tell our story and try to spread the word, so people can make informed decisions. If they think there is some value to these drugs, so be it. But go in with your eyes open, understanding what the downside is. 'Cause the downside could be very great.'[59]

Like Tom Woodward, London general practitioner Dr Iona Heath is concerned that too many people with ordinary life experiences are being too quickly offered a label and a drug. She is particularly worried by simple screening checklists and questionnaires that ask people if they have been feeling sad, blue, unhappy or down in the dumps—the sort of questions to which many of us might answer yes. Heath stresses that while it is important for doctors to be diagnosing and treating genuine mental illness, these kinds of screening tests are so broad they may wrongly label healthy people as sick in too many instances. She points out that much depression will be relatively mild and can pass within a matter of months, yet according to some estimates millions of people are prescribed these antidepressants for several years or more.[60]

Dr Heath says that what is important is for physicians to take time to listen to patients, many of whom in her view don't want to have their complaints reduced to a simple problem with levels of serotonin in the brain. She sees many sources of emotional distress in her daily work, including people experiencing serious pain, the loss of a loved one, a job under threat, an abusive partner, or a damp, overcrowded and dangerous home.[61] Many people struggle to make sense of their suffering and many people develop the skills to cope.

Heath, who works with the Royal College of General Practitioners as well as the *British Medical Journal*, rejects the 'pill-for-every-ill' model, where the patient is characterised as 'broken' and the physician is there to 'fix' him or her. Instead, she sees the interaction with her patients as part of a much richer relationship. Her goal is to come to mutual agreement on the extent to which a person may want to see their difficulties as a medical problem that might require treatment. And if treatment is called for, she draws from a very large bundle of solutions, including medications and talking therapies, for which there is good evidence of effectiveness.[62] She will sometimes suggest people write things down or tell stories about their suffering and distress, and she might even recommend dancing classes or doing more exercise—strategies not as heavily promoted as the biochemical approaches pushed by company detailers.

Studies in several nations show that roughly 80 per cent of doctors still regularly see drug detailers, though GPs like Dr Iona Heath and Canadian Dr Warren Bell do not.[63] A family physician in Salmon Arm, a small rural town in the interior of British Columbia, Bell grimaces as he talks about the early flattery and friendship offered to him by the company detailers when he was a young intern. 'I was basically offended, deeply offended by the fact that people would be nice to me not because of who I was, but because of the role I play in society. I think it was my first contact with people who were treating me as a political entity rather than a person. It really did irritate me.'[64]

What Bell did as soon as he started practising medicine in the community was cut himself off from the drug industry's marketing, completely. He has no logos in his office, and has never seen a drug salesperson, ever, in his 27 years of medicine. He chuckles at the thought of his colleagues 'bemused and hopelessly imprisoned within the world of pharmaceutical bafflegab ... even quite intelligent, quite knowledgeable people can't step beyond it, because they're in this sea of drug company logos'.[65]

Bell and Heath aren't the only ones who have disentangled themselves from the influences of drug company marketing. The New York based group No Free Lunch has been running a global campaign along those lines for some time, featuring its slogan 'Just say no to drug reps' and its high-profile 'pen amnesty' that encourages doctors to send back their drug company pens and other paraphernalia.[66] The activist group has already enjoyed some considerable success. Inspired in part by No Free Lunch, a few years ago the 50 000-strong American Medical Student Association mounted its own 'PharmFree' campaign calling for an end to all forms of free lunch.[67]

Back at the American Psychiatric Association congress in New York, it seems No Free Lunch is yet to have a big impact. Tonight the psychiatrists are scheduled to listen to a thought-leader in the Sheraton's Imperial Ballroom tell them about anxiety disorders.[68] Cultivating a stable of thought-leaders is a key part of the industry's marketing strategies, whether for depression or any other condition. The quality of that stable depends a lot on the groundwork of drug reps like Michael Oldani, who would often assess a young doctor's potential for influencing his peers, first-hand, as part of his daily rounds.

Promising prospects might be singled out by a detailer as a potential thought-leader, and then given some small speaking assignments to test them out. Later, if they've proven their worth, they might be paid to speak regularly in small local settings about the latest new drug in the pipeline. With a bit of luck the thought-leader could eventually find themselves on a drug company's 'speaker's bureau' earning thousands of dollars for making presentations to their international peers about the latest new disease, at high-profile events like the APA congress in New York.

So important are the alliances with thought-leaders that some marketing firms actually calculate the 'return on investment' a drug company can reap from these sorts of presentations.[69] A thought-leader's performance can be tracked by secretly measuring the impact of their messages on the prescribing patterns of those being 'educated'. Oldani remembers from his time in the industry that the best spokespeople were those who appeared to deliver a balanced message—never crudely cheerleading for a drug. Attendees at such educational or scientific sessions would never know they were being marketed to. The most accomplished of his thought-leaders—or 'product champions' as they are also known within the industry—could really work the crowd, and 'sell without selling'.[70]

By any objective analysis, one of the reasons the SSRI antidepressants were embraced by prescribing doctors so fulsomely all over the world for so long was because the hard work of detailers like Oldani was backed with the credibility of psychiatrist thought-leaders in the pay of the drug makers. When comparing the scientific reality of these drugs' modest benefits and serious harms against the enthusiastic marketing messages espoused for more than a decade, many within psychiatry must today feel a sense of shame. And while their specialty may be more entangled than most, the same web of financial ties exists across virtually the entire medical landscape. When it comes to educating doctors with doughnuts, few medical specialties have been left behind.

For a condition like depression, trying to separate the marketing from the science has not always been easy, because many people do suffer with genuine mental disorders, many can be helped greatly with medications, and many with serious problems are not getting the treatments they need. Moreover, many of the doctors working closely with the drug companies are highly motivated to act in the best interest of patients—and their ties with industry may reflect a shared professional interest rather than an inappropriate commercial relationship. And complicating matters even further is the ongoing argument over what is 'unmet need' and what is 'met un-need' in relation to depression and other mental illness.

Sometimes, however, the most natural and normal processes of life are being sold as medical conditions to be treated with drugs. And sometimes that marketing is made even more powerful and effective by the intangible magic of celebrity selling.

# Working with celebrities

*Menopause*

The summer of 2002 brought good and bad news for Lesa Henry, the busy public relations chief at the drug company Wyeth, and the woman helping to market one of the best-selling drug regimes of all time—hormone replacement therapy. The good news was that she'd just picked up an advertising industry award for her work using celebrities to promote drugs, and she'd been named one of the top 25 marketers of the year. The bad news was that scientists had just discovered long-term use of hormone replacement therapy was doing women more harm than good.[1]

In the world of drug marketing, Wyeth's Lesa Henry is seen as well ahead of the game. She was one of the first to recognise the value of celebrities for 'educating consumers' about health conditions, and the drugs that go with them.[2] One of Wyeth's major coups had been hiring supermodel Lauren Hutton to help raise public awareness about a 'health condition' otherwise known as the menopause—the time in a woman's life when her periods, and her fertility, come to an end. Hutton's famous face has fronted a massive marketing campaign promoting both the 'dangers' of the menopause, and the 'promise' of Wyeth's hormone pills. As director of communications within the company's Women's Healthcare division, Henry was leading the way for the industry, according to the judges who gave her the award, 'in appropriately using celebrity spokespersons in an innovative, results-oriented communications effort'.

Celebrities have become central figures in drug company campaigns to change the way we think about the common ailments of life. Baseball stars help transform fears about sexual performance into pills for sexual dysfunction, and football heroes now help sell shyness as a symptom of a mental illness. For their trouble the stars are paid anything from $20 000 to $2 million, yet the exact size of these pay cheques are well-kept secrets.[3] What's more, many of the talk shows and the tabloids will portray these celebrities as being engaged in worthwhile 'awareness-raising' activities, while making no mention of the fat fees flowing to the stars behind the scenes. One of the most cynical campaigns of all has been Wyeth's attempt to inflame fears about the menopause at the same time as scientists have been documenting the dangers of the company's menopause drugs. The supreme irony is that hormone replacement therapy, after finally being properly studied, would ultimately be shown to cause some of the very health problems it was supposed to prevent.

A milestone in the campaign to 'educate' consumers about menopause was a cover story in 2000 in *Parade*, the weekly magazine inserted into newspapers across the United States.[4] Seen by an estimated 70 million Americans every Sunday, it is arguably one of the most widely read magazines on the planet, and a cover story here is a marketer's dream.[5] Photographed with two other beaming celebrities, the sexy Hutton adorned the *Parade* cover along with the headline, 'Live Longer, Better, Wiser: This year's indispensable guide for every one of us'. Blurring the lines between news and advertising, Hutton not only appeared on the magazine cover and in its main article, she also featured as the centrepiece of a Wyeth advertisement in the same issue— talking about the consequences of 'estrogen loss' at menopause.

The Wyeth advertisement detailed a horrifying list of what apparently lies ahead for women after the menopause: Alzheimer's disease, heart attacks, colon cancer, cataracts, teeth loss, night sweats, vaginal dryness, bone fractures and more. 'Talk to your doctor,' urged Hutton's reassuring image, 'because the more you know about menopause and its associated estrogen loss, the more you'll want to take an active interest in your health.'

Just a few pages away from the advertisement was an article called 'Celebrities Reveal Their Secrets', where the 55-year-old supermodel and health advocate shared her tips for feeling good and looking fabulous. First she praised the virtues of apples, fish, pasta and yoga. Then came the most important part of Hutton's message. 'My No. 1 secret is estrogen,' she said. 'It's good for your moods, it's good for your skin. If I had to choose between all my creams and makeup for feeling and looking good, I'd take the estrogen.' US FDA regulations forbid Wyeth executives from making such one-sided claims about the company's hormone drugs in their advertising, with no mention of side effects, yet their paid celebrity is apparently not under the same FDA constraints.

Selling menopause as a fearful time of hormone *loss* lays the groundwork for selling the promise of hormone *replacement*. As the industry magazine *DTC Perspectives* rightly recognised when it anointed Lesa Henry one of the top marketers of the year: using celebrities brings results. And Lauren Hutton is not the only star in the Wyeth stable. Soul diva Patti LaBelle and actress Cheryl Ladd have also been on the payroll.[6] Not surprisingly, Lesa Henry won that same industry award a second time round, the following year.[7]

Wyeth strongly defends the use of celebrities, arguing that the women are prompted to participate in educational programs because of their own experiences, and their desire to share those experiences with other women. In relation to the awards, a Wyeth spokesperson said the company was pleased when employees are recognised for their professional achievements.[8]

'These campaigns are extremely effective in reaching consumers,' says celebrity-broker Amy Doner Schachtel. Working from her office in New Jersey, the attractive former drug company public relations expert has moved to the leading edge of medical marketing.[9] Sometimes juggling two phones at once, she connects high-profile celebrities with big-name drug companies keen to educate the public about common conditions. 'Just one segment on a national talk show, or one print article in a major newspaper can tremendously impact patients' decisions to seek treatment,' she says. The goal of these company-funded celebrity campaigns, as she stresses repeatedly, is to drive patients into doctors' offices to seek treatment. Schachtel has helped find celebrities to raise awareness about irritable bowel syndrome, depression and social anxiety disorder. She's worked with *West Wing* heart-throb Rob Lowe, country singer-songwriter Naomi Judd and television mega-star Cybill Shepherd. 'People look up to celebrities,' she says, 'because they trust them.'

Hutton's role, like that of other celebrities, was not to create a condition, but rather to help sell a certain perception of one.

In this case the Wyeth advertisement featuring her was helping to persuade women that the menopause was not simply a natural part of life, but rather a condition of 'estrogen loss' which brought an increased risk of deadly and frightening diseases, and required a visit to a medical doctor. This picture of the menopause is by no means a new one, but in recent years Wyeth's reasons for promoting it have intensified, as the world has learnt more and more about the dangers of the company's hormone pills. By the time of the famous *Parade* front cover in the year 2000 the preliminary findings were starting to flow from a massive government-funded study of long-term use of the drugs. As we would all later learn, the combined form of long-term hormone replacement therapy—one of the most prescribed drug therapies ever—was doing more harm than good to the millions of women around the world who were taking it: slightly *increasing* their risks of heart attacks, strokes, blood clots and breast cancer.[10]

Promoting a woman's natural change of life as a medical condition of 'estrogen loss' has a history dating back several decades at least. And just like today, drug company–backed celebrities were at the centre of the action. In the mid-1960s, New York gynaecologist Dr Robert Wilson published the landmark work *Feminine Forever*.[11] The book's cover declared a revolutionary breakthrough: 'the discovery that menopause is a hormone deficiency disease, curable and totally preventable' means that 'every woman no matter what her age, can safely live a fully-sexed life for her entire life'. Excerpts were published in *Look* and *Vogue* and it sold 100 000 copies in a matter of months.[12] The book became a bestseller, and Wilson a celebrity physician. 'Instead of being condemned to witness the death of their own womanhood during what should be their best years', said the book's preamble, 'they will remain fully feminine—physically and emotionally—for as long as they live'.

> ... menopause is a hormone deficiency disease, curable and totally preventable ...
>
> *Feminine Forever,* 1966

The central claim of *Feminine Forever*—and one that echoes through Hutton's celebrity scripts almost forty years later—was that menopause is a condition that requires medical help. It is a *deficiency disease* to be fixed with hormone pills. 'With estrogen therapy,' proclaimed Wilson, 'her rapid physical decline in post-menopausal years is halted. Her body retains its relative youthfulness just as a man's does.' A host of scientific articles were used to support Wilson's claims about the miracle properties of estrogen. While it was clear the pills could offer short-term benefits in terms of symptom relief, their long-term risks and benefits were simply unknown.[13]

Against the backdrop of the emerging women's movement of the 1960s and its language of emancipation, Wilson's book argued that his revolutionary view of menopause, and its treatment, was a way of helping to liberate women—particularly sexually. He attacked a predominantly male medical profession that had failed to appreciate menopause 'as a serious physical and mental syndrome'. By acknowledging the sometimes severe suffering of his menopausal patients, Wilson firmly aligned himself with women, standing courageously against the 'indifference' of male physicians who dismissed women's suffering as simply a state of mind.

Similar charges are regularly levelled against the medical profession from within the women's movement. Just like Wilson, advocacy organisations like the National Women's Health

Network criticise clinicians who dismiss the problems experienced by women at midlife as 'just' menopause. Echoing his arguments, the feminist group urges clinicians to be more sensitive to reports of the uncomfortable changes that many women experience at menopause, and to try to offer remedies for them.[14]

Yet that same women's group is scathing about the celebrity book *Feminine Forever*, and Wilson's claims that menopause is a disease. 'Menopause has become medicalized', the group claims. 'This approach is not useful to women.'[15] The Washington, DC based network is one of the few high-profile consumer outfits in the US that remains totally independent of pharmaceutical industry funding and support. Acknowledging the need for effective remedies for menopausal symptoms, and for good, accurate information about staying healthy, the group strongly objects to the view that the normal change of life is a deficiency disease. 'Menopause is a natural bodily function, not a disease, and does not automatically require treatment.'[16]

Sociologist Susan Bell has traced the medicalisation of menopause back well before the book *Feminine Forever*—to the 1930s, when a small group of elite medical specialists started to define a woman's change of life as a medical problem and label it as a deficiency disease.[17] Coincidentally, the same group of physicians was researching a new drug called DES—one of the early synthetic forms of the female hormone estrogen.

According to Bell, there were benefits for women from the process of thinking about menopause as a medical condition: complaints of hot flashes (hot flushes), sweats and other symptoms were now legitimised and explained by modern medical science, and in some cases relieved with medical therapies, instead of being dismissed as figments of women's imagination. But for Bell, the downsides of medicalising menopause far outweighed the benefits. Once menopause was defined as a deficiency disease, its treatment with estrogen was not only legitimate, it became an obligation—a line of thinking that echoes today with supermodel Hutton urging women to take an *active interest* in their health. And many readers will already have made another connection here. Just as modern long-term hormone replacement therapy is now being exposed as toxic and harmful, the 1930s drug DES was ultimately found to be a dangerous carcinogen linked to birth defects in the daughters of some of those who took it.[18]

Both doctors and drug companies have much to gain from the construction of menopause as a condition that requires treatment and, as occurs with other conditions, elements within the two groups worked closely together on this one.[19] The perfect illustration is perhaps *Feminine Forever*—the book that helped sell to generations of women the idea that they could treat their disease of *deficiency* with hormone *replacement*. What wasn't clear to many of those who read the late Dr Wilson's bestseller was that his celebrity book tours and his scientific work testing estrogen were in part sponsored by the drug company that manufactured the hormones, Ayerst Laboratories, which ultimately became Wyeth—the same company that sponsored Hutton's celebrity selling nearly four decades later.[20]

While this alliance between parts of the medical profession and drug companies is sometimes referred to as the 'menopause industry', some writers are keen to point out that the process of transforming a woman's change of life into a medical condition is not part of a dark commercial conspiracy. Rather, there is a complex interplay of images and ideas back and forth between society and the world of medicine, fed by deep-seated and widespread anxieties about ageing, femininity and sexuality.[21] While there may be no conspiracy here, this does not stop critics from calling for a halt to what they see as medicine encroaching way too far into ordinary life—and taking too much power away from ordinary people as a result. Two researchers, Susan Ferguson and Carla Parry, recently argued there was an urgent need to 'demedicalize the language and experience of menopause', and describe and understand it as a natural and healthy process.[22]

Groups like the National Women's Health Network see themselves as doing exactly that—advocating a view of menopause as a natural process, at the same time as exposing the marketing campaigns that reinforce the idea of a disease of deficiency or loss.[23] The group's director of programs and policy is Harvard graduate Amy Allina—a strong critic of the marketing of menopause.[24] She says Wyeth's campaign featuring Hutton 'plays off the celebrity worship in this country'. Allina boasts an extraordinary collection of drug ads including Hutton's *Parade* appearance that come in very handy whenever she speaks publicly about the way menopause has been sold, and is still being sold to women. 'We use the ads to show how drug companies expand the market for HRT,' she says. 'They all promote the idea that there is something wrong with women's bodies, there's something wrong with getting older, and these drugs are going to fix you.'

'This wasn't a change, it was a catastrophe', says a middle-aged woman in one ad from a medical magazine of the 1970s. Another features a large close-up photo of the joyless face of a very depressed woman, with three words printed starkly beside her in bold type: Estrogen Deficient Woman. That ad urges the physician to Treat Her With Premarin, and Keep Her On Premarin, the Wyeth drug that would become one of the biggest-selling pills of all time. Looking over the ads with Allina in her downtown office, one doesn't know whether to laugh or cry.

While company advertisements were urging physicians to Keep Her On Premarin, early studies were already suggesting women taking the drugs were at an increased risk of endometrial cancer. Public controversy over the use of hormones was growing, and in fact it helped create the very network where Amy Allina works today, a quarter-century later. Following those initial cancer findings, a second drug called progestogen (or progestin) was added to estrogen, to make a combined form of hormone replacement therapy, sold by Wyeth as the popular Prempro with the promise of being safer than estrogen alone.

By the late 1980s and into the 1990s millions of women worldwide would start taking this combination hormone replacement therapy—or HRT—promoted on the basis of evidence suggesting that not only could it help relieve symptoms, but that in the long term it might reduce a woman's risk of bone fracture, heart disease, and cognitive decline.[25] Essentially HRT would be seen as the elixir of life.

Much of that evidence was from the beginning weak scientifically, and many of the promises would later prove utterly false. Yet the fiction that HRT was a panacea was reinforced at company-sponsored medical meetings and scientific conferences all over the world, including the international menopause congress held in Sydney's famous harbour one springtime in the mid-1990s.[26] Not only did industry heavily sponsor the congress, individual companies, including Wyeth, were able to fund almost half of the scientific sessions, just as the maker of antidepressants helped fund the psychiatrist meeting in New York. On each afternoon of the four-day conference, the symposia were all drug company funded, including a Wyeth session on brain function and hormone replacement therapy. To help the international delegates understand the latest science about menopause they were also offered a sumptuous smorgasbord of Sydney social engagements, including trips to the celebrity landmark the Sydney Opera House and romantic harbour cruises. Post-congress tours explored the tropical rainforest, the Great Barrier Reef, and Uluru.

While some of the thought-leaders at Sydney Harbour that year were still singing the praises of hormone replacement therapy for the menopause, and organising or attending conferences sponsored by drug makers, others were offering much more sober assessments of the state of the existing evidence. That same year as the Sydney conference, two doctors in the United Kingdom published a letter in a medical journal strongly questioning the ability of long-term HRT to reduce a woman's risk of heart disease, and suggesting much safer options might include more exercise, a healthier diet and stopping smoking. 'The menopause is a normal physiological state', they wrote, 'not a disease'.[27]

At the time of that Sydney meeting, combined hormone replacement therapy had been widely used since the 1980s, yet it was not until 1998 that a rigorous top-quality study, called the HERS trial, actually assessed its long-term risks and benefits.[28] Until then, these drugs were being taken by women who were essentially unwitting participants in a giant uncontrolled global experiment.

The HERS trial was a particularly significant landmark because it was among the first of what's called a *randomised controlled trial* of these drugs—the form of study that is now considered a gold standard in science for evaluating how well a treatment works. It might sound like an awkward scientific term, but a randomised controlled trial is a relatively simple yet very powerful way to test drugs or other treatments.

A group of people are randomly divided into two groups.

One group is given the drug, and the other group, called the control group, is given a placebo or dummy pill. Then at the end of the trial the health of both groups is compared.[29] In the HERS trial, a group of almost 3000 older women who already had some form of heart disease were randomly divided into two groups—one group received combined estrogen plus progestin—HRT—while the control group received a placebo. The trial was run by researchers at the University of California, San Francisco, and funded by Wyeth. Its results were startling.

Researchers found that after four years, the group of women taking the drug had done no better than the group who were taking the placebo. The drug had failed to prevent any heart attacks—contrary to a lot of what women had been led to understand for a decade or more. More worrying still, in the first year of the study, a slightly higher number of women had had heart attacks in the group taking hormone replacement therapy.[30] Before this, the studies purporting to show that the drugs reduced the chance of heart attacks were mainly *observational studies*—rather than the more reliable randomised controlled trials.[31] But despite this frightening new evidence about a popular medicine, coming from a top-quality trial, the HERS study received remarkably little public attention—and certainly no celebrity endorsements.[32]

In fact, rather than focus people's attention on the important new scientific findings about HRT's lack of long-term effectiveness, in that same year, just a few months before the publication of the HERS trial results, Wyeth unleashed a worldwide campaign to remind women and their doctors of the dangers of 'estrogen loss' at the menopause. Inflaming fears about the disease would serve to counter what Wyeth marketers knew would be growing fears about its drugs.

Wyeth wrote to physicians across the US, not to warn of the mounting concerns about HRT, but to advise them of a new patient education campaign designed primarily to 'educate women about all the consequences of estrogen loss at menopause, and the different, sometimes serious, effects it can have on their bodies'.[33] The second aim of the campaign, according to the Wyeth letter, was to encourage women to see their health care provider 'to learn more about menopause and . . . estrogen loss'. The excerpt from the patient education material that was attached to the letter to doctors featured the sketched image of a naked woman surrounded by the frightening array of threats to her health associated with 'estrogen loss': Alzheimer's, heart attacks, etc . . . virtually the same list that appeared surrounding the image of supermodel Hutton in the *Parade* advertisement.

The letter to doctors is important not only because it reveals Wyeth's growing commercial need to reinforce public fears about the menopause, but also because it sheds light on the shared interests of doctors and drug companies. A well-funded 'awareness- raising' campaign that urges women to see their health care providers about a natural event they will all experience is clearly going to be good for the business of doctors, as well as drug companies.

Like many modern marketing campaigns, Wyeth's new wave of promotion was global, and eventually reached the shores of distant Australia around the same time Lauren Hutton was adorning the front cover of *Parade* magazine. In Australia the marketing of menopause at the dawn of the new millennium would become a textbook case of selling sickness.

At two minutes past two one afternoon in mid-July 2000, a facsimile arrived at the Sydney newsroom of an influential national newspaper.[34] Like dozens of faxes that arrive in newsrooms around the world every day, this one was from a global public relations firm, advising journalists of the latest important piece of health news. This fax was from the Manhattan-based Hill & Knowlton, announcing the launch of a new national awareness campaign about menopause 'devised by a group of experts' from the Australasian Menopause Society. As part of the campaign, the fax explained, the Australian experts had developed a free information booklet for patients, and a series of consumer seminars would soon be held around the nation.

This Aussie campaign was no small affair. A week after the fax, newspapers ran advertisements encouraging women to attend seminars with medical experts talking about the consequences of 'estrogen loss', and what to do about it, at towns and cities across the country.[35] Like the press release, the newspaper ads featured the name and logo of the Australasian Menopause Society.

What both the faxed release and the newspaper ads failed to mention was that the US-based Wyeth was funding the Australian campaign, and it was part of the company's global marketing effort to boost sales of HRT—the drug regime soon to be hit by a hurricane of bad news. Contrary to the suggestions in the Hill & Knowlton press release, the Australian experts from the menopause society did not devise the so-called 'educational materials' being distributed to the public. Drafts of the materials, including the patient information booklet, had come from Wyeth and its PR team, Hill & Knowlton, before being revised and signed off by the Australian experts—a fact admitted months later by the menopause society president.[36]

At least one of the key images in the supposedly independent patient information booklet—notably the sketch of the naked female—was lifted directly from the Wyeth ads running at the time in the United States. Similarly, it listed the now familiar health threats to women at the menopause: Alzheimer's disease, heart attacks, and so on. The front page of the booklet featured the name and logo of the Australasian Menopause Society, and while Wyeth's funding was revealed in tiny print on the back page, its role in developing and distributing the bookle and orchestrating the wider 'awareness-raising' campaign was not disclosed.

The company-funded patient booklet distributed to Australian women in 2000 stressed the many purported 'dangers' of menopause, yet it failed to mention the latest evidence about the dangers of Wyeth's HRT. Under the section about the benefits of HRT, the booklet stated that observational studies suggested the drugs reduced the risk of heart disease. It did not reveal that one of the first top-quality randomised controlled trials, the HERS trial, had suggested the drugs had no such benefit. Yet the HERS trial results had by then been known for two years. Similarly, the booklet totally failed to inform women of the well-proven risk of blood clots associated with the use of these drugs.[37]

Here was another model example of astro-turfing, the use of corporate money to try to create the appearance of a grassroots campaign. In this case, biased and unbalanced marketing materials were signed off by so-called Australian experts and dressed up as independent patient information. Yet again marketing masquerading as education. And what's worse, the web of company sponsorship was hidden in some of the campaign's dealings with the media and the public. Perhaps most importantly, despite clearly misleading materials being promoted to the public about one of the biggest-selling drugs of all time, virtually no one within the medical establishment would bat an eyelid, and no one within the health authorities would take any action to hold those responsible accountable.

What made that campaign even more misleading was that early findings from the much bigger and far more important study were by then also ringing alarm bells about HRT. The timing here is critical. In mid-2000, as Wyeth's latest wave of marketing was washing around the world, capturing the front cover of *Parade* magazine with its paid celebrity Lauren Hutton and flooding Australia with supposedly independent materials, the first frightening findings were already starting to surface from the enormous randomised controlled trial set up almost a decade earlier by the US federal government. It was called the Women's Health Initiative, and its findings would turn established medical wisdom on its head.

The HERS trial, published in 1998, had been conducted among women who already experienced some form of heart disease. But the Women's Health Initiative was the first large, long-term trial of the hormone drugs among *healthy* women. And it was much bigger, involving more than 16 000 women, making its findings far more relevant to a broad range of women. The US National Institutes of Health had launched it in the early 1990s, following pressure for such a rigorous trial from women's groups like the National Women's Health Network. The US taxpayer was funding it and Wyeth was providing the pills.

In early 2000, before Wyeth even kicked off its Australian campaign, the researchers running that giant Women's Health Initiative trial had written an extraordinary letter to the thousands of women taking part. The letter informed them that the study participants taking the combined version of HRT were in fact experiencing slightly more 'heart attacks, strokes and blood clots' than those women taking the placebo—or dummy pill.[38] This was an historic finding—backing up what the HERS trial had found two years earlier—and seeming to contradict much of what was widely believed within the medical world. The increase was only slight, and it was hoped that over time, as the trial continued, it might disappear. But it was still cause for major concern, given that the drugs were supposed to be reducing women's risks, not increasing them. For women taking part in the trial this must have been alarming news, particularly because as part of the trial design they were not even aware whether they were taking the real drugs or the placebo.

Ultimately, those increased risks associated with the drugs did not disappear. Two years later the trial was stopped early because hormone replacement therapy was found to be doing more harm than good. In mid-2002, the first results of the Women's Health Initiative were published in the *Journal of the American Medical Association*, sparking front-page headlines around the world.[39] A small benefit in terms of reduced risk of fractures and colon cancer was outweighed by increased risks of heart attack, stroke, blood clots and breast cancer.[40]

For every hundred women taking combined hormone replacement therapy long term, the drugs were *causing* one extra serious adverse event—including heart attacks and strokes.[41] Rather than preventing heart disease, the drugs were causing it. Among the older women in the trial, over five years the drugs doubled the risk of developing 'probable dementia', from roughly 1 per cent to 2 per cent.[42] Rather than prevent Alzheimer's, the drugs appeared to be causing more of it. Apart from the slight reductions in fractures and colon cancer, the long-term health benefits of these drugs simply did not exist. The promise to fix *hormone loss* with *hormone replacement*, the very basis of Wyeth's award-winning celebrity campaigns, had proved utterly false.

What's more, the claims that the drugs alleviated many of the symptoms associated with the menopause—the reason many women start therapy—were also thrown into some degree of doubt when further findings from that same trial were released. As one part of the huge Women's Health Initiative, the researchers had tested how well HRT improved quality of life. They looked at effects on general health, vitality, mental health, and sexual satisfaction. After three years of treatment they found there were 'no significant benefits in terms of any quality-of-life outcomes'. However, among a subset of those in the study, the younger women, aged 50–54, who experienced moderate to severe symptoms, the drugs offered some benefit with hot flashes (hot flushes) and sleeping problems.[43] Importantly, there is a strong body of good evidence that these drugs are very effective in reducing the frequency and severity of hot flashes (hot flushes) for many women.[44]

These extraordinary findings have brought a mix of shock and disbelief, and forced many physicians to face the fact that their beliefs about the long-term health benefits of hormone replacement therapy were based on flawed science, and were sustained in part with the help of celebrity awareness-raising campaigns funded by the drug makers. However, some company-funded medical groups have been particularly slow to acknowledge the new scientific reality. A full two years after the release of the groundbreaking HERS trial in 1998 that found no heart benefits for women taking HRT, the influential American College of Obstetricians and Gynecologists was still recommending that women take HRT to 'reduce the risk of cardiovascular disease'.[45] Similarly, the results of the Women's Health Initiative have been criticised by many researchers as being flawed, despite its rigorous quality and enormous size.

Some observers like Amy Allina believe there has been a concerted campaign to try to minimise the impact of these two important studies on both public understanding and doctors' prescribing habits. She points out that company-funded medical groups are trying to suggest the Women's Health Initiative results are of limited relevance, particularly to younger women. She worries that good science is again being undermined by marketing. Certainly it is the case that our knowledge about the risks and benefits of HRT, like all scientific knowledge, is evolving, and it is important to place the findings of these latest studies in the context of all the relevant data. But that said, few unbiased observers would question the assertion that the publicly funded Women's Health Initiative is one of the biggest and the best trials so far conducted in this field. Despite the criticisms of that study, and the ongoing defence of the drugs from those who have long championed them, the rates of prescriptions for HRT have fallen dramatically since 2002.[46]

Ironically, as the dangers of hormone replacement therapy have become better known, and rates of prescriptions of HRT have fallen—in spite of the concerted campaign to defend the drug—other companies selling different medicines or alternative therapies have attempted to muscle in on the 'menopause market', often also enlisting stars to help out. In one case celebrity broker Amy Doner Schachtel helped hire Cybill Shepherd to raise awareness about menopause on behalf of an Australian company that makes a popular soy-derived supplement.[47]

'A partnership between a celebrity and a brand has an intangible sort of magic,' said a senior marketing executive recently, offering tips to her peers in the pharmaceutical industry.[48] One tip was to have celebrities appear on talk shows or do media interviews, rather than straight advertising. Why? Because the 'great advantage over advertising is that the airtime is practically free, and there is no fair balance to worry about'.[49] The now infamous endorsement of estrogen in the *Parade* magazine article made no mention of the side effects of the drug, presumably because there was no fair balance to worry about.[50] Neither did the article mention the celebrity's paid work for the company which markets estrogen.

'This is an outrageous circumventing of public health protections,' says Allina, arguing that in her view, if paid celebrities appear in public hawking a disease or a drug, without disclosing their links to the manufacturer, it's equivalent to 'outright deception'. Yet celebrities being paid by drug companies have been under no clear regulatory requirements to disclose accurate information about the nature of the condition or the therapy they might be promoting. Similarly, there are no legal requirements for them, or for the media outlets in which they appear, to disclose the link with the drug manufacturer, even though the public may sometimes be misled into thinking the star is independent.[51] Until the health regulators awake from their dreamy slumbers, these star-studded marketing campaigns will continue to dazzle consumers around the world, and the complexity of the science will continue to get lost under the bright lights.

For many observers, the appropriation of a woman's change of life is the perfect illustration of the dramatic transformation of a normal human experience into a treatable medical condition. The stars in this drama now include 'A list' celebrities with strong ties to the drug companies. As we'll see, they also include some of the world's best-known patient groups.

# Partnering with patients

*Attention deficit disorder*

The rolling green fairways of the Norbeck Country Club shimmer in the welcome sunshine of a long overdue spring. A good hour's drive from the sirens and stress of downtown Washington, DC, the manicured private golf course sits amidst the wealthy suburbs of the state of Maryland. The silence here, like the surrounding affluence, is striking. Being May, the quiet is interrupted by the occasional bursts of birdsong, and on this particular Monday afternoon, by the gentle sounds of middle-aged male golfers teeing off at the start of the annual CHADD charity golf classic. CHADD stands for Children and Adults with Attention-Deficit/Hyperactivity Disorder—the energetic patient advocacy group that now boasts 15 000 members and 200 affiliates across the United States.

A scene of such tranquillity might seem an unlikely setting for an ADD charity event, but really the location is perfect. White suburbs like those around the country club are amongst the healthiest and wealthiest places on earth, yet they are also considered the centre of the ADD epidemic. In a neighbouring state, in some school years, up to 20 per cent of young white boys are now taking speed-like stimulants for their ADD.[1] In other parts of the world, such as Perth on Australia's west coast, rapidly rising rates of drug use have also generated great concern.

Growing global controversy about both the nature and extent of attention deficit disorder has not slowed the rapid growth in the use of ADD drugs. According to those who study this phenomenon, in the decade from 1990 production of the drug Ritalin rose almost 800 per cent. By 2000, with under 5 per cent of the world's population, Americans were consuming 80 per cent of the stimulants manufactured worldwide.[2] That same year a leading scientific journal revealed a dramatic increase in the prescription of these drugs to toddlers.[3] But despite growing disquiet, medication use among kids shows no signs of abating, as drug companies aggressively market new medicines to rival the ever-popular Ritalin. As with many other conditions, much of that marketing promotes the disease itself, not just the drugs, and who better to help out with such 'awareness-raising' than company-sponsored patient advocacy groups.

Partnering with patient groups has become a key element of marketing strategies for every major medical condition, and with virtually every major drug company. A survey from Britain estimated that two-thirds of global health charities and patient groups now accept support from drug or device manufacturers, though it is often hard to know exactly how much they receive.[4] With ADD, as with other conditions, company-funded consumer groups provide a service to their sponsors by helping to paint a picture of an underdiagnosed medical disorder best treated with drugs and by giving a human face to that disorder.

Unlike many other groups around the world, to its credit

CHADD clearly discloses exactly how much it gets from drug companies. It receives almost $700 000 annually, which is just under one-fifth of its total income of around $3 million.[5] There is little doubt that CHADD, and groups like it, can play a valuable role in providing support to thousands of members and their families. Yet at the same time it is also providing a valuable service to its drug company sponsors. In this case, helping to promote and reinforce a particular view of this controversial disorder.

The celebrity on hand at the CHADD charity golf classic in Maryland was Johnny Holliday, a high-profile sports broadcaster on radio and television in the US, known for his coverage of the Olympic Games. He had come to the country club to play a round of golf and act as master of ceremonies for the evening's celebrations. Explaining that he lived not too far away, Holliday said he was happy to help out with the event for free, because his daughter had once suffered with ADD, discovered in her case in eighth grade. 'I know the frustration she went through and her parents went through,' he told a reporter from the *British Medical Journal*.[6] As for drugs, Holliday said, she had only taken her medication intermittently during school time, mainly to help with tests. 'It really did the job,' he said, before jumping back into his golf cart and adding with fatherly pride that she had just graduated from college with honours.

Few would argue there are some children who have severe and debilitating symptoms of hyperactivity, inattention, or impulsiveness, who may benefit greatly from a medical label, medical care and medication. But there is much less agreement about how best to describe or deal with the difficulties faced by vast numbers of children who can't sit still, or who drift off in class. Because of the uncertainty and disagreement about the nature of this disorder, commonly cited estimates of the numbers of children suffering

ADD range widely, from less than 1 per cent to one in ten kids.[7] As with depression, there is much scientific uncertainty about whether these difficulties are primarily due to biological and chemical problems in the brain, or are the result of a complex interplay of physical, social, cultural and economic factors.

Mountains of scientific research have been published on these questions, but there remain strongly conflicting views on what all that research actually means. Some scientists insist there is now a consensus—that attention deficit disorder is a widespread and proven biological disorder, and that the debate is over.[8] Others, publishing in exactly the same scientific journals, insist the debate is very much alive. In stark contrast, these researchers claim there is great uncertainty about how to define this disorder, there is no reliable medical test for it, and no strong evidence that it is biologically determined.[9] Even the National Institutes of Health in the US, one of the biggest biomedical research houses in the world, concludes that the causes of the condition remain speculative, and there is not yet enough evidence to say with certainty that ADD is a brain disorder.[10]

It's obvious that viewing ADD as a biochemical disorder greatly benefits the companies selling chemicals that purport to fix it. Less obviously, drug companies are using a multitude of marketing tactics to influence the wider public debate, to make sure that particular view dominates. As we will see, one powerful form of that influence flows directly through partnerships with patient groups like CHADD, whose high profile is due in no small part to the longstanding supply of funds from industry.

It's clear that accepting sponsorship doesn't mean a group's credibility is compromised or that it is crudely told what to do. But it's also clear that drug companies tend to fund patient groups whose public positions are in tune with their own marketing messages, in order to help amplify those messages and make them resonate. Despite the widespread scientific uncertainty and legitimate ongoing debate about ADD, both CHADD and its drug company partners promote the condition as a common 'neurobiological' disorder to be treated primarily with drugs.[11]

Back at the country club, the lead sponsor of the CHADD charity golf classic was a drug company called Shire, whose name appeared on several strategically placed signs in and around the club on that sunny Monday in May, and on a giant banner dominating the banquet room where Johnny Holliday was to work as volunteer master of ceremonies. A relatively recent entrant to the pharmaceutical industry, the global company Shire boasts headquarters in London and Philadelphia, and it sells more than half a billion dollars of an amphetamine called Adderall every year.

According to a presentation that its chief executive officer, Matthew Emmens, gave for potential investors a few months before the golf classic, the company had high hopes its sales figures would grow exponentially in the coming years.[12] One of the slides presented by the CEO at a merchant bank meeting in New York featured a graph of Adderall sales, surging from just $10 million in 1996 to almost $520 million six years later. This single amphetamine product constitutes more than 40 per cent of the company's total revenues.

Another slide from the same presentation displayed a pyramid representing the marketplace as Shire saw it. The pyramid was divided into different layers representing the different categories of people that the drug company was seeking to influence. In the top two layers of the pyramid was the small elite group of medical decision-makers—the thought-leaders—that Shire was working with through its sponsored education efforts and other strategies. At the bottom of the pyramid, in the biggest layer, were the great bulk of patients Shire was attempting to influence with direct-to-consumer advertisements. In the middle of the pyramid was a layer titled 'Medical Societies' and 'Patient Advocacy Groups'.

Not only does Shire fund CHADD events like the golf classic, it is also a sponsor of the group's annual conference, and it supports the group's magazine, *Attention*,[13] which is distributed to thousands of patients, families and physicians. So where does Shire sit on the scientific controversy about the nature and extent of ADD? There is no debate, no controversy, no question: this is a 'neurobiological disorder'[14] affecting between 'three and seven percent of school age children'.[15]

Long before Shire's drug Adderall hit the market, CHADD was set up in Florida by a small group of families and psychologists.[16] Two decades later it is one of the highest profile patient advocacy groups in the US, and perhaps the world. CHADD's massive annual conference now opens with special two-day workshops offering parents CHADD-certified training in how to provide CHADD-approved support and education to other families. The organisation's extensive website declares it a 'success story, inspired by the desire of countless parents to see their children with AD/HD succeed'.[17] Certainly the group has inspired the creation of many similar advocacy outfits in Australia and elsewhere.

While acknowledging there is some degree of scientific uncertainty about causes, CHADD's position is that the disorder 'has a very strong neurological basis'.[18] As for its treatment, while it is seen as important to combine different approaches including talking therapy, according to CHADD, medication is 'the most effective foundation for treatment'.[19] More than an advocacy group, CHADD is akin to a highly energised political or religious organisation. A leading series of articles in the group's magazine *Attention* recently bore the title 'ADHD: Building a social movement'.[20]

Since its beginnings the patient group has built that social movement with support from drug makers and their money. Famously CHADD accepted three-quarters of a million dollars in the early 1990s from Ciba-Geigy, the chemical company that manufactured Ritalin. In the $500-billion world of the prescription drug business, less than a lousy million may not sound like much at all. Yet anyone who has ever tried to run an advocacy group would well appreciate the value of such an investment, particularly in a young organisation still finding its feet.

Tracking the exploding use of Ritalin and other ADD drugs at that time, the US government's Drug Enforcement Administration took a strong interest in the work of this particular group, warning on one occasion that: 'The relationship between Ciba-Geigy and CHADD raises serious concerns about CHADD's motive in proselytizing the use of Ritalin.'[21] Similarly, some of those concerned about soaring rates of drug use have raised alarms about the obvious conflicts of interest such sponsorship carries.

The group's CEO, Dr Clark Ross, declined requests to discuss CHADD's relationship with its pharmaceutical company sponsors. However, clearly sensitive to the appearance of conflicts of interest, the group publicly discloses the full extent of company sponsorship. Moreover, its interactions with industry are governed by a set of 'ethical principles' outlined on its website.[22] The site also shows that the group's revenue comes from multiple sources, with almost half from membership dues and government.

Just like the financial relationships between drug companies and doctors, the links between companies and patient groups can operate in ways that are subtle and complex. Often the partnership is a coming together of like-minded allies, rather than an opportunity for a company to clumsily curry favour with an innocent group of hardworking patient activists. There is often a *confluence of interests* that creates a powerful force in the public debate. The problem is that the public is usually not aware of the way these special partnerships are working to transform public perceptions about diseases and disorders. Perhaps one of the best examples of such a transformation is happening now, before our very eyes: the promotion of a new condition called adult ADD as a major public health problem.

One of the most important messages that the Shire chief imparted to potential investors at the merchant bankers' meeting in New York was that a whole new 'adult market' was about to open up, assuring healthy growth in drug sales for many years to come.[23] In a slide titled 'Adult ADHD', Shire showed estimates that there were 8 million potential adult patients in the US, of which only a tiny fraction were currently being treated. While it wasn't stated explicitly in the slides, potential investors would be well aware that children are only children for a decade or so—the lifespan of an adult's potential drug-taking is much, much longer.

Coincidentally, the same month as the Shire presentation suggesting there may be 8 million potential new adult drug users, CHADD's drug company-sponsored magazine *Attention* ran a feature story entitled 'Dads with ADHD'. About the same time as adult golfers were teeing off for the Shire-sponsored CHADD charity classic, Shire was releasing the results of a survey at the giant American Psychiatric Association congress in

New York, detailing what were described as the devastating emotional difficulties facing millions of adults with ADD.[24] Shire was of course also one of the sponsors of the psychiatrists' congress, setting up a large display in the exhibit area, tastefully decorated with potted palms and fresh white flowers.[25] At the time of these marketing activities, Shire did not even have regulatory approval to promote its drug to adults, though according to the fine print of the CEO's presentation to investors, many doctors were already prescribing its drug for adults 'off label'— contrary to its existing approval which was only for children, but within the bounds of the law.[26]

The first drug company to get the green light for the adult ADD market was not Shire but Lilly, whose ADD drug Strattera sold more than a million prescriptions in its first six months in 2003.[27] Unlike Ritalin and Adderall, Lilly's Strattera is not an amphetamine or stimulant, which means the rules governing its marketing are a little looser.[28] But just like Shire, Lilly also provides funds to CHADD and, just like Shire, its marketing helps sell new ideas about the disorder as well as the drug.

> Distracted? Disorganized? Frustrated? Modern Life or Adult ADD?
> Many adults have been living with Adult attention deficit disorder (Adult ADD) and don't recognize it. Why? because its symptoms are often mistaken for stressful life.[29]
>
> Lilly ad in *US News & World Report*

As the industry's ADD marketing machinery is shifting towards adults, CHADD's too is stressing that ADD can be a lifelong disorder. At CHADD's 2004 annual conference there was a focus on making sure the public understood this to be a 'lifespan' disorder.[30] 'Medications for Adults with ADHD' was even the title of one of the planned presentations.[31] And as it turns out, key drug company sponsors of the conference include Shire, Lilly and Novartis (the company that now makes Ritalin)—who are all competing aggressively for a share of this expanding, and now maturing, market. The Shire advertisement in the CHADD conference program was not particularly subtle in its marketing to adults: 'Already Done with my Homework Dad!' says a cute child in a baseball cap who might be as young as five years old, with the tag line underneath the picture reading, 'Now the whole family has time to learn more about AD/HD!'[32]

What was happening with the ads, the conferences, the surveys and the golf charity event is what some in the industry call the 'branding' of a condition. Vince Parry is the Manhattan-based marketing professional who specialises in helping pharmaceutical companies to 'brand' medical conditions, the way one might brand chewing gum. One of his clients is Lilly.

Expanding on what he calls the 'art of branding a condition' Parry says drug companies will often bring the key players together—the thought-leaders, the local physicians and the patient groups—to help define, refine and brand new conditions. 'By bringing them together, you're fostering a consensus about the condition, about the importance of the condition and about the best possible ways to address the condition.'[33]

For Parry, a common aim in his marketing work for drug companies is 'elevating the importance of an unknown condition'. One example he points to is ADD, previously considered a condition almost exclusively affecting children. 'Recently, there's been a lot of work done realising that adults have it too,' he says. '... people are having the same problems at work as adults as they were as children in schools. So there's been a lot of talk lately about reframing a discussion about that condition to maybe split it up into ... a childhood condition as well as an adult condition. It's raising the level of awareness about something we don't even know we have until we began looking into this further.'[34]

Vince Parry's insights into how pharmaceutical companies help to shape public perceptions about conditions are invaluable, because the strategies are often hidden from public view. Men and women like him with expertise in advertising, marketing and public relations working from chic offices in Manhattan, London, Toronto or Sydney are being paid to fundamentally change the way we think about our bodies, our health and the conditions we supposedly suffer. The pro-drug messages hammered out in these marketing offices are camouflaged as 'awareness-raising' exercises and then transmitted far and wide, through massive advertising campaigns, sponsored medical education, and PR campaigns that generate much media reporting. And integral to many of these 'awareness-raising' activities are company-sponsored patient groups.

In Parry's mind there is little doubt that drug companies take a lead role in what he calls 'branding' conditions. He should know, because he works with them. The more you listen to this industry insider, the more you realise that what companies might describe as awareness-raising activities are really designed to change awareness—in ways that serve the 'marketing needs' of their latest products, as Parry explains it.

> There's a couple of ways that manufacturers of pharmaceuticals and health care products approach someone such as myself or other people in the branding business. It could be a direct request from them saying that, you know, there's a particular condition, you know, such as ADHD for example. And we've identified another aspect of that, we'd like you to help us work with the community and the professional and patient community to come up with a name that

really suits this and come up with a condition that addresses our needs.

In other cases, it happens just as a general discussion that you're having with them about the marketing needs of a particular product ... And it might be something we volunteer and say, 'You know, we think it would be a good idea, instead of going to this complicated process, if we can simplify this aspect of the process. Have you ever thought of taking this condition and branding this particular condition by giving it a name that can be recognised?' So, there are two ways they can engage us.[35]

Just weeks after Parry made those comments, one of America's leading news magazines *US News & World Report* ran a dramatic cover story, under the banner headline 'Adult ADD'.[36] Featuring the face of a beautiful young blue-eyed white woman, the magazine cover story offered readers a scoop on the latest from medical science: 'Living with Adult ADD. New hope for coping with the distraction and anxiety.' The eight-page article inside seemed to pay little attention to the wider scientific controversy about the nature and treatment of ADD, and read more like an excited industry promotion of the next big market than the serious investigative journalism for which the magazine has a well-deserved reputation.

The reigning theory, according to the magazine piece, was that the disorder was caused by 'faulty biochemical communication in the brain'. Four per cent of adults suffer this disorder, said the article, and less than one in four of them know they have it. Medication was deemed so important, according to one quoted expert, it was 'necessary all the time for nearly every aspect of life'. Lilly's new drug for adult ADD, Strattera, was mentioned early on in the article, along with the news that it had achieved sales of $370 million in its first year. A few pages later, the magazine ran a Lilly advertisement for Strattera, which featured a headline strikingly reminiscent of the magazine's front cover: 'Distracted? Disorganized? Frustrated? Modern Life or Adult ADD?'

Like many media articles on medical conditions, the *US News & World Report* piece featured the harrowing personal stories of sufferers, the gritty anecdotes from 'real' people that make journalism live and breathe. And like a lot of media articles, those personal stories were used to reinforce an argument that yet another grave condition remains underdiagnosed and under-treated, essentially the same message being heavily promoted by drug companies and the sponsored patient groups including CHADD, though a view heavily contested by other scientists and researchers around the world. Surprisingly, despite the synchronicity between the magazine article's key arguments and those of CHADD, there was no mention of the group, or any quoted spokespeople in the piece.

One of the important roles of advocacy groups is to serve up patients to media outlets giving them a steady stream of real people, to help reporters craft stories that will impact emotionally on their readers. CHADD explicitly sees part of its role as providing 'physician experts and families dealing with AD/HD for news and feature articles, television segments, or radio interviews'. A quick check with the organisation's media liaison staff revealed CHADD had in fact supplied at least one of the adult patients reported on in the *US News & World Report* story.[37] But the published version of the magazine story had somehow failed to mention that the adult in question also happened to be CHADD's director of public policy.

CHADD's acceptance of drug company funding and its dealings with the media are in some ways just par for the course, when compared to what most other groups are doing. As the global survey of health charities from Britain suggested, around two-thirds of these groups accept industry funds. Similarly, many work in alliance with industry to use the media to promote the need for greater recognition of their particular condition and more resources for treatment. But as Parry the marketing man makes clear, the alliances between companies and patient groups have another purpose, at least for the companies involved: to help change the way the public thinks about medical conditions in order to maximise the sales of medicines. The aim, he says, is to create an inextricable bond between the condition and the drug. And it works. Think ADD and you think medication. And it is for this reason that independent-minded consumer groups like the Amsterdam-based Health Action International believe health advocacy groups should attempt to minimise and even sever their sponsorship ties with health care corporations.[38]

Parry is not the only industry insider who is upfront about the value to industry of these relationships with patient advocates. Another insight comes from the industry magazine *Pharmaceutical Executive*, which published a special report by PR practitioner Teri Cox called 'Forging Alliances, Advocacy Partners'.[39] According to Cox, advocacy groups help companies provide the media with patients for their stories, they help defuse the arguments of industry critics by offering positive messages about drug companies, and they even help influence the decisions of policy-makers and regulators.

Importantly, for Cox, all company activities, including lavish product launches, medical education, and disease awareness campaigns can benefit from having 'respected third party advocates as members of the pharma marketing team'. Note the fact that the patient advocates are described as members of the drug company's 'marketing' team. Accepting commercial sponsorship almost always ties the recipient, whether they like it or not, into the sponsors' marketing machinery.[40]

In her article Cox also describes a fascinating shift in the nature of these alliances in recent years, quoting a senior PR expert from a global drug company. 'Gone are the days when companies just handed out big checks to groups with no discussion afterward,' said the PR expert. 'Now we seek opportunities with groups that not only help them achieve their goals and objectives, but also help us move our business along.'[41] While ADD drug maker Shire has said publicly it gives money to CHADD because the company feels an obligation to do so, there are quite obviously more self-interested motivations as well.[42]

Some drug firms are becoming highly organised about how they record and analyse their alliances with patient groups. One even created a web-based tool to track every event, every funding opportunity, and every key contact person for all of its patient group 'partners', including notes that documented each 'transaction, interaction and activity'. Teri Cox concludes that such a comprehensive strategy is needed to strengthen the alliances with patient advocacy groups at a time when 'the pharma industry needs all the friends it can get'.[43]

Working with groups of patients, in this case parents, to help get the marketing messages out, is not new to the industry, though the alliances may certainly have become more sophisticated and better funded. In the days before CHADD was set up, the promotional tactics of Ritalin maker Ciba-Geigy included presentations to parent–teacher associations and other parent groups, at a time when concerns about increasing rates of drug use were already emerging.[44] A sociology professor writing in the mid-1970s described officials in some states as being alarmed that between 5 and 10 per cent of elementary school children were using medically prescribed amphetamines including Ritalin 'to control their fidgety restlessness or lack of attention in the classroom'.

The professor went on to argue that this was another example of the medicalisation of human problems. 'The increasing tendency to define unpleasant human feelings and troublesome behaviour as a "disease" to be corrected with drugs may serve to (1) diminish pressures to seek more fundamental approaches to the real sources of the drug user's distress, and (2) individualize and depoliticize complex social problems.'[45] The rhetoric may sound a little dated to some but the concerns about medicalisation are more relevant than ever, as both prescription drug use and corporate influence in medicine have grown astronomically in the decades since these observations.

The complex causes of the ADD epidemic are the subjects of many other books and articles and much public debate. One voice in that debate is Dr Lawrence Diller, a pediatrician who practises in an affluent suburb of San Francisco and has written extensively on the topic.[46] Diller had been prescribing stimulants for young boys with hyperactivity for many years, but through the 1990s he started to see a very different candidate for the diagnosis of ADHD: kids across a much wider age range with milder problems and less impairment, often good students simply not meeting their potential.[47] 'I began to wonder if boyhood, at least in my community, had become a disease,' he muses. Comparing rates of stimulant use between different towns and cities, Diller suggests 'the ADHD/Ritalin epidemic appears to be a primarily white middle-upper middle class phenomenon'.[48]

A long-time observer of CHADD and someone who has met with members of its board, Diller feels drug company funding, though influential, hasn't bought fundamental changes in the group's direction. Rather he believes the money has enabled CHADD 'to become a more effective lobbying tool for industry'. In response to arguments put by CHADD that it can accept funding and remain independent, Diller has this to say: 'It's the same thing as the doctors and medical researchers saying we're independent, yet all the studies show money influences research. It's naïve to believe money doesn't have some influence.' While he says there is a spectrum of opinions about the disorder within CHADD, and that at a local level the group can do some good work, on the whole the group's official position is 'way too medication focused and brain based'.[49]

Diller, also an assistant clinical professor at the University of California, San Francisco, does not dismiss the role of neuro-biological causes in severe cases of hyperactivity or impulsiveness, but he argues that economic, social and cultural factors are playing a big role in contributing to the modern epidemic. He points to increasing educational pressures on kids and a growing acceptance in the post-Prozac era that many of life's difficulties are caused by chemical imbalances in the brain. At the same time class sizes have been growing, putting pressures on teachers too, and patient–physician consultation times have been shrinking, reinforcing the move to the quick fix.[50]

The final key factor Diller identifies as highly significant: a change to federal disability laws in the US, which meant that if a child had a diagnosis of ADD, it could lead to special edu-cational services for that child at school. As it happens, CHADD makes much of the fact that a diagnosis of ADD can bring special help at school, and nowadays, for adults, special help in the workplace.[51]

And while all that has been going on, psychiatrists have been quietly broadening the definition of ADD that appears in their manual, the *Diagnostic & Statistical Manual of Mental Disorders* (DSM), drawing in more and more children and adults and thus widening the pool of potential patients. Lists of 'symptoms' that appear in the DSM and overlap with very common behaviours—including things like 'often talks excessively', 'often does not seem to listen', 'is often forgetful'—make it easy to understand concerns that many ordinary kids might be ending up with a medical label.[52] Some researchers have actually done studies comparing the definitions, looking at how many kids each definition defines as sick. The results of this research are stunning.

One American study found that when the definition in the psychiatrists' manual in 1980 was compared with the definition published in 1987, 50 per cent more children received a diagnosis of ADD under the newer definition.[53] The same kids, a new definition; many more of them classified as sick. A study in Germany compared the 1980 definition to the 1994 definition, and found the numbers of children receiving the diagnosis of ADD jumped more than 60 per cent.[54]

Of course, the elephant in the room in this story is the fact that amphetamines like Ritalin can have positive effects on attention and focus not only for kids or adults diagnosed with this disorder, but for virtually everyone—even horses—according to Dr Judith Rapoport, a senior ADD researcher at the NIH. One of the many scientists working for public institutions who are convinced ADD is a neurobiological disorder, Rapoport is currently involved in an ongoing long-term study looking at the brain development of those diagnosed with the condition. More than twenty years ago it was Rapoport who did some groundbreaking research showing amphetamines had effects in normal kids as well as those who were hyperactive—a finding that has stood the test of time and is still cited today in the scientific literature. 'These drugs have the same effect in healthy and ADHD kids. Amphetamines seem to improve anyone's attention—whether they have a problem or not. Whatever the task is, you do it better. Football players and racehorses have known this for a long time.'[55]

Many proponents of the notion that ADD is a widespread and severe neurobiological disorder have used the fact that children do better on stimulants as confirmation that a particular diagnosis is valid and correct. But evidence suggesting stimulants can help pretty well everyone rather undercuts that argument.[56] This self-reinforcing—but sometimes false—confirmation may be another explanation for the continuing explosion in the numbers of people being diagnosed and using drugs. In the opening year of the twenty-first century, sales of stimulants for ADD were among the fastest growing categories of drugs.[57] In the first three years of this century the use of ADD drugs by kids under five jumped 50 per cent.[58] And now, with the marketing of adult ADD, those increases in the rates of drug use are set to soar much, much higher.

Just a few months after the *US News & World Report* cover story, Shire's drug Adderall was approved for adult ADD, and the company excitedly announced its marketing campaign was ready to roll immediately.[59] The marketing was certainly immediate, and some of it was to take a fascinating form. Two weeks after the approval, the American Medical Association bombarded medical journalists with a series of email alerts, advising them to attend important media briefings. The powerful AMA publishes some of the world's leading medical journals, and for many journalists it is a highly respected source of news.

The first AMA briefing was specifically about ADD— and two of the key topics to be discussed were adult ADD and medications. The sponsor of this AMA media briefing was Shire, who supplied the AMA with an 'unrestricted educational grant' for the event. The second event was the AMA's science writers' conference, billed as bringing journalists news about the 'most urgent medical issues' of the day. At the top of the list of topics in the email alert was ADD. The keynote speaker on ADD was a paid consultant for Shire, who had also done work for five other drug companies.[60] If the promotion of adult ADD continues as aggressively as it has started, and the lifelong drug use that it encourages occurs, exploding use of these pills will continue to make Shire shareholders very, very happy for a long time to come.

What long-term value the drugs might offer those actually taking them is less clear. Many of the clinical trials have been relatively short and poorly run, though several good long-term trials are currently under way.[61] But whatever the outcomes of those studies, notwithstanding the importance of offering care to children and adults with severe and debilitating problems, there appears to be another fundamental distortion of our health priorities at work here. In the era of the global AIDS crisis, ADD is surely not as serious a public health issue as company-sponsored patient groups like CHADD claim, and it is certainly not one of the most 'urgent medical issues' as communications about the company-sponsored AMA meetings have claimed. Without blaming or judging anyone, it can be argued that the ADD epidemic has enabled millions of families from Perth to Providence to supply a safe dose of speed to their kids, often, to help them do better at school. Similarly, any reasonable assessment would suggest the epidemic is not due simply to faulty biochemistry, but rather to a much more complex mix of many factors—including the well-funded 'condition branding' designed by Vince Parry and his colleagues in Manhattan.

In this age of globalisation, is it conceivable that we in the wealthy developed world will continue to spend billions every year diagnosing and medicating children whose symptoms include *often fidgets with hands or feet* and prescribing lifelong speed to adults who *drum their fingers*,[62] when each year millions of children and adults just across our borders will die early from preventable and treatable life-threatening diseases? Surely this is one obscenity too many.

Yet it is not just with controversial conditions like ADD where we are arguably squandering billions medicalising and treating the symptoms of normal life. With much more established 'diseases' like high blood pressure there are very lively debates about whether this is a condition at all, or simply one risk factor for future illness, and whether too many people are being given a medical label, and an expensive drug, when for some avoiding both may be much better for their health and the public's purse.

# 5

# Making risks into medical conditions

*High blood pressure*

The parking area is full at the town hall centre in White Rock, a tiny coastal retirement town south of Vancouver. White Rock is where Canadian seniors come to live out their days amid beautiful mountain and ocean scenery, close to snow and surf. While most Canadians are chattering through the frosty winter in the east, retired boomers living in White Rock brag that they live in one of the few spots in the country where they can go downhill skiing in the morning and salmon fishing in the afternoon.

On this mild evening, as the last stragglers of mostly retired people take their seats, two men are engaging in a little playful banter as they set up their overhead projector. The taller, younger one, James McCormack, is a doctor of pharmacy. He's cracking a few jokes at the expense of his sidekick, Dr Bob Rangno, a medical doctor who specialises in medications. Rangno and McCormack have driven here from Vancouver, where they are members of the Therapeutics Initiative at the University of British Columbia, a group that works to educate physicians, pharmacists—and sometimes the general public—about the best ways to use prescription drugs.[1]

Tonight's lecture is about the frightening subject of heart disease, but the full house of senior citizens is in for a treat. Unlike a lot of what they normally hear, this presentation is not designed to inflame their fears but, rather, to better inform them. One of the first things they learn is that having high blood pressure, as many of them do, is not a disease in its own right, but instead it is one factor than can raise their risk of future heart attacks and strokes. Like cholesterol, blood pressure attracts a lot of attention, because it can be easily modified with drugs.

In the coming hours, a sense of surprise and anger will sweep the room more than once, as many of these seniors will for the first time start to get a realistic sense of how much their blood pressure actually increases their chances of future heart disease, and by how much drugs can decrease those chances. Many will head off into the night feeling that high blood pressure—or hypertension as it is called medically—is not the bogeyman they once thought it was. As Dr Bob says to James while they are still warming up the crowd, 'As I always tell my patients, high blood pressure is better than no blood pressure at all.'

Interest in hypertension runs high among the elderly, because according to current definitions almost all of them have it. Under recent US guidelines, more than 40 million Americans are categorised as having 'high blood pressure' and an estimated 90 per cent of those over the age of 55 will someday have it if they don't already.[2] As with other conditions, the definition of what constitutes high blood pressure is regularly revised, and the notch on the dial that describes 'high' seems to creeep lower over time.

With lower levels for what is considered to be 'high' blood pressure, vast new numbers of otherwise healthy people are given the medical label of having 'hypertension', are considered 'at risk' of heart disease, and are being pushed in the direction of drugs. These ageing Canadian boomers and others like them around the world make up what the pharmaceutical industry hopes will soon be a $40 billion global market in blood pressure medicines.[3] The first part of McCormack and Rangno's often-delivered talk is designed to help people understand some of the basic statistical tricks used to sell those medicines to otherwise healthy people.

James McCormack always starts his presentation with a scenario like this.[4]

'Now imagine that you were just told by your doctor that you have this "risk factor" for cardiovascular disease, maybe it's something like high blood pressure or high cholesterol.

'We have a drug that will treat this risk factor, it has no side effects and its cost is covered by a plan. I am going to present you the results of three different studies and I want to ask you if you would be willing to take this drug every day for the next five years based on the results. There is no right or wrong answer—it is your decision.'

At this point James normally projects this overhead:

**Would you take a drug every day for five years if it ...?**
A. Lowered your chance of having a heart attack by 33%?
B. Lowered your chance of having a heart attack from 3% down to 2%, a difference of 1%?
C. Saved one person in a hundred from having a heart attack but there is no way to know in advance who that one person will be?[5]

'Okay, so how many would take the drug given the results of the first study, study A?' James asks. About 80–90 per cent of the seniors in the audience usually thrust their hands into the air.

'In scenarios B and C?' Around 20 per cent of the people in the audience raise their hands.

James and Bob pause to let this sink in before they deliver the punchline.

'I hate to tell you this but you've been fooled because what we've just told you is the exact same study results reported to you three different ways.'

A collective 'huh?' often rises from the crowd. Some of the seniors roll their eyes in disbelief. Some are annoyed or confused. But by this stage in the presentation many of them are normally sitting on the edge of their seats. They all want to hear more.

Bob takes the mike from James.

'Okay, so here's the trick, but don't feel bad, we fool doctors with this all the time. You see, if your risk of a heart attack is 3 per cent to start with, I could give you a pill to reduce that by 33 per cent, down to 2 per cent. See? Two is *33 per cent less* than three. But it is also a 1 per cent difference. As even mathematically challenged people like James know, if you have 3 per cent and you go down to 2 per cent, that's a 1 per cent difference. Simple, right?'

There are often still a few frowns scattered among the audience.

James continues. 'Let's put it this way, instead of your risk of a heart attack, let's talk about buying a dress. Let's say the regular price for a dress is $300 and it's on sale for 33 per cent off, what do you pay?'

'Two hundred dollars,' several people in the audience shout back.

'That's right, and if the dress was only $3, and that was 33 per cent off, what would you pay? Two dollars, right?'

By now, when Bob and James scan the sea of grey hair in front of them they can usually see the audience starting to get it. 'Jeez, you caught on more quickly than the doctors we presented this to earlier today!' Bob adds with a chuckle.

The reason this revelation is so important is that drugs are often promoted using this statistical gimmick that exaggerates benefits. Advertisements to doctors and patients will claim, for example, that a drug offers a 33 per cent reduction in the risk of heart attack, without explaining that in actual fact you may have to take the medicine for five years in order to lower your risks from 3 per cent to 2 per cent. As Bob and James explain each time they give their lecture, in *relative* terms that is a 33 per cent reduction. In *absolute* terms that's a 1 per cent reduction, from 3 per cent to 2 per cent. Several studies have shown that people are less likely to take a drug if they are given the absolute figures. Sadly, many media stories about medications also tend to use the more exaggerated version, and simply fail to provide the more informative absolute figures.[6]

In some ways the promotion of these medicines has to exaggerate their benefits, because they are often being targeted at generally healthy people who may feel there is nothing actually wrong with them. With high blood pressure the pool of potential patients who are otherwise healthy has recently been expanded. The new official US guidelines have listed a new category of illness called 'prehypertension'.[7] According to those guidelines, anyone with a systolic blood pressure of 120 to 139 or a diastolic of 80 to 89 'should be considered as pre-hypertensive', and therefore require lifestyle changes—though some observers see drug use increasing as a result.[8]

Under the latest version of the guidelines, published in 2003, the number of people classified as having a medical condition has increased by an estimated 50 million, further growing the potential markets for high blood pressure medications.[9] And because the desired targets for blood pressure are now so low, if you accept these new guidelines many people may need to be taking multiple medications to get their blood pressure down to those target levels.

But some specialists in the field are not so enthusiastic about the aggressive push to get everyone's numbers lower and lower. A strong supporter of the role of medications, Wake Forest University's Professor Curt Furberg is increasingly troubled by the lowering of the definition of 'high' blood pressure, which has over time redefined millions more healthy people as sick. With a sense of exasperation in his voice he says the newest guidelines have 'gone too far'.[10] As for the level at which he considers a person to have an 'illness', Dr Furberg says that he personally doesn't believe it a good idea to treat someone with a blood pressure of 160 who was otherwise younger, healthy and at low risk. This highly respected heart specialist takes the view that blood pressure is just one measurement, and one risk factor, and that you have to look at the totality of a person's risks, 'whether they smoke or exercise, their cholesterol levels and so on, and then decide when and if the patient needs treatment'. But, he adds, 'under the new guidelines you'd have to treat someone at 160'.[11] More broadly, Furberg worries that medicine is becoming far too compartmentalised—with too much focus on the numbers for blood pressure, or cholesterol, which can take attention away from seeing the person as a whole.

As with the cholesterol guidelines, the high blood pressure guidelines were written by a panel riddled with major conflicts of interest. Nine of the eleven co-authors of the latest guidelines received speaker's payments or research funding from, consulted for, or owned stocks in a long list of drug companies.[12] One of them declared financial ties to 21 companies.

There is no suggestion these ties have caused the authors to write the guidelines in a particular way. The problem is one of perception. Moreover, according to Furberg, the whole debate about high blood pressure is skewed by the influence of what he describes as the 'hypertension mafia', the thought-leaders who he says constantly push lower and lower targets for blood pressure control. He says the danger is that recommendations can end up being based on opinions and beliefs instead of the best science.[13]

Controversy over the definition of high blood pressure is nothing new to this lanky, laconic, Swedish American. In the mid-1990s Furberg was invited to participate on the panel that was writing the sixth version of the guidelines. When he and a handful of other researchers asked the federal government's National Institutes of Health to require that the panel members disclose their links with drug companies, their request was not met. He and his colleagues boycotted the panel and the guidelines were published without any disclosures.[14]

Taking such a principled stand may have had an effect on the process, because when the next version of the guidelines emerged they came with a long list of disclosures. But for Furberg, who recently received an award from the university in Sweden where he studied for his 'courageous efforts to promote honesty and integrity in research', this latest disclosure does not go far enough.[15] Even though the financial ties reported are so extensive they take up one third of a page, what is missing is any hint of the magnitude of money these researchers are accepting. 'If someone takes $1500 from a few companies—I don't see a real problem,' says Furberg, who himself works on occasions as a paid consultant or speaker to the industry. 'If someone is getting $100000 a year I don't trust a word they say.'[16] Moreover, he argues that researchers should be obliged to disclose both their past financial ties, as well as any potential future relationships currently being negotiated.

This is not the first time blood pressure has stirred up controversy. The most widely publicised case occurred in 1999 when international consumer advocates Health Action International and a group of more than 800 concerned physicians wrote stinging letters to the Director-General of the World Health Organization (WHO), Gro Harlem Brundtland.[17] The critics argued the WHO blood pressure targets were not based on the best available evidence at the time and were set too low, and that WHO had failed in its responsibility by relying too heavily on one drug company study. According to the complaints, WHO had endorsed recommendations that would be used 'to encourage an increased use of anti-hypertensive drugs, at great expense, and for little benefit'. Brundtland wrote back saying 'there should be no conflict of interest in our partnership with private industry', though concerns about the way the WHO develops guidelines remain.

Back at White Rock, British Columbia, Bob Rangno and James McCormack have just finished explaining that a hypothetical heart medication might lower someone's risk from 3 per cent to 2 per cent. By about now they are commonly interrupted by an audience member, perhaps an elderly gent who stands up and asks: 'Look, you're talking about such small numbers, surely the risk of having a heart attack if you've got high blood pressure or high cholesterol is more than 3 per cent, isn't it?'

'That's a *very* good question,' Bob will respond. 'In fact it's the most important question anyone told to take a drug needs to ask. If your doc is telling you that you need to take a drug to lower your risk, don't you think you need to know what your "risk" is to start with?'

'So let's figure out what it might be,' says James. The interaction, which James has acted out many times, goes something like this.

'Excuse me sir, can you tell us how old you are?'

'Sixty-five.'

'Do you smoke?'

'Nope.'

'Ever had a heart attack?'

·'Nope.'

'Angina?'

'Nope, don't even know what that is.'

'Okay,' James will say to the audience, 'let's take an average 65-year-old man, like this gentleman. He's a non-smoker, never had a heart attack or angina but he's been told he's got "high" blood pressure. Let's say for argument, somewhere around 160 over 90 or so. If his doctor thinks he is at high risk, what do you think this man's chance is, over the next five years, of having a heart attack?' James then asks the crowd.

'Put up your hands if you think it is less than 10 per cent.' No hands.

'Okay, 10 to 20 per cent?' Only a few hands.

'Twenty to 30 per cent? Thirty per cent to 40 per cent?...' It's not till James hits 40–50 per cent that most of the audience raise their hands.

'So I'd say that most of you believe that "high" risk is some-where between 40 and 50 per cent.'

People nod.

'Well this is normal—and even doctors get it wrong—but you have estimated his risk to be almost ten times what it actually is. Because you see, the risk of a non-smoking, 65-year-old man with elevated blood pressure having his first heart attack over five years is about 5 to 6 per cent.'

To make it even clearer James then uses the 'identical twin brother' explanation to show how much someone's raised blood pressure might affect the chances of a future heart attack.

'Let's say Bob and I are identical twins . . . the same genetic material,' says James.

'God forbid,' Bob groans.

'And Bob's got "normal" blood pressure and I've got "high" blood pressure,' says James.

'So my "high" blood pressure increases my risk of a heart attack by about 2–3 per cent over Bob's. In other words, my risk over five years is about 5–6 per cent because I've got high blood pressure and Bob's is 3–4 per cent, because he doesn't.'

'You're kidding, that's all?' someone might ask.

'It is what it is,' says James. 'We can reduce it by 1–2 per cent back closer to the risk your twin brother has, with diet, or drugs, but we will never get it down to zero or likely even back to your dear twin brother. And of course, it will be higher if you are a smoker and have diabetes and so on. But your doctor needs to be able to tell you what your risks might be based on your own situation.'

In closing the segment, Bob suggests: 'So once you know what your risk might be, and you learn how much a drug can lower that risk, the questions you now have to ask are: do I want to take this drug every day, pay the money, visit the pharmacy every month and maybe deal with some side effects that aren't that pleasant? Those are the things you need to ask.'

And the rest of the 'Bob 'n' James Show' continues into the night—as the duo banters about the numbers from clinical trials, answering people's questions about what their actual risk might be, and how much the drugs many of them are already taking can reduce those risks.

People file out of the auditorium at the end of the night, some of them having discovered that this 'major' risk factor—high blood pressure—which they have come to dread, doesn't seem that big at all. And for many of them, they've also had the twin discovery that the benefits of the long-term drugs they are taking are somewhat less impressive than they had previously believed.

Yet as the University of British Columbia duo's show rolls on through small conference halls around the province, so too does the much larger high blood pressure marketing machine, which provides a living for a lot of vested interests besides drug companies. For a physician, for example, a diagnosis of 'hypertension' can create a lifelong patient. In fact, physicians—who do most of the checking, prescribing and rechecking of your numbers—have a considerable stake in treating this condition. For a busy doctor, strapping on the cuff and taking a patient's blood pressure is an ideal clinical encounter: it's easy, quick and fairly well paid for the short time spent. Doctors like doing it, patients come to expect it, and the rate at which it is done is skyrocketing. In Canada, a country of around 30 million people, there were more than 17 million patient visits to office-based physicians for high blood pressure in 2001—an increase of 30 per cent in just four years.[18]

While it may not be fully appreciated by the people being tested during those consultations, the way blood pressure measurements are taken is also the subject of great controversy. The irony of ironies is that physicians themselves may often be the cause of their patients' raised blood pressure in the first place. People get nervous in the presence of authority (the doctor) and their blood pressure goes up, a phenomenon so well known within the medical community it even has a name—'white-coat hypertension'. Some researchers even suggested recently that physicians shouldn't be measuring blood pressure, because they so rarely measure it accurately, and that trained and monitored observers or automated devices might do a better job.[19]

While many physicians are strong believers in the value of regular testing and aggressive treatment of high blood pressure, others like Dr Malcolm Kendrick are heretics on the issue. A general practitioner from Macclesfield, a small town outside of Manchester, England, Dr Kendrick is a self-declared sceptic who approaches medical research with an eye for evidence and a penchant for parody. He argues, baldly, that 'almost everything written about treating blood pressure is wrong'.[20]

Kendrick was particularly stunned when he read the current official American recommendation to mass screen children for high blood pressure, starting at age three.[21] 'When I read it, I found myself clutching my chest and making small panting noises, unable to articulate my feelings. Perhaps I should have taken my blood pressure at that point, I am sure it would have been at the level where my brain was in danger of popping like a ripe tomato hit by a large hammer.'[22]

Like a modern-day medical Jonathan Swift, Dr Kendrick has a 'modest proposal'. He asks, 'Why should we leave blood pressure screening until the age of three and expose children to unnecessary medical risks for the first thirty-six months of life?' His proposal? 'Let's get started the moment the umbilical cord is cut.'[23]

While it may be easy to poke fun at the idea of mass screening three year olds as being a little over the top, older people do face greater risks of succumbing to heart attacks and strokes, and it makes sense to 'do something' to try to lower their blood pressure. Many researchers would agree that for many people who are otherwise healthy, the best thing to do first, based on the evidence, is to try to alter one's lifestyle—getting more exercise, quitting smoking and modifying one's diet.[24] Yet if drugs are required what does the evidence say about which one to use?

As luck would have it, an enormous long-term scientific study comparing several different drugs can help to answer that question. Like the giant Women's Health Initiative that tested hormone replacement therapy, this trial was funded mainly by the US federal government, with some support from the pharmaceutical industry. It was called ALLHAT, it had more than 40 000 participants, and the chair of its steering committee was Dr Curt Furberg.[25] The historic study compared four different sorts of drugs—including the oldest and cheapest, the newest and most expensive. The drugs were compared in terms of how effective they were at reducing heart disease, how safe they were, and how much they gave value for money. A core question posed by the ALLHAT study was, 'Do the more expensive drugs add value?'[26]

The end result was very bad news for the pharmaceutical industry, but good news for pretty well everyone else. The oldest, cheapest drugs—low-dose diuretics (or thiazides)—not only did as well as the newer ones at lowering the chances of heart attacks and strokes, but came out marginally ahead because they were slightly better at preventing heart failure.[27] On the question of cost, the old drugs won hands down, because they are off patent and available as generics: treatment with these pills is so low it is almost free. In Canada it's been estimated that taking a daily dose of a diuretic for ten years might cost as little as C$40, yet the newer, more heavily promoted and marketed medicines, like the popular Norvasc, would cost up to 200 times as much.[28]

According to the ALLHAT study's finding, there would still be people who would benefit most from one of the newer pills, or from a combination of drugs, but for a lot of those who require a drug to lower their blood pressure, the older diuretics would be just as effective, probably safer and a lot cheaper. The historic study conclusions were published in a paper in the *Journal of the American Medical Association (JAMA)*: the diuretics were 'superior' in preventing one or more types of heart disease and were 'less expensive'.

Putting these findings into practice could save literally billions of dollars for health systems around the world, because at the time the study was published the newer, more heavily promoted drugs dominated prescribing habits. Yet the release of results from this major study barely affected the number of prescriptions being written for the newer, more expensive pills. Why? Because rather than good science, it is the roar of the promotional machine, from the detailers to the television drug ads, that influences what a lot of doctors prescribe to their patients. After a brief burst of publicity when the study was first published in *JAMA* in late 2002, the dust soon settled, and it became clear that marketing would again trump science.

At least that's what Curt Furberg, one of the study's key researchers, believes. Soon after the publication of the findings of the massive trial, Pfizer, the maker of Norvasc, issued press releases that 'ignored' some of the study's key findings, according to Furberg. The company was claiming its drug was as good as the old diuretic, he says, but because it was more or less equally as effective, but much more expensive that the older drugs, 'it was actually inferior'.[29]

In 2003, the year following the publication of the ALLHAT study, Pfizer sold almost $5 billion worth of Norvasc, making it the best-selling blood pressure medication and the fourth biggest revenue-generating drug in the entire world.[30] Pfizer clearly has a strong financial interest in ignoring or playing down the study's key findings, and it seems that is what the company did, according to reports at the time. Shareholders would presumably expect nothing less.

According to an article in the *British Medical Journal*, when Pfizer staff learnt through a research agency that doctors' awareness of some preliminary ALLHAT results was minimal, 'they took steps to avoid sullying that lack of awareness'.[31] And when Pfizer representatives heard that Curt Furberg was presenting early data about one of the company's drugs from the ALLHAT trial at a scientific conference in San Francisco, the company organised for visiting international heart specialists to go out on a sightseeing trip rather than hear the presentation. An internal Pfizer memo quotes staff congratulating their colleagues on the masterful plan. 'The good news is that they were quite brilliant in sending their key physicians to sightsee rather than hear Curt Furberg slam Pfizer once again!'[32]

It has become clear from the solid scientific evidence produced by studies like ALLHAT that collectively the world is wasting billions on the most expensive blood pressure drugs. According to another study published in *JAMA*, almost a quarter of that spending could be saved if physicians stuck to the cheaper therapies.[33] A similar study undertaken by publicly funded researchers in Norway had more conservative estimates: the United Kingdom could save more than $100 million, and the United States could save between $500 million and a billion dollars per year.[34] An Australian study estimated taxpayers could save up to A$100 million a year by using more of the older but equally effective medicines.[35] Even the official US guidelines—despite their authors' extensive conflicts of interest—state that for many people with 'uncomplicated' high blood pressure, the cheap diuretics should be the drugs of first choice 'either alone or in combination' with other drug classes.[36]

In the initial period immediately following the publication of ALLHAT, Curt Furberg and others had high hopes for change. They were planning to mount a massive publicly funded pro-motional campaign—to counter the industry's spin—and educate doctors about the value of the older cheaper drugs. Just two years later those hopes had evaporated, the counter-spin campaign has not materialised as envisaged, Furberg has resigned from the project in frustration, and this vital scientific data has already started to gather dust.

In the meantime, the propagation of the faith continues, as the demon of high blood pressure is damned even from religious pulpits. In the US the first Sunday in May is dedicated to the annual 'Church High Blood Pressure Sunday', and used as an opportunity to get faith-based organisations preaching the gospel about the seriousness of this condition.[37] On that one day, some churches from within all denominations convert their sanctuary basements to mini-clinics, encouraging their patients—er, parishioners—to head downstairs after the sermon for a blood pressure test and dietary advice with their post-service tea.

While pharmaceutical industry backing often helps sponsor educational programs, there is a real enthusiasm on the part of public health agencies to also get in on the blood pressure act. In the US the publicly funded National Institutes of Health sponsors many events to promote public education, and it recommends that church-based blood pressure awareness activi-ties should have clergy who endorse the activity enthusiastically.

The obvious danger is that in the midst of the religious fervour, the fine details of the science can get lost. Details like the $500 million-plus that could be saved in the US annually if doctors based their prescribing more on scientific evidence and less on promotion. Details like the figures Bob Rangno and James McCormack showed to their audience, demonstrating that even with 'high' blood pressure, a person's risk of future heart disease is much lower than many might think. Details like the actual or *absolute* benefits of long-term drug therapy, which can be far more modest than people are led to believe by TV commercials or lazy journalists. The difference is that Furberg and the University of British Columbia researchers are not preaching fear or promoting drugs, they are trying to better inform everyone about their risks and how best to manage them.

The maverick Dr Malcolm Kendrick says it's time the orthodoxy about blood pressure lowering is more rigorously questioned. He argues that the way the official guidelines are colonising whole new groups of healthy patients should be something of a clarion call that society needs to heed. And for him, the guidelines on blood pressure are an example of a much bigger problem, where the idea of 'normal' is being more and more narrowly defined, so that 'more and more people slip from the category of healthy into unhealthy'.[38] For Kendrick the words of Bob Rangno ring a lot truer than a lot of the religious orthodoxy: '. . . it's better to have high blood pressure than no blood pressure at all.'

That reassuring message, though, could not be further from the fear-mongering of the pharmaceutical industry's promotion, which is sometimes so audacious it advertises diseases that may not even exist.

# 6

# Advertising disease

*Pre-menstrual dysphoric disorder*

An anonymous woman tries to disentangle a shopping trolley from an interlocked row of them, outside a suburban store. She is frustrated and angry. She becomes even more exasperated when another shopper enters the frame, calmly unhooks a trolley and glides smoothly on her way. Watching this TV advertisement unfold, it might look like the woman is experiencing little more than a normal bout of tension or stress. But the folks at the drug company Lilly know better. This woman may need a powerful antidepressant because she is suffering a severe form of mental illness called pre-menstrual dysphoric disorder—a new condition approved in the United States just months before the advertisement's broadcast.

> Think it's PMS? It could be PMDD.
>
> Lilly TV commercial

Columbia University Professor Jean Endicott tells us PMDD is a psychiatric condition suffered by up to 7 per cent of women. Brown

University Professor Paula Caplan claims the condition has essentially been invented, and there is no strong scientific evidence to distinguish it from normal pre-menstrual difficulties. Even worse, argues Caplan, using a medical label to explain away the severe distress some women experience in the lead-up to their period runs the risk of masking the underlying causes of their suffering.

In the US, the FDA has accepted that the condition PMDD exists and has approved Lilly's Prozac and several similar antidepressants for its treatment, yet in other parts of the world it is not even a recognised disease. It is simply not listed as a separate disorder in the World Health Organization's International Classification of Diseases.[1] And even in the US, despite the hard work of Endicott, Lilly and others, PMDD still only has a partial listing in the psychiatrists' manual of diseases, the *DSM*, and is therefore not strictly seen as a fully official category of illness.[2]

Yet this scientific controversy is invisible in the avalanche of television and magazine advertisements about PMDD in the US—much of it targeting young women. The $500-billion pharmaceutical industry has identified another new mega-market—women of childbearing age—and the world of marketing demands simple, clear messages. The emotional ups and downs preceding your period are no longer a part of normal life—they are now a telltale sign you could have a psychiatric condition. As Caplan puts it, by watching these ads 'women are learning to consider themselves mentally ill'.[3]

A friendly and hardworking academic, Jean Endicott operates from a small office buried in the basement of a psychiatric hospital in New York city. In stark contrast to Caplan, she insists PMDD is a genuine disorder that can be 'very disabling', and often not properly diagnosed or treated. She welcomes drug company efforts to have the condition taken more seriously. It was Endicott who led the key scientific meeting—funded by Lilly and attended by company representatives—that paved the way for two of the most important developments in the life of this young disorder: FDA acceptance of the condition, and approval of Lilly's antidepressant as the first drug to treat it. As to the appropriateness of drug companies advertising disorders like this on television, Endicott is a strong believer. 'I think it educates people.'[4]

The pharmaceutical industry in the US now spends more than 3 billion dollars a year on direct-to-consumer advertising, promoting its most lucrative brands. Promotional budgets that once exclusively targeted doctors with doughnuts and free samples, and cultivated thought-leaders, are now aimed very much at the general public as well. Prime-time television news bulletins are dominated by drug ads.[5]

Increasingly, however, these commercials are not just selling drugs, but also the diseases that go with them. The shopping trolley ad for PMDD is part of a new form of TV advertising, designed to introduce millions of people to previously unheard-of conditions. While the advertising claims made about the benefits and risks of medicines are regulated by law—albeit very loosely—claims about diseases remain a virtual free-for-all.

The US and New Zealand are the only developed countries in the world that allow full-blown advertising of drugs to consumers. However, many nations—including Australia, Canada and Britain—allow companies to sponsor disease 'awareness-raising' campaigns that involve advertising and other media attention. With prescription drug expenditures rising dramatically in many nations, and a growing view that these disease 'awareness-raising' campaigns are really only a form of back-door drug advertising, debates about tougher regulation of all these marketing activities have been taking place everywhere.

In Britain these issues have been treated so seriously a major parliamentary inquiry has investigated them, and in New Zealand there has been a strong push within the national government to tighten the rules on the advertising of both drugs and diseases. In Canada, Australia, and across Europe, national governments are juggling growing consumer concerns about this mass marketing with the pressure from the pharmaceutical industry and sometimes part of the media industry as well to open up the airwaves, just as they are in the US.

One of the world's best-known and most informed critics of the industry's advertising is Australian general practitioner Dr Peter Mansfield, who helps run a globally recognised group called Healthy Skepticism, from his base in Adelaide. According to the indefatigable Mansfield, trying to find good consumer information about health is like searching for a needle in a haystack. Drug company advertising, says Mansfield with his trademark smile, 'just makes the haystack bigger'.[6]

Until very recently, much of the criticism of advertising has focused on the way ads can mislead people about the risks and benefits of new medicines—not surprisingly many commercials tend to exaggerate benefits and play down side effects.[7] In fact, the FDA, which regulates drug advertising in the US, frequently writes to drug companies warning them their advertisements are so misleading they may have broken the law. As it turned out, Lilly's shopping trolley commercial was one that attracted such a letter. In this case the FDA alleged the ad was 'lacking in fair balance' because it minimised information about the drug's side effects.[8] In the end, as is usually the case, Lilly was simply asked by the FDA, politely, to withdraw the offending ad. Despite repeated violations across the industry, and tens of millions of Americans being regularly exposed to misleading information about the risks and benefits of widely prescribed drugs, companies are not fined and executives are not held accountable.[9]

These days, though, another theme has emerged in the analysis of pharmaceutical industry advertising. Researchers are finding more and more ads are helping sell the idea that everyday human experiences are symptoms of medical conditions requiring treatment with drugs. Together with colleagues, the Dartmouth Medical School duo Drs Steve Woloshin and Lisa Schwartz recently analysed 70 drug company ads in ten popular US magazines. They found that almost half tried to encourage consumers to consider medical causes for their common experiences, most often urging them to consult a physician.[10] The ads targeted aspects of ordinary life including sneezing, hair loss, or being overweight—things many people could clearly manage without seeing a doctor—and portrayed them as if they were part of a medical condition. The researchers speculated that advertising was increasingly medicalising ordinary experience, and pushing the boundaries of medical influence far too wide.

Watching these trends closely is Canadian researcher Dr Barbara Mintzes, who included in her PhD at the University of British Columbia in Vancouver a rigorous examination of drug company advertising. She also discovered that many ads now promote medical conditions, rather than just drugs, and are helping to medicalise life, as she puts it. 'To an unprecedented degree they portray the educational message of a pill for every ill—and increasingly an ill for every pill.[11] It's a shift from a drug that's approved to treat people who are actually suffering from an illness to the idea that you just take a pill to deal with normal life situations.'[12]

Mintzes is particularly outraged by the promotion of PMDD, which has been aggressively advertised in magazines read by teenagers, as well as in TV commercials. In her view it seems designed to make younger women feel there is something wrong with the normal emotional fluctuations they experience in the lead-up to their monthly period. While accepting that for some people the problem can be severe, Mintzes worries that the ads paint a shallow picture of what it means to be a young women. 'There is pressure on people to be someone other than who they are.'[13]

With all treatments there is a balance between benefits and harms. For someone who is very sick, the chances of a great improvement may easily outweigh the risks of side effects from a drug. The antidepressants like Prozac that are being prescribed for PMDD carry many side effects, including serious sexual difficulties, and for teenagers an apparent increase in the risk of suicidal behaviour.[14] Such risks might be worth taking for someone severely debilitated by chronic clinical depression, but for a woman arguing with a boyfriend, or frustrated by a shopping trolley?

'When you're giving drugs to healthy people you're shifting the balance,' says Mintzes. 'If you're already healthy, the likelihood of benefit becomes much, much smaller and then there's a concern that what we are actually doing at a population level is causing much more harm than benefit through drug treatment.'[15]

New York professor Jean Endicott bluntly rejects the concern that PMDD is an example of ordinary life being medicalised. 'It's an insult to suggest that women with less severe symptoms would even be seeking treatment. Women are not running around saying, "Give me a pill for everything".'[16]

Looking for good hard scientific evidence to help settle this difference of opinion is difficult. Mintzes's view is based on a belief that the aggressive promotion of conditions like PMDD is causing too many otherwise healthy people to see themselves as ill and opt for drug therapies that may cause them more harm than good. Her research has added to a body of evidence showing that these ads do in fact drive many people into doctors' offices, and that some doctors will prescribe the advertised drugs even when they may doubt their appropriateness for the problem at hand.[17] But there have been few, if any, large studies that rigorously investigate whether direct-to-consumer advertising causes unnecessary medical labelling or leads to inappropriate or harmful prescription of drugs. What is crystal clear, however, is that these ads boost drug sales.

Industry executives argue that the most powerful case for direct-to-consumer advertising is evidence of underdiagnosis and undertreatment among those people with serious health problems, including high cholesterol, high blood pressure, depression and, presumably, PMDD.[18] In a special issue of the *British Medical Journal* devoted to the topic of medicalisation, and titled 'Too Much Medicine?', two senior officials from the drug company Merck wrote that the rules governing drug advertising should be loosened in Europe to help fix the urgent problem of undertreatment. They claimed there was little good evidence to support the view of Mintzes and others that advertising leads to inappropriate prescribing or harm: 'unfounded fears' about advertising, they wrote, were restricting peoples' rights 'to have all the information they need to make informed choices about their health care'.

One of the weaknesses in this argument is the failure to acknowledge the controversy and uncertainty surrounding the definitions of the common conditions said to be massively underdiagnosed. If the estimates of the numbers of people suffering these conditions and requiring treatment are inflated to start with, as some observers consider to be the case with high cholesterol and depression for example, then claims of wide-spread undertreatment deserve to be taken with extra-large doses of scrutiny and scepticism. With PMDD, claims of under-diagnosis and undertreatment make little sense if the condition itself doesn't even exist.

A major report on medicines prepared for the European phar-maceutical industry, as part of the push to loosen the advertising rules there, claimed there is strong evidence of undertreatment in many conditions including heart disease, Alzheimer's, depression and cancer.[19] Two Italian researchers analysing that report, however, directly countered those claims, arguing that the industry's report selectively cited the scientific evidence—making reference to studies showing undertreatment, but overlooking studies that demonstrate examples of overtreatment. 'Not a single study on overuse . . . is quoted, and only research looking at under-use is mentioned', wrote the Italian researchers.[20]

There is little doubt that many people in genuine need are not getting the medical attention or medication they require, particularly among the poor of wealthy nations and the wider developing world. Whether spending billions advertising disorders like PMDD on television and in women's magazines is the best way to correct that problem is highly questionable. Undertreatment may often have more to do with a lack of money or access than a lack of information. And as to the claim that advertising is the best way to inform, educate, and encour-age more choice, the high-profile deputy editor at *JAMA*, Dr Drummond Rennie, disagrees. 'Direct-to-consumer adver-tising has got nothing to do with the public's education and it has got absolutely everything to do with . . . boosting product sales.'[21]

The recent history of the controversial young disorder PMDD also has a lot to do with boosting product sales—in this case antidepressants. Taking a closer look at that history offers some fascinating insights into how a new condition is brought into the world, and the various players who nurture it in the years leading up to its debut on the world stage in highly produced TV advertisements. And just to underline how controversial this disorder really is, the European health authorities ultimately stopped Lilly promoting Prozac for PMDD, because it was 'not a well established disease entity across Europe'.[22]

Like the notion that menopause is a disease of estrogen deficiency, scholars trace the origins of the modern concept of PMDD back to the 1930s, when the term 'pre-menstrual tension' was first being coined. By the 1960s the medical community was describing a 'pre-menstrual syndrome' (PMS) that featured common symptoms like fluid retention, irritability and moodiness. Writing about the history of PMS, feminist researchers Joan Chrisler and Paula Caplan find there are so many different definitions as to make any one overall definition almost impossible. What's more, they counted up almost 150 symptoms supposedly associated with the condition. 'The concept of PMS is so vague and so elastic that almost every woman can see something of her own experience within it', they wrote.[23]

Examining references to PMS in popular culture and the medical literature Chrisler and Caplan found that it was very much a western notion, with most medical research having been done in Europe, North America and Australia. While women everywhere experience tension, irritability or water retention prior to monthly periods, many do not believe this is abnormal or feel any need for professional intervention. The two authors argue that long before PMDD was created, the widespread use of the term PMS had already medicalised women's menstrual cycles—the cycle itself had become the medical problem that needed to be solved.

While clearly critical of what they see as a strong example of unnecessary medicalisation, the pair acknowledges that many women may feel their concerns will not be taken seriously if they aren't given a medical explanation. Similarly, they argue, many people may see the medical discussion of PMS as being friendly to women, and cast those who reject the idea of the medical label as being insensitive and uncaring.

Against this backdrop of uncertainty and debate about the very definition and meaning of PMS, in the mid 1980s a small group of psychiatrists and others working with the American Psychiatric Association came together to try to define a new condition. The idea was to separate out normal pre-menstrual complaints from a severe form of mood disturbance that came and went every month, but was serious enough in some women to be disabling and warrant treatment. The group was pulled together by the imposing figure of Dr Robert Spitzer, the man then responsible for revising the psychiatrist's bible, the *Diagnostic and Statistical Manual of Mental Disorders (DSM)*.[24]

Each time the *DSM* is revised, new disorders are added and over the last few decades the numbers have expanded dramatically. Physically, the book started out as a slim volume, but has since morphed into a massive tome. Under the direction of Robert Spitzer—Jean Endicott's colleague at the New York State Psychiatric Institute—the numbers of new conditions listed in the *DSM* exploded. So keen was he on adding new diseases to the manual, the now elderly Spitzer confesses to having been teased by some of his younger colleagues as being someone who never saw a disorder he didn't like.[25] PMDD was one of the most controversial disorders ever added, and it was known at first by the very awkward name of late luteal phase dysphoric disorder (LLPDD) when Spitzer's committee sat down to discuss it back in the summer of 1985.

According to Spitzer's account of the heated debates of the time, even within his committee there were disputes about whether to include this supposed new mental disorder in the *DSM*. Part of the concern was that so little was known about its causes, or how to treat it—criticisms acknowledged by Spitzer and his colleagues. Yet ironically, this lack of knowledge became one of the powerful reasons to create the new condition, with enthusiasts arguing that a listing in the *DSM* would facilitate more research on its causes and treatment.[26]

Another key concern raised from the beginning by some of Spitzer's committee was that because all women experience some degree of pre-menstrual symptoms, there was a danger the psychiatrists were going to label aspects of ordinary life as a mental disorder. Again acknowledging the concern, Spitzer and his supporters responded that similar arguments could be made about many established mental disorders. For example, they argued, depression was simply an extreme form of sadness. Spitzer's point was that with these sorts of disorders, a lot of care must always be taken in defining the boundary between what is normal and what is sick. But Spitzer did not explain how those boundaries are supposed to survive the whirlwind of mass marketing deliberately designed to blur them. While the strict criteria for a disabling impairment might look like a reasonable boundary on paper in front of a group of psychiatrists, in the real world of drug promotion a woman having trouble with a shopping trolley becomes the definition of a new disorder seen by tens of millions across America.

Despite the objections of two of its members, Spitzer's original committee recommended including the condition then known as LLPDD in the *DSM*. The recommendation sparked a chorus of criticism from some women's groups and professional societies—underlining the premature nature of such an addition. The compromise solution was to include the new disease, but only in the appendix to the manual, as a disorder requiring further research. It was therefore not even an *official* category when the next version of the manual was published in 1987.[27]

Six years later, in preparation for the following revision of the *DSM*, another committee revisited the same debate. Despite reviewing hundreds of studies, committee members found there was still much uncertainty about how to define this condition. There was still no consensus about whether it existed as a separate mental disorder, and more research was needed to resolve the dispute. At that time the name late luteal phase dysphoric disorder was replaced with pre-menstrual dysphoric disorder, but the disorder would remain listed in the appendix of the *DSM* as a condition requiring further research.

There was, however, another highly significant development at this point. Despite the ongoing doubts and disputes within the committee, the publishers of the manual took the unusual step of classifying PMDD as a bonafide depressive disorder and listing it in the main body of the *DSM*, at the same time as it was still listed in the manual's appendix as a tentative unofficial condition needing more research. While appearing somewhat contradictory this move was important commercially because it gave PMDD a precious item number—allowing doctors to prescribe drugs to treat the condition, and health insurers to fund them.[28]

It was here that the rifts between the scientists debating this

new condition became major disagreements. Psychiatry professor Sally Severino—a member of the committee trying to define
the new condition—says it was at this point that she parted
company with her colleagues Spitzer and Endicott. 'The data did
not prove PMDD existed as a valid diagnosis,' she said. 'The
decision to make it a depressive disorder was driven more by
politics than science.'[29] Making the condition look more like a
legitimate mental illness, Severino explained, opened it up for
lucrative research funding from pharmaceutical companies. 'As
far as I was concerned the decision was not based on anything in
the data we looked at.' So does PMDD really exist? 'That's a
good question,' she laughed.

What happened next would help push an unknown, unofficial and for some, an unreal condition from the back pages of
the psychiatrist's manual into glossy magazines and television
screens everywhere, thanks to Lilly, the company best known
for its blockbuster antidepressant Prozac. By the late 1990s
Prozac—whose chemical name is fluoxetine—was about to lose
its patent, and Lilly stood to lose hundreds of millions of
dollars because of the emergence of cheaper generic competitors.
Winning approval for the drug for a new disease might re-
energise sales of this blockbuster chemical.

In late 1998 Lilly helped fund a small meeting, impressively
titled as a 'Roundtable' of researchers, which came together and
discussed PMDD. The meeting of just sixteen key experts took
place in Washington, DC, and it was attended by a group of
FDA staff and at least four Lilly representatives. The chair was
Columbia University's Jean Endicott, who had by then been
pushing for the acceptance of this disorder for over a decade.
This time, though, Endicott had a giant pharmaceutical
company on her side.

Within twelve months the minutes of that 'Roundtable' would appear in a medical journal article claiming there was now a scientific consensus that PMDD was a 'distinct clinical entity'.[30] Even though the article appeared in a very minor journal, its publication would lend credibility to the claims that this was a real disorder and help convince the FDA to approve Lilly's drug for the treatment of PMDD just a few months later. Despite requests, neither Lilly nor FDA officials would talk publicly about the Roundtable meeting. They have offered no explanation as to how a company-sponsored gathering can apparently play such a key role in regulatory acceptance of a new condition and simultaneous approval of that sponsor's drug. While the Roundtable was obviously designed to help win regulatory approval for Prozac's new use, it was also designed to try to end the scientific uncertainty about whether PMDD really exists. As it turned out the meeting only served to highlight the continuing uncertainty and controversy.

The meeting was held in the shadow cast by just one company, Lilly. It was supported by just one company, and representatives from just one company were in attendance. Turning down repeated requests for interviews, Lilly has refused to answer one of the most critical questions here: what role did it play in transforming those Roundtable meeting minutes into a medical journal article that helped provide the scientific rationale for the approval of the company's antidepressant for this controversial condition? Company-sponsored ghost-writing of scientific articles is widespread within the medical establishment, particularly within the world of psychiatry.[31] Asked about the fact that drug companies were now funding such vitally important scientific activities—where the very existence of new disorders was being debated—Endicott said simply, 'It's a way of life.'[32]

Critics like Paula Caplan argue no important new scientific evidence had emerged since the early 1990s to prove this was a separate condition, so at the time of the Roundtable in 1998 PMDD still didn't deserve the status of a separate mental disorder. Psychiatrist Sally Severino agrees. Jean Endicott disagrees and says there was significant new evidence, though not a lot of it. Yet even with the limited new evidence that Endicott points to, it is clear even from the published journal article that enormous uncertainties still existed about this so-called disorder—even among the tiny group of hand-picked experts who attended the meeting.[33]

Endicott's summing up at the conclusion of the Roundtable had an important qualification, hinting at lingering doubts. 'Most present are convinced (maybe in different ways) that PMDD is a distinct entity.' But despite the doubts and disagreements the Lilly sponsored meeting had two important bottom-line conclusions, both highly favourable to the meeting's sponsor: there was now an alleged consensus that the disorder existed, and most people present thought there was sufficient evidence to support the use of antidepressants like Prozac to treat it.

By Christmas of 1999, a meeting of advisers to the FDA had voted unanimously to approve Lilly's fluoxetine for the treatment of PMDD. Soon after the FDA formally gave Lilly the green light to market its drug for PMDD and Lilly organised a launch to do just that. But in an extraordinary turn of events, the pill was not launched under the name Prozac. Lilly had done some sophisticated market research with doctors and potential patients, and as a result it had decided to re-paint Prozac with attractive lavender and pink colours and rename it Sarafem.

For specialists in pharmaceutical marketing like Vince Parry, the story of PMDD and Sarafem is a great example of a company 'fostering the creation of a condition and aligning it with a product'.[34] He worked for Lilly on the campaign, which he describes as helping to 'build awareness for both the condition and the drug'. To kick it off, he says, the company sponsored a 'pre-launch initiative' to raise awareness of the condition. 'By changing the brand name from Prozac to Sarafem—packaged in a lavender-coloured pill and promoted with images of sunflowers and smart women—Lilly created a brand that better aligned with the personality of the condition for a hand-in-glove fit.'[35]

With Sarafem and PMDD, Parry explains, Lilly's market research investigated how best to brand both the drug and the condition, to come up with language women felt most comfortable with. PMDD, he says, 'has a certain kind of personality that they can see themselves in . . . even the advertising that was done to support it, the women weren't sort of these spooky women who looked depressed. The advertising featured women who were confident, self-assured, were unafraid of asking for help and recognising that this is a condition they shouldn't feel ashamed of or anything . . . all those things are developed in conjunction with the very patients themselves to make sure that there is a lock and key result.'[36]

Somehow, though, despite Parry's and Lilly's best efforts, the *personality* of both Sarafem and PMDD became a little confused, partly because of some strong negative reactions to the shopping trolley ad screened across America. Even the industry-friendly FDA reacted, arguing that the TV ad trivialised the seriousness of this alleged new mental disorder by associating it with normal pre-menstrual problems. In a letter to Lilly the FDA was particularly critical of the catchy tag line, 'Think it's PMS? It could be PMDD.'[37]

The letter stated that the ad never clearly defined the difference between PMS and PMDD, and it therefore 'broadens' the condition unreasonably. While the FDA had clearly accepted the view that PMDD exists, ironically its criticisms of the ad reinforced the concerns of those who felt ordinary life was being made into a medical condition. Says drug researcher Barbara Mintzes, 'These ads are really selling the magical solution that you won't have to deal with something that was a normal part of life any more.'[38] Says psychologist Paula Caplan, 'In a nutshell, you see them taking a very common kind of experience and making that very thing into a mental disorder.'[39]

Caplan's concern that serious problems were being trivialised comes from a different perspective than that of the folks at the FDA. She worries that a psychiatric label of PMDD can be used to cover up or mask the real sources of pain and anguish for some women at the time of their period. Such sources may include a history of violent relationships, stressful life circumstances, poverty, or harassment—problems that clearly cannot be fixed with a pill.[40]

Despite the concerns, the marketing of both the new condition and the antidepressants to treat it has continued apace in the US. In Europe, however, Lilly's marketing of Sarafem/Prozac (fluoxetine) for PMDD came to a very abrupt stop. In mid-2003, following deliberations about standardising product labels across Europe, the central drug regulator issued a devastating statement raising serious questions about the disorder's existence. It also fiercely criticised the quality of the company's clinical trials that purported to show the benefits of the drug.

A panel from the European Agency for the Evaluation of Medicinal Products noted that 'PMDD is not a well-established disease entity across Europe. It is not listed in the International

Classification of Diseases and remains only a researcher diagnosis in *DSM IV*. But their next finding was the most powerful reason advanced for halting the promotion of Prozac and PMDD, and it echoed the now familiar arguments of feminist critics. 'There was considerable concern that women with less severe pre-menstrual symptoms might erroneously receive a diagnosis of PMDD resulting in widespread inappropriate short and long-term use of fluoxetine.'[41]

The regulators then vigorously criticised two of Lilly's key studies of Prozac/fluoxetine for PMDD, finding them to have major deficiencies. The trials were too short, the patients were not representative of those who would be prescribed the drug and, worst of all, it was not exactly clear what the trials were measuring so the results were of questionable value anyway. The damning findings of this panel were in stark contrast to the conclusions of the Lilly-sponsored Roundtable of experts in the US: the European regulator was not at all convinced there was enough evidence to justify the use of Lilly's Prozac for PMDD.

Paula Caplan welcomed the move. 'I think it's a wonderful decision,' she said. 'This kind of scrutiny of the science or lack of science behind trials of drugs is all too rare and it is to be praised.' Jean Endicott was not at all impressed, saying the decision did a disservice to women. Lilly was forced to inform physicians in Europe of the regulator's decision banning Prozac for PMDD via letters, a decision that a spokesperson described as 'unfortunate'.[42]

While the FDA may have criticised Lilly's initial round of ads, the US regulator has gone on to approve several other similar antidepressant medications for PMDD, including Pfizer's Zoloft and GSK's Paxil. And as with many new drug approvals these days, they are accompanied by much company-funded 'awareness-raising' about the disorder the drugs have been approved to treat. Pfizer's marketing of PMDD even employs some of the words and concepts used by Lilly.

> Are you giving up days to what you think is PMS? If you are, it could be PMDD.
>
> > Zoloft ad

It's likely these more recent advertisements have not received the same level of scrutiny from the regulators as the initial Lilly ad received back in 2000. Soon after winning office that year, the Bush administration appointed an attorney to be the official counsel for the FDA who had in the past worked as a legal counsel on the side of the drug companies against the FDA. His arrival brought new procedures requiring that any warning letters to be sent to drug companies had to be first approved by his office, where inevitably a bottleneck formed. The steady stream of warning letters to companies slowed to a trickle, sometimes sent so belatedly they did not arrive at the company's offices until well after the offending ad campaign had finished.[43]

GSK's advertisements for Paxil and PMDD are even more blatant in their attempt to blur the boundaries between ordinary life and mental illness.

> I always thought it was just PMS. Now I know otherwise.
> Grouchy? Emotional? Irritable? It may be PMDD.[44]

As advertising campaigns like these are clearly targeting relatively normal and healthy women experiencing common problems, the issue of side effects becomes ever more important. For these three drugs, serious sexual problems are a major and common side effect. And as the world has learnt, many years after its original approval, with Paxil side effects can be particularly worrying, including withdrawal problems that are in some cases severe.[45]

But the problem of withdrawal is just one of many challenges to the blockbuster Paxil—also known as Seroxat and Aropax. One of the world's top-selling antidepressants, the drug was also one of the biggest money-spinners ever for the giant Anglo-American pharmaceutical company GSK. A large part of Paxil's extraordinary success was because it has been approved to treat more conditions than almost all of its competitor antidepressants.

The most controversial of those conditions, though, was ultimately not PMDD, but another obscure psychiatric disorder the drug giant has pushed into the spotlight with claims it affects one in eight people. To help launch the new disorder, GSK turned to one of the world's giant communications corporations. That company would run what would become an award-winning public relations campaign, and produce an historic case study in selling sickness.

7

# Shaping public perceptions

*Social anxiety disorder*

Deborah Olguin first heard about social anxiety disorder from a television commercial. She was unemployed at the time and having a lot of trouble coping with job interviews. Each interview seemed to go worse than the one before and Deborah found herself becoming more and more nervous and agitated. Then she saw an advertisement about a new condition called social anxiety disorder and a medication called Paxil. 'I just thought, well, maybe this will help me with my job interviews,' she says, looking back a few years later. 'I pretty much diagnosed myself.'[1]

A resident of a small trailer park community in southern California, Deborah took herself off to her local physician. 'I told him what was going on and that I'd seen these commercials on television and asked him if he would give me a prescription. He did, and I started taking Paxil.'[2] Two months later, her anxiety alleviated, Deborah landed a job working in real estate, where she stayed for the next four years. 'I think taking the

119

medication helped me be able to work with the public in a comfortable way.' With her successful self-diagnosis of social anxiety disorder, Deborah was at the frontier of medical science—her condition had only just been pushed from the shadows of obscurity into the glare of the public spotlight, and the powerful antidepressant Paxil had just become the first drug ever approved to treat it.

In the space of little more than a year Paxil's manufacturer GSK took a little-known and once-considered rare psychiatric condition and helped transform it into a major epidemic called social anxiety disorder—claimed at one point by the company to affect one in eight Americans.[3] The transformation would ultimately help rack up sales of Paxil worth $3 billion a year, and make it the world's top-selling antidepressant. The ads Deborah saw on TV were just the tip of the iceberg, the most visible part of a multi-layered campaign to fundamentally reshape public perceptions about shyness and uneasiness in social situations. To pull it off, the pharmaceutical giant turned to WPP, one of the world's big communications corporations, and that company's public relations subsidiary, Cohn & Wolfe.

'We're not only tapped into the latest trends, we set them,' boasted the team at Cohn & Wolfe.[4] With headquarters on New York's Madison Avenue, it is one of a select group of PR houses that specialise in unconventional ways to market pharmaceuticals. Set up in the 1970s, the firm rose to global prominence when it won the PR work for Coca-Cola's Olympic Games sponsorship. Now its list of corporate clients includes household names in fast food, oil and drugs—Taco Bell, ChevronTexaco, and GSK.

With a division dedicated entirely to health care and pharmaceuticals, Cohn & Wolfe has developed very special skills. Not only does it market drugs, it can also help drug companies with the tricky process of seeking FDA approval. 'But it is often the work we do cultivating the marketplace prior to approval,' says the website, 'that demonstrates the true power of our communications efforts.'[5] This was the power that GSK harnessed to help sell a little-known disorder to the world.

Despite their enormous influence around the globe, public relations firms are largely invisible to those of us whose minds they change. Cohn & Wolfe is actually only a brand name anyway, since it is a subsidiary of the giant WPP Group, a global conglomerate that sells advertising, PR, branding and other services to many of the world's biggest corporations—including tobacco company Philip Morris—generating revenues of more than $6 billion a year.[6]

As the public relations industry saw it, GSK specifically hired Cohn & Wolfe to *position* social anxiety disorder as a severe condition.[7] This occurred *before* Paxil was even approved for the treatment of this condition, in order to give Cohn & Wolfe time to start 'cultivating the marketplace'.[8] The campaign would have two clear objectives. The first was to generate extensive media coverage about social anxiety disorder, always making the link between the condition and the drug. The second and far more important aim was to make sure Paxil would outsell Zoloft—the blockbuster antidepressant that was then number two to world leader Prozac.[9] To put it bluntly, the public was to be educated about a new condition by a campaign whose primary goal was to maximise sales of a drug.

In keeping with modern public relations techniques, the PR firm helped orchestrate what looked like a grassroots movement to raise public awareness about a neglected disorder. The awareness-raising campaign was based on the slogan, 'Imagine being allergic to people'. Posters that featured a sad-looking man and listed commonly experienced symptoms were distributed across America. 'You blush, sweat, shake—even find it hard to breathe. That's what social anxiety disorder feels like.' The posters appeared to come from several medical and advocacy groups under the umbrella of the Social Anxiety Disorder Coalition: all three members of the 'coalition' rely heavily on sponsorship from drug companies. Calls from the media to the 'coalition' were handled by Cohn & Wolfe.[10]

Just as we have seen with the promotion of ADD and other conditions, advocacy groups earn some of their drug company sponsorship dollars by providing suffering patients to talk to deadline-sensitive journalists. And that is exactly what happened in this case—with the PR firm organising teleconferences with sufferers. What Cohn & Wolfe describe as 'aggressive media outreach' also involved the distribution of video news releases, press kits, and the setting up of a network of spokespeople. The outreach to the media apparently worked wonders: stories were generated everywhere from the high-class *New York Times* to the lowbrow *Howard Stern Show*—from the glossy *Vogue* to the much-watched *Good Morning America*.[11]

No awareness-raising campaign is complete without medical expertise, and in this case it came from University of California psychiatrist Dr Murray Stein. Among others, Stein offered flattering praise for Paxil in the company's original press releases about social anxiety disorder—described as a condition where people are sick with the fear of social settings that might involve being scrutinised and evaluated by others.[12] The press release explained that the condition 'is not just shyness', but a much more distressing disorder that interfered with normal life. 'Social anxiety disorder can be thought of in some ways as being a real extreme of shyness,' says Stein, who helped run the key company-funded trials of the drug for this disorder, and who has since maintained ties to the manufacturer.[13] At last count, on top of his university job, Stein has worked in recent years as a paid consultant to no less than seventeen drug companies, including GSK.[14]

What was at first just a trickle of media stories about social anxiety disorder soon became a steady stream. The market was being well and truly irrigated—as part of Cohn & Wolfe's cultivation program. In early 1999 the FDA gave GSK the green light by approving Paxil for this new disorder, pushing the marketing campaign into overdrive. A barrage of direct-to-consumer advertisements, just like those for PMDD, introduced a generation to a psychiatric condition they'd never heard of before. TV commercials that featured disturbing images of people with intense fears of social situations were seen by tens of millions of Americans, including Deborah Olguin, unemployed, watching TV from her trailer park in California.

The following year Cohn & Wolfe was recognised for its innovative work on the social anxiety disorder campaign, winning an award from the Public Relations Society of America. According to the commendation, the PR firm had successfully used psychiatrist experts, third-party representatives and patient testimonials, and 'educated' reporters, consumers and physicians about the new disorder—generating '1.1 billion media impressions' in just one year. The award was particularly warranted because the 'heightened public awareness of Paxil and social anxiety disorder' had helped boost sales of the drug so much so that it had surpassed Zoloft and was temporarily tied with Prozac—a major achievement within the industry.[15]

But had people like Deborah Olguin and the millions of others watching really been *educated*? She was certainly not warned that five years later she would still be taking Paxil because of horrendous withdrawal symptoms that occurred every time she tried to stop. She was not told that while social anxiety disorder would help make Paxil one of GSK's top money-spinners, the prohibitive costs of her monthly prescription would regularly send her driving for hours across the border to Mexico seeking affordable pills. Likewise, Olguin was never informed of evidence suggesting Paxil was associated with an increase in the risk of suicidal thinking and behaviour in children and adolescents—evidence that when it finally became public would cause British health authorities to virtually ban the drug for youngsters. To describe the GSK-funded Cohn & Wolfe's PR campaign as *education* is a grotesque fiction. The fact that it also generated so much sycophantic media coverage may well justify the PR award and excitement on Madison Avenue, but it is also a timely indictment of the flaccid culture of much medical reporting.[16]

There is little doubt that for some people antidepressants including Paxil can be beneficial and even life-saving. But for others like Deborah Olguin, the drug honeymoon is soon over. 'I don't want anybody to ever go through what I have gone through with this medication,' she said. Ironically, her problems with the drug first started when she stopped taking Paxil because she couldn't get to a doctor to renew her prescription. A few days later she began feeling anxious and nervous, experiencing weird sensations she described as electric zaps going through her brain. When she finally got the prescription refilled, the symptoms went away. After the same thing happened on a second occasion when she was unable to get a prescription for several days, she started to think the drug might be causing the problem. Her doctors simply told her to keep taking the medication, though she became determined to try to stop. 'There was one point I went around ten days without the drug and I was totally not functioning. Not functioning at all. It was horrible, it was just horrible.'[17]

Initially denied by GSK, and overlooked by health authorities, long-term campaigns by consumer activists and others have forced official recognition of Paxil's withdrawal problems. One of the key campaigners has been British activist Charles Medawar whose site, Social Audit, has played an important role in raising public awareness.[18] While there is still debate about how many people experience difficulties stopping—it could affect one in four users—with some, like Deborah, withdrawal symptoms can be so severe they are unable to stop at all.[19] With millions of people taking Paxil worldwide, even if just a small proportion experience serious problems that's an awful lot of people.

It wasn't just that comprehensive and accurate material about the drug's side effects were left out of the award-winning Cohn & Wolfe campaign. Material from the PR firm also missed out important information about the *condition*, only telling part of the story. The widely recognised name for this condition is *not* social anxiety disorder at all, but rather social phobia. Social phobia has long been considered a rare psychiatric condition that causes a very small proportion of people to avoid social situations. It was first described in modern times by French researchers at the end of the nineteenth century.[20] Try looking for a condition called social anxiety disorder in many current textbooks of psychiatry and you won't find it.

The international manual of mental illnesses simply does not list a condition called social anxiety disorder.[21] In the bible of US psychiatry the name is only mentioned in brackets after the official title—Social Phobia (Social Anxiety Disorder). The US psychiatry manual's authorised list of symptoms describing the condition still appears under the heading 'Social Phobia',[22] and the accompanying guidebook appears to make no mention of any condition called social anxiety disorder.

Trying to find out exactly how GSK came to choose the name social anxiety disorder to create those I.I billion 'impressions' in the media is not easy, because neither Cohn & Wolfe nor GSK will answer questions. It seems certain, though, that marketing considerations were part of the company's motivation in selecting one name over another. According to psychiatrists who specialise in this field, the two different condition names suggest two quite different views of the underlying problem and how it might best be treated.

To put it simply, an *anxiety* disorder is seen as being more able to be treated with drug therapy. Something called a *phobia* is considered to be a condition more amenable to the idea of talking therapies. 'Industry could, by preferring the term social anxiety disorder, give the impression that this disorder necessarily requires drug treatment,' says British psychiatrist Dr David Baldwin, who has worked on company-funded trials of the antidepressants but like many of his colleagues still strongly prefers the term 'social phobia'.[23]

The other important difference is that a lot more people can be categorised as being ill if you apply the definition of an anxiety disorder rather than a phobia. This is because with the definition of social phobia, which still holds weight in much of the world outside North America, there is an emphasis on the patient having to *avoid* situations that cause fear, in order to be diagnosed with this condition and defined as being sick.[24] With the definition of social anxiety disorder being pushed in the United States a person doesn't necessarily have to avoid the social situation to attract the label, it is enough that they fear it and that that fear causes them anxiety and distress.[25] In other words the threshold for diagnosis is lower with an anxiety disorder, and the potential pool of patients much bigger.

The marketing guru Vince Parry didn't work on this GSK campaign, but he sees it nevertheless as a good example of branding a condition. 'I'd say that the area that has been most ripe for condition branding has been anxiety and mood disorders,' said Parry, explaining that for these disorders there is no blood test a person could take—so the diagnosis is made with a checklist of symptoms.[26] In the past we had 'jitters, stage fright, inability to feel comfortable in a crowd. These were normally called shyness or extreme shyness,' he says. But now we have a medical condition called social anxiety disorder, which is a 'general feeling of sort of uneasiness among other individuals that might limit your ability to participate'. Importantly, Parry's vague description of the symptoms of this new condition— experienced by vast swathes of the entire population—reinforces the arguments of critics who suggest we are witnessing a blurring of the boundaries between normal life and treatable illness.[27] For Parry, who earns his living helping drug companies design and promote new disorders, or spruce up old ones, this blurring is not unhealthy. On the contrary, he suggested cheerfully, it makes people feel better about themselves. 'When people can identify and see themselves as these individuals [with this condition], they don't judge themselves as harshly. They know they can go and get help and as a result they can pursue their career dreams, or their relationship options without feeling like there's something really, really wrong with them.'[28] It seems that before becoming healthy we must all recognise we are sick.

Not all attempts at branding conditions are as successful as the Cohn & Wolfe campaign. When another drug company tried to promote social phobia a few years earlier it failed miserably.

Some of the action took place in Australia, where a less experienced PR firm was hired to cultivate the social phobia market—on behalf of Swiss giant Roche, at the time keen to promote its antidepressant drug Aurorix for the condition. One of the classic press releases from that effort claimed that a million Australians were suffering from a little-known but soul-destroying psychiatric disorder called social phobia.[29] But this key 'fact' was an extremely shaky foundation for the campaign, because among the population of 18 million or so there was nothing like a million Australians suffering with this disorder. Official government estimates at the time suggested a third of that number, and even that was probably an overestimate.[30] As it turned out, Roche couldn't even find the small number of social phobia patients needed to enrol in clinical trials of the company's drug, and the clumsy PR campaign was quietly abandoned.

Roche's plain-talking managing director in Australia, Fred Nadjarian, would later claim to have been 'taken in' by estimates given to him by his marketing staff of how widespread the condition was supposed to be. 'I thought there might be a big market,' says Nadjarian, 'but when we tried to recruit [for the trials] we just weren't able to.' Warning that behind every statistic there is a vested interest—whether it be a professional society, a self-interested researcher or a drug company—Nadjarian urged that more healthy scepticism was needed all round. 'A lot of disease estimates are blown out of all proportion,' he said. 'The marketing people always beat these things up.'[31]

With this particular condition—whether it's called social phobia or social anxiety disorder—the estimates of how many people legitimately suffer it range from less than 1 per cent to 16 per cent.[32] As with many other conditions, the bigger the supposed prevalence, the easier for drug companies to claim that there is massive underdiagnosis and that millions are suffering in silence without needed treatment—and to use that claim as the key justification for massive PR campaigns like the one run by Cohn & Wolfe.

In Europe the estimates of how many people have medical conditions are often lower than in the US, which is certainly the case with this condition. Yet even in the US there is a remarkable variety of estimates—and some rapid changes in those estimates have taken place in recent years. Just two decades ago, senior American psychiatrists cited evidence suggesting social phobia may affect roughly 2 per cent of the population in any given 6 month period.[33] By 1998, around 13 per cent—or one in eight—Americans suffered from social anxiety disorder, according to an estimate in drug company advertising material. So what's happened?

First the list of symptoms that define social phobia (social anxiety disorder) has steadily expanded in key revisions of the psychiatrist's manual, the *DSM*, essentially widening the pool of those defined as sick. Second, those new broadened definitions have been used in high-profile surveys of the population that have come up with dramatically higher estimates of how many people have serious mental disorders, including social phobia/social anxiety disorder. Third, a drug company trying to push its product took some of the highest estimates and used them as part of a massive PR campaign.

As with other conditions like ADD, recent revisions of the *DSM* have widened the definition—expanding the number of social situations a person can fear to qualify for the disorder, and removing the need for *avoidance* of those situations as a strict criterion. One major survey based on those expanded definitions, the one conducted by Harvard Professor Ron Kessler, estimated that 13.3 per cent of people suffered this disorder at some point in their life—the source of the one-in-eight claim by the Paxil manufacturer.[34]

> Social anxiety disorder is a lot more common than you may think . . .
> I out of every 8 Americans suffers from social anxiety disorder.
> The good news is that it is treatable.
>
> Company patient brochure[35]

When researchers led by Dr William Narrow revised those inflated estimates downwards, the biggest drop for any single condition occurred with social phobia (this survey did not use the term social anxiety disorder). Narrow's revised estimates suggested that in any given year the figure would be under 4 per cent—and possibly significantly lower.[36] Based on their reading of all the scientific literature, some leading psychiatrists suggest the true proportion of the population suffering social phobia is less than I per cent.[37]

Asked about the selling of social anxiety disorder, Narrow said that in his view some of the Paxil TV commercials had accurately described the intense fears experienced by people paralysed in social situations, but he worried that the aggressive marketing campaign could potentially make common shyness seem like a mental illness. Using figures like 'one in eight' is counterproductive, he said, because 'unrealistic numbers really trivialise the disorder'.[38] In its marketing the company has since used lower estimates, with some commercials suggesting that more than 10 million people have the disorder, rather than the 30 million or more implied by the one in eight figure.

GSK's social anxiety disorder campaign appears to be another case where those with mild illness, or sometimes none at all, are being told they may have a serious psychiatric disorder. As we saw with attempts to paint menopause as a condition of hormone deficiency requiring treatment, part of the selling strategy here has involved the calculated use of celebrities, including in this case the US football phenomenon, running back Ricky Williams. Despite his success on the field, Williams is apparently a very shy person. Like Deborah Olguin in her trailer park in California, he only realised he had the mental illness after watching a TV commercial.[39]

In the summer of 2002, a blaze of publicity revealed that Williams—who played for the Miami Dolphins—was suffering from social anxiety disorder. Stories appeared in the *New York Times* and the *Los Angeles Times*, and there was a segment on the *Oprah* show, one of television's most sought-after venues. The celebrity sports hero told the national network NBC, 'I've always been a shy person.' What some of the media stories disclosed, but others somehow failed to mention, was that at the time Williams was being paid by GSK to help raise public awareness about social anxiety disorder.[40] He was also taking Paxil. The celebrity media appearances, rather than the result of any intelligent journalism, were simply the latest wave of a now three-year-old PR campaign to change perceptions about a condition. Coincidentally that same year Paxil itself would become a major celebrity, pushing briefly past both Prozac and Zoloft to become the world's top-selling antidepressant.[41]

Asked at the time whether the football star's comments about being shy were part of a deliberate attempt to medicalise shyness, a GSK spokesperson said, 'It's an important point, but I don't think so.' He added that there was a big difference between shyness and social anxiety disorder, which he described as an underdiagnosed and undertreated condition. 'We're very pleased to be working with Ricky. He's got an important message, he's got an inspirational story, encouraging others who might have the symptoms of social anxiety disorder to seek treatment.'[42] With symptoms that include sweating, blushing or a pounding heart, clearly a lot of people may be driven to 'seek treatment'— in this case a polite euphemism for seeking Paxil.

The point here is not to play down the genuine suffering of those who are extremely fearful of public speaking and other social situations. Rather, the aim is to expose the way drug marketing, masquerading as education or awareness-raising, attempts to so profoundly reshape our views about what constitutes treatable illness, and at the same time channel people towards the latest pill.

The day after that Williams television interview on NBC, the same network broadcast a segment billed as providing tips for shy people. During the show an expert told the vast viewing audience that for 'social anxiety disorders or even a public speaking problem, medication may be helpful'. Though the GSK spokesperson said the football star was 'not hired to sell product', an increase in Paxil sales may not have been an entirely unexpected outcome of Williams's media appearances and the follow-up stories they provoked.[43] Curiously, given he was not hired to sell product, he did offer a very fulsome endorsement to Paxil just over a year later in a company press release about a new formulation of the drug. 'As someone who has suffered from social anxiety disorder, I am so happy that new treatment options, like Paxil CR, are available today to help people with the condition.'[44]

While the celebrity Ricky Williams might be happy with his Paxil, and presumably happy also about his deal with GSK, thousands of others like Deborah Olguin are taking legal action against the company, alleging they were not warned of the drug's potential to cause withdrawal and dependence. The tall, tanned and tenacious Karen Barth Menzies is the lead attorney from the Los Angeles law firm Baumhedlund coordinating the legal action. 'We've had 10 000 people call us now, and all of them for the same things,' she said. 'I started taking this drug, I had no idea that I could become addicted to it, and now I'm addicted.'[45] While GSK concedes some people experience problems when they abruptly stop the drug, it rejects the notion that Paxil causes dependence and people get hooked. It is strongly defending the action. But the problem of withdrawal is not the only one facing Paxil and GSK.

One of the key expert advisers to the LA law firm is the high-profile psychiatrist Professor David Healy, from the University of Wales. While he sees value in the antidepressants, including Paxil, Healy has argued that too much ordinary life is being transformed into medical illness—and that the promotion of social anxiety disorder is a classic example of the problem. 'We're changing the experience of what it means to be human,' he said.[46] 'If you've got a very severe problem and I treat you with a pill like Paxil, I may save your life, I may save your marriage, I may save your career. But if you don't have that, if you've got a very mild problem, then making you a psychiatric patient and putting you on a pill may pose more risks than leaving you untreated.'[47]

Over the past decade Healy has become increasingly angered by the mismatch between the marketing of the antidepressants and the scientific reality—particularly in relation to the question of suicidal behaviour. As a result of his work with the legal case Healy got special access to the GSK corporate archives, where he claims to have seen evidence of Paxil's withdrawal problems in the company's own scientific data. What's more, he says that the trials of Paxil in depressed children showed that the drug caused a slight increase in the risk of suicidal thinking and behaviour. Healy's discoveries helped fuel global alarm, and growing consumer and media activism that ultimately forced health authorities in Britain, the United States and elsewhere to open investigations into the safety of the whole class of new anti-depressants, with some extraordinary outcomes, as we saw in chapter 2.

After a close examination of the GSK-funded trials of Paxil in children and adolescents with depression, the regulators in the UK and the US finally uncovered the fact that potentially impor-tant behaviours had been mislabelled in those company trials under the term 'emotional lability'. Forced to go back and relook at the data from their own trials, GSK then reported that there was in fact a higher incidence of suicidal thinking and suicide attempts among the children taking Paxil compared to the children taking a placebo or dummy pill.[48] When authorities broadened their investigations to look at several of the other similar antidepressants, they found similar dangers.

At the same time as looking at side effects, the regulators also decided to investigate the supposed benefits of the anti-depressants. To their shock they found that when all of the company-funded trials in children with depression were reviewed and summarised, there was no good evidence that the antidepressants were any better than a placebo.[49] Yet prescrip-tions to the young had been skyrocketing.[50] In the US alone, 5 million prescriptions a year were being written for Paxil and Zoloft for people under eighteen.[51] Against the backdrop of an exploding scandal, and claims of fundamental weaknesses in drug regulation, the authorities finally reacted. In 2003, with the exception of Prozac, the British authorities recommended against using these drugs for children. In 2004 in the US, in the heat of a presidential race, the FDA finally required 'Black Box' warnings on the labels of all antidepressants, including Prozac, a move likely to slow rates of prescriptions at home and elsewhere in the world.

In mid-2004, the New York Attorney-General, Elliot Spitzer, launched his own legal action against GSK, very publicly accusing the company of fraud. He alleged the drug company concealed data about both the dangers of Paxil and the lack of evidence of benefit in depressed children, and it had therefore misled doctors and the public.[52] Within three months GSK had settled the case. While it rejected the charges as unfounded, it did agree to pay $2.5 million to avoid the cost of protracted legal action with the state of New York.[53]

In court documents the company argued that because Paxil was not officially approved for use in children (it was being prescribed by doctors off-label), GSK had therefore been legally restricted from distributing all the information from its clinical trials.[54] Yet, according to press reports, an internal GSK memo sent to its drug detailers in 2003 specifically advises the company's sales representatives not to discuss the potential link with suicidal behaviour with prescribing doctors.[55]

Around the same time as the New York Attorney-General's allegations, GSK announced the creation of a new register of its trials, to allow more public scrutiny of the results whether they are favourable or not. The GSK register is one part of a worldwide move towards a global register of all trials, an initiative pushed by reformers for decades that may bring a long overdue transparency to industry-funded medical science.[56] While some observers hope these developments will herald a new era of openness and accountability within the drug industry, it is far too early to make that call yet.

Creating a publicly accessible register of trials will make it harder for companies or researchers to conceal unfavourable study results, but it will do nothing to control the marketing campaigns designed to change the way we think about medical conditions. Cohn & Wolfe, the subsidiary of the giant WPP communications group, exquisitely executed GSK's social anxiety disorder campaign, generated a billion media impressions, sent sales of Paxil through the roof, and picked up an industry award for its efforts. Unless the regulatory environment changes, the PR world will be emboldened by this successful model, Cohn & Wolfe will do so again, and most likely so will the firm's competitors, who will help to foster the creation of conditions not even yet imagined by Vince Parry. One of those competitors, the Manhattan firm Manning Selvage and Lee (MS&L), had this to say in a recent advertisement pitched at pharmaceutical company executives:

> At MS&L, we have a new and higher purpose.
> We don't just change perceptions,
> because perceptions can be fleeting.
> What we do—in every sense of the words—is this:
> Change Minds[57]

As we saw with depression, part of the 'awareness-raising' about social anxiety disorder was designed to narrowly portray the condition as being caused by a 'chemical imbalance' in the brain, to be fixed with chemical solutions like Paxil.[58] Company suggestions that one in eight people have a psychiatric condition that 'may be related to an imbalance of a chemical' are as absurd as they are false. A more rational public discussion of the causes of social unease—one truly seeking to educate people rather than propagate sales—would take a very different approach.

A recent textbook about social anxiety suggests an analysis of its causes might fruitfully begin 'not with the reasons why particular individuals are shy or anxious, but with investigation of cultural influences on patterns of social interaction'.[59] The editors of the book, which collates the work of different researchers from around the world, suggest a first step towards understanding is asking, 'What is the nature of a society that produces widespread social unease among its members?' A question, according to the book's editors, that provokes speculation and research about cultural phenomena like competition, our definitions of success, and changing patterns of how we relate to one another—rather than chemical imbalances in the brain.

The push to suggest that the 'cause' of this condition lies within the individual, whether for biological or psychological reasons, clearly distracts all of us from a broader understanding of the complex sources of social anxiety—whether it is defined as a mental disorder or not. While this is not the only condition where this is the case, it serves as a strong example of a much wider problem. The messages coming from the pharmaceutical industry's marketing machinery try to keep the public focus on a narrow range of chemical *solutions* to health problems. But they also keep the focus on a narrow range of *causes*.

There is a growing body of scientific evidence that suggests the health of individuals and populations is determined by many more factors than their serotonin levels and how many medicines they consume.[60] Factors that relate to education, environment, the economy, and inequality have big influences on health. To keep pushing the attention of the public, and their decision-makers in government, towards such narrowly defined chemical causes and pharmaceutical solutions is to potentially miss out as a community on much safer, cheaper and far more effective ways to reduce the burden of genuine illness and help make more people healthier and happier. Perhaps one of the best examples of the public debate being skewed in this way is the current obsession for testing bone density in order to prevent fractures.

# Testing the markets

*Osteoporosis*

It was a bright winter morning in Edmonton, the capital of the Canadian province of Alberta. The ground was coated with a fresh blanket of snow that had fallen overnight. With no bird tracks yet tracing the tops of the snowdrifts the world looked so smooth, so beautiful, so uncomplicated. Or so thought Wendy Armstrong, a former nurse turned health advocate as she looked out her kitchen window and picked up the phone.

There was only one message left overnight on the Alberta Consumers' Association's answering machine. An Edmonton woman in alarmed tones asked: 'What the heck is going on?' She was talking about something she'd heard on the radio. It sounded like an advertisement but she wasn't sure. A popular sports announcer on a local radio station was hectoring his listeners as if he was calling a hockey game. 'C'mon, are you worried about that dreaded disease called osteoporosis that's sweeping the nation? Then get down to Saint Mike's and get your bone density test today. And Alberta Health will even pay for it.'[1]

This hectoring by the local sports announcer was in fact the start of a global decade-long campaign to drive women into clinics to get their bone density tested. The campaign was enthusiastically supported by the drug companies, who make money selling the drugs for the condition, and the specialist doctors called radiologists, who make money doing the tests. Using a raft of sophisticated public relations techniques, this informal alliance has tried to convince a generation of healthy women that they are at risk of breaking a bone at any moment and that their very lives are in peril, stalked constantly by the 'silent thief' of osteoporosis.

What the campaign propaganda usually leaves out is that the value of these bone density tests is highly controversial, the drugs are often of modest benefit yet carry serious side effects, and whether this is a disease at all is open to question. The loss of bone density is something that occurs in many people as they age—it is a natural, normal process, except in very rare cases. Having bones with particularly low mineral density does increase a person's chances of a future fracture, but it is just one among a series of factors that do—including whether or not there are loose mats in your house and whether you might need better glasses. When a group of independent Canadian researchers and doctors based at the University of British Columbia examined all of the scientific data about osteoporosis a few years ago, they concluded that the widespread promotion of bone density tests to women was a classic case of 'the marketing of fear'.[2]

Hip fractures due to falls are a huge public health issue affecting millions of elderly people around the world every year.[3] A hip fracture can be devastating to an individual, and costly to a health system. They usually don't happen until someone is quite elderly, and are often associated with the closing chapter of life. There are many ways to try to prevent hip and other fractures, including changes in lifestyle, diet, and household arrangements, but in recent years there has been a narrowing focus on the measurements of bone density, coinciding with the release of new blockbuster drugs that slow its loss. Like ice covered by a snow drift, falls—one of the main reasons people break their hips—have stayed buried under mounds of enthusiasm from those pushing the testing and the drugs. In 2003 Americans spent $1.7 billion on just one osteoporosis drug to slow the loss of bone density—Fosamax—yet it's highly likely the nation only spent a tiny fraction of that on public awareness campaigns to try to prevent elderly people falling.[4]

Because osteoporosis essentially has no symptoms, drug companies have had to work hard to convince women to take the condition seriously. The key to selling has been to instil enough fear to drive people into clinics to get tested for the 'disease' and then to get them into treatment. Central to the industry's campaigns have been marketing specialists like Kym White. A PR professional with the New York office of Ogilvy Public Relations, the confident White has spent nearly twenty years advising the world's major health care, pharmaceutical and biotechnology companies on PR, including how to mount successful 'disease awareness' campaigns.

Kym White recalls early market research on osteoporosis that uncovered a major problem for the pharmaceutical industry: basically the average person in the street wasn't really all that worried about it. In fact, in the early 1990s, few people had even heard about osteoporosis and if they had, it was largely dismissed as something that hunched-over little old ladies had. This signalled to the PR world that osteoporosis needed a makeover. She explains: 'What needed to be done in the field of osteoporosis—for all the companies that had a stake in that disease—was we needed to convince women who were much closer to the age of 50 that osteoporosis was something that they needed to be thinking about then, because there were steps they could be taking in their fifties and in their sixties, to make sure that they didn't end up being that little old woman that they saw on the street.'[5]

One of the companies with a big stake in osteoporosis was Merck, which launched a drug called Fosamax in 1995, the first 'blockbuster' in a new generation of osteoporosis drugs. Even before its drug hit the streets in the US, Merck was subsidising the distribution of the bone density testing machines needed to ensure that women would get the diagnosis for which Merck's drug would be prescribed—a brilliant strategy that earned the company accolades for its business acumen.[6] One analyst noted simply: 'The more physicians who are capable of reliably diagnosing osteoporosis, the more prescriptions for Fosamax are likely to be written.'[7]

Coincidentally, just a year or so before Fosamax's launch, a new definition of the condition called osteoporosis had been written by a study group of the World Health Organization.[8] That group decided that 'normal' bone density was the bone density of a young woman (a thirty-year-old)—a definition that automatically made the bones of many older women 'abnormal'. In an extraordinary moment of candour the authors admitted that the decision about where to draw the line defining osteoporosis is 'somewhat arbitrary'. They then proceeded to write a definition that automatically defined 30 per cent of all postmenopausal women as having a disease. Under these rules an X-ray would be used to scan bone density. If a woman had a little bit of bone loss compared to the bones of a young woman, then that would constitute 'pre-osteoporosis'—or osteopenia. A little bit more bone loss, and a woman would be diagnosed and labelled as having a 'disease' called osteoporosis.

While this definition is now widely accepted within medicine, it has also generated strong criticism from those like the independent group of researchers at Canada's University of British Columbia, who see it as another example of turning an aspect of ordinary life into a medical condition. Helping fuel that criticism is the fact that two other drug companies funded WHO study groups' deliberations, sponsoring the key meeting where the definition was finalised.[9] With the imprimatur of the WHO, this definition established an international benchmark, which has gone on to spawn the mainstream measures of the diagnosis and treatment of osteoporosis around the world, from Alberta to New South Wales.

Based on the WHO definition, groups like the National Osteoporosis Foundation in the US tell us that this 'debilitating disease' is a 'major public health threat for an estimated 44 million Americans', or more than half of the entire population over 50 years old. That 44 million figure includes 10 million who qualify for the diagnosis of the 'disease' 'osteoporosis' and another 34 million estimated to have low bone mass or osteopenia, putting them 'at risk' of osteoporosis.[10] Like many other ostensibly independent groups, this osteoporosis foundation has received support from drug companies.

For independent-minded health researchers like Australian Professor David Henry, this corporate-sponsored approach to understanding the problem of bone loss and fractures is simply wrong. The head of a multidisciplinary team of public health scientists and medical doctors based at the University of Newcastle in Australia, Henry is appalled by the attempt to turn so many healthy women into patients. He believes the use of figures like 44 million promote fear rather than understanding and positive action. When people define osteoporosis as a 'disease' that needs to be treated, rather than seeing fractures primarily as a public health problem that might benefit from changes in lifestyle and diet, says Henry bluntly, 'that is disease-mongering'.[11]

While the grossly inflated figures may draw sharp criticism from some, they unquestionably help the pharmaceutical industry to claim that this 'disease' is widely underdiagnosed and undertreated. Which is exactly what Merck has done. In its communications to shareholders, the company has emphasised the treatment gap, saying that 'fewer than 25 percent of women with osteoporosis in seven major markets have been diagnosed and treated'.[12]

Back in Edmonton, Wendy Armstrong witnessed first hand how the whole osteoporosis machine kicked into gear around the time of those hectoring radio announcements. In 1994 in Alberta, a province of almost 3 million people, there were just over 2500 bone density tests done. By the time Merck's Fosamax had hit the Canadian market two years later, that number had increased more than fivefold, to over 13 000.[13] The climb in bone density testing helped bring on the explosion in sales of osteoporosis drugs,[14] creating a global market for the pharmaceutical industry currently worth $5 billion annually, but predicted by some to reach over $10 billion in a few short years.[15]

While the tests were certainly building drug sales, some of the scientists were becoming more and more uncertain that this strategy of focusing on testing and drugs was the best way for individuals or communities to prevent fractures. A landmark 1997 report from the British Columbia Office of Health

Technology Assessment based in Vancouver examined the entire body of evidence for bone density testing to try to find out what the scientific data was showing. The authors, those same independent researchers from the University of British Columbia, concluded: 'Research evidence does not support either whole population or selective bone mineral density testing of well women at or near menopause as a means to predict future fractures.'[16]

The conclusion strongly contradicts the marketing messages urging widespread testing, and it is well backed up by other scientific evidence, and similar conclusions from other researchers elsewhere around the world. A large Dutch study, published in the *British Medical Journal* the same year, found that a person's loss of bone density actually only contributes about one-sixth of their overall risk of a future hip fracture, and that several other factors such as the strength of muscles and likelihood of falling have a big influence.[17] In other words bone density is only a relatively minor component of a person's chances of future fracture. The Dutch researchers concluded that slowing the loss of bone density with drugs can help reduce the risk of a hip fracture, but it is just one factor and it only makes a 'limited contribution'.

In 1999, again in the *British Medical Journal*, Professor Terence Wilkin from the University of Plymouth argued strongly that based on his reading of the scientific evidence, the widely used tests were not good predictors of future fractures.[18] Rather than manage osteoporosis by numbers, Wilkin wrote, there should be more focus on other strategies like preventing falls among the elderly. Most disturbingly, he presented evidence suggesting that other changes in the bones—relating to their architecture rather than their density—may have a much bigger impact on a person's chances of a future fracture. He concluded there was no benefit in widespread testing for bone mineral density, and suggested that while there was a role for drugs to prevent fractures, their benefits may be just as great if women started taking them much later in life than many of them currently do—in other words much closer to the time when fractures are more likely to occur.

In a short piece criticising Wilkin's article, Professor Richard Eastell from the University of Sheffield said he believed it was 'reasonable' to use a test for bone mineral density to assess someone's risk of future fracture, and to make decisions about whether to recommend drugs. Yet his endorsement of widespread testing was lukewarm to say the least, conceding that the narrow focus on bone density 'ignores the importance of other determinants of bone strength and of factors that increase the risk of falls'—including things like low body weight and smoking. While Eastell's links with the pharmaceutical industry were not specified in the *British Medical Journal*, they were disclosed elsewhere at the time: he was an adviser to four drug companies.[19]

Yet despite the uncertainty and debate about how reliably the bone density tests can predict whether a person goes on to have a fracture, their uptake has continued to expand dramatically. In Vancouver, British Columbia, at the Women's and Children's Health Centre, one of the early Canadian champions of testing, Dr Brian Lentle, runs the hospital's quality program for bone density testing. As a radiologist he has had a front-row seat watching the massive growth of this testing industry in the very Canadian province that produced some of the harshest scientific criticism of its use.

Lentle disagrees strongly with the conclusions of the landmark 1997 report by the University of British Columbia researchers, and says that bone density testing is an important service people need access to because of its ability to help diagnose osteoporosis. But he adds that over the years, the enthusiasm behind the marketing of the tests has gone too far, and that 'a lot of the tests that are being done shouldn't be done'.[20]

Dr Ken Bassett, a medical doctor, researcher and anthropologist and one of the co-authors of the 1997 report, recalls the immense controversy that ensued in Canada when it came out. Even though he and his colleagues were attacked in the medical and popular press, largely by those with a stake in promoting bone density testing and osteoporosis drugs, the science behind their report has never been refuted. While many company-sponsored websites urge women to get their bones tested, whenever independent scientists look at the evidence behind the tests they tend to find the same thing: the tests are not good predictors of future fractures.[21]

Even seven years later, authors of new Canadian guidelines on osteoporosis concluded 'there is no *direct* [in original] evidence that screening reduces fractures', merely *indirect* evidence that testing helps identify women with the condition, and that treatment for the condition can reduce the risk of future fracture.[22] On the basis of their reading of the evidence, the authors of the latest guidelines recommended that routine screening should not start until age 65.[23]

Some public health departments in Canadian provinces tried to stem the tide of the invasion of bone density machines. Similarly, some were initially reluctant to reimburse the X-rays with public funds, precisely because of the lack of evidence of the benefits of testing, as pointed out in the 1997 British Columbia Office of Health Technology Assessment report and by others.[24] Yet that didn't stop the rapid uptake of bone density testing: champions ignored the uncertainty and controversy surrounding the evidence and worked with patient groups, drug companies, private radiology and menopause clinics to plant the seeds of fear far and wide.

Some of the strategies for the campaign drew on the expertise of those with a specialty in changing minds, like the PR professional Kym White. She explains the importance of the work done at the grassroots level, which is often organised with the help of public relations agencies. Those 'grassroots' activities include providing speaker's kits to women's health groups, promoting book signings at stores like Barnes & Noble, and educational events raising awareness about the value of bone density testing. For White, while company sponsorship often plays a role in these activities, companies also have a 'shared agenda' with the other players about the main messages that need to be communicated. Yet independent health advocates like the Alberta Consumers' Association, and independent researchers like those at the University of British Columbia, do not share the same 'agenda' or agree at all with White as to what are the 'main messages'.

Importantly, public relations companies also helped orchestrate what's called 'third-party' groups to lobby governments so women have access to affordable bone mass measurement. The use of 'third-party' organisations that appear to be independent is a well-established PR technique for trying to put corporate messages into other mouths. The 'legislative component' of these campaigns targeted government and health insurance plan decision-makers who needed to be convinced to fund bone density tests. The rationale was simple, according to Kym White: 'If the test wasn't paid for, there were a lot of women who, even if their awareness was heightened, weren't going to seek that test.'[25]

One of the vehicles used to put bone density measurement higher on the legislative agenda around the world was the

'Osteobus' funded by drug companies and local osteoporosis societies. Over the past decade or so these mobile bone density testing buses travelled across Europe, North America and the Middle East, disseminating 'comprehensive information about osteoporosis' and 'empowering people to take responsibility for their own health'.[26] It came with 'videos, posters and medical experts on-hand to answer questions' and it rolled into communities that may have never heard about osteoporosis, offering citizens the sponsors' version of this disease. The bus got itself on the agenda of political decision-makers in some cases by literally driving into their parking lots.

The Osteobus appeared at Israel's Knesset, home of the Israeli parliament, parked itself across from the headquarters of the World Health Organization in Geneva, visited Brussels, headquarters of the European Parliament and educated members of the Legislative Assembly of Ontario, Canada's largest province. Getting politicians on board for bone density tests is not only a unique way to sell the merits of the technology, but it gave those tests traction in the minds of key health decision-makers. In Poland, the Osteobus won an important PR award from the International Public Relations Association.[27]

According to White, it is all of these sorts of promotional activities that really paid off: 'I think what we've succeeded in doing, certainly, was really putting osteoporosis higher on the agenda, certainly for public funding.' So high in fact that the number of bone density tests done in the province of Alberta went from around 13 000 in 1996 to over 90 000 by the year 2000.[28] While that dramatic increase may be of concern to health advocates like Wendy Armstrong at the Alberta Consumers' Association—well schooled in the scientific uncertainty surrounding the test's value—there seems to be no stopping the juggernaut.

If you think you are healthy, you just haven't had enough tests.

Dr Bob Rangno

As it has rolled on, the PR campaign appears to be targeting younger women. A recent issue of the magazine *Health* featured a front-cover headline: 'Brittle Bones at 30: It could happen to you.' The story profiled a group of women who 'discover' that their bodies are already wracked by the 'silent thief' and are thankful that they are learning about their risk of future fracture. As is typical in such profiles, this story came with a sidebar mini-questionnaire where anyone answering with 'yes' at least twice is encouraged to consult their physician. In the same issue of this magazine was a three-page ad for Merck's Fosamax, now available in a new 'once weekly' formula, which marketed the drug by marketing the test: 'Ask your doctor if a Bone Density Test is right for you.'[29]

These types of ads beg the question: how well do the drugs actually work? How much prevention is packed into these kinds of pills for women who have been told their bone density isn't what it should be? As it turns out, the actual risk of a major hip fracture, and the genuine benefits of these drugs, are both much smaller than you might think if you listen to all the frightening statistics. As with other conditions like high cholesterol, it is those at very high risk of a future illness who can benefit most from drugs that reduce those risks. For most relatively healthy people at low risk, taking a powerful drug over the long term could do more harm than good.

One of the key studies of Fosamax that attracted a lot of attention at the time the drug was hitting the market was a Merck-funded study called the Fracture Intervention Trial.[30] It compared the drug to a placebo over four years. According to many advertisements, widely read newspaper reports and much-watched TV broadcasts, that study found that the drug reduced the risk of hip fracture by 50 per cent—an extremely impressive figure for women, their doctors, and Merck's potential investors. But taking a closer look at the study reveals a very different picture. Firstly, it was only women at 'high risk' of a future fracture who were included in the published study—in other words, older women who had already experienced at least one fracture. This is a much smaller group than the tens of millions of healthy women targeted by the promotion of bone density tests.

Among the women in the study taking the placebo, two out of a hundred, or 2 per cent, had a hip fracture during the trial. Among the women taking the drug, 1 per cent had a hip fracture. In *relative* terms the drug reduced the risk of a hip fracture by 50 per cent—from two to one. In *absolute* terms it is a 1 per cent reduction. Yet most media coverage never supplies these much less impressive absolute numbers. A study of five years' worth of media coverage of Fosamax found that among the newspaper and television stories that featured statistics about this drug, more than 80 per cent of stories only used the much more impressive relative numbers—'the drug cut the risk by 50 per cent'—without giving people any indication of just how small this benefit was in absolute terms.[31] While that Fosamax study was only in 'high risk' women, the results of a much larger government-run trial show that for most healthy women the long-term benefits of drug therapy are minuscule in terms of reducing the risks of hip fractures.

Before Fosamax, it was hormone replacement therapy that was sold to women as the panacea for fighting osteoporosis and preventing fractures. In 2002, when the giant publicly funded Women's Health Initiative study reported its results on HRT, the actual benefits of taking long-term HRT were finally out in the open for the world to see. Among the women taking a placebo, roughly twelve in a thousand had a hip fracture over the seven years of the study. Taking HRT reduced that risk from twelve in a thousand to about eight in a thousand: in relative terms an impressive 33 per cent reduction; in absolute terms a 0.4 per cent reduction.[32]

With such modest benefits, the costs and risks of drugs become much more important. We now know HRT came with the risks of increased heart attacks, strokes, blood clots and breast cancer. The side effects of Fosamax are not so serious, but can still be very troubling. Due to its potentially corrosive nature it is linked to severe damage to the oesophagus and stomach. Its other known adverse effects include diarrhoea, flatulence, rashes, headaches and muscular pain.[33] In 1996, the first full year it was on the market, there were more than 6000 formal adverse drug reactions reported to the US government, the most reports made about any single drug that year.[34] Since that time Merck has re-released Fosamax in a once-weekly formulation, rather than as a daily tablet—for 'convenience', according to the company.[35]

Luckily, there are several safer ways of preventing fractures in the elderly than taking long-term potentially troublesome pills. What seem to be most successful are programs that try to prevent the traumatic event that usually precedes a hip fracture: a fall. Fall prevention programs, weaning the elderly off large multiple-medication regimes, fixing footpaths and improving eyewear are all ways to try and reduce hip fractures.[36]

One of the disturbing concerns raised about the mass promotion of both the tests and the drugs is that labelling people as having osteoporosis may actually cause them to stop taking the preventive measures that may help reduce their future risk of fractures. For example, people who are told they have diseased and brittle bones may stop exercising for fear of fractures, even though exercise is proven to help develop muscle and balance and works as a key foil to falling and fracturing a hip. So the rush to measure, label and treat a woman's 'risk' factors may, for some women, be causing more problems than it is solving. Until large long-term studies of bone density testing and the osteoporosis drugs are done, many of these nagging questions will remain.

Somehow, though, the non-drug approaches can't seem to compete with the continued zeal for bone density measurement and drug treatment. Even Brian Lentle, now the President of the Radiological Society of North America, representing the very specialists who have done so well from the testing explosion, believes some doctors are too enthusiastic about the tests he says should be reserved for women at high risk.

One independent scientist who continues to question the value of the whole screening and testing approach to conditions like osteoporosis is Dr Ken Bassett. As a physician, he describes how wearying it is in the actual practice of medicine to know the scientific evidence about bone density and fractures, and to then spend a lot of time rebuffing patients who ask for what he considers to be mostly useless tests. With deep frown lines, Bassett says he uses a lot of his energy as a doctor 'trying to resist the pressure to have a routine cholesterol test on a young, healthy woman or man, trying to resist having bone density tests, when I know that it will for the most part lead to a misleading labelling of a person[37] ... What I think is the problem, and the one where I think we've failed as a society ... is in this whole area of how many healthy people are now having tests, labelling themselves at risk, altering their behaviour, and using up limited social resources to use medicines that we are blandly assuming are doing more good than harm.'[38]

Health advocate Wendy Armstrong agrees with Bassett that too many healthy people are being labelled as patients, but rejects as a 'modern urban myth' the argument that consumers are to blame for the rising use of drugs and tests of dubious value. Her anger rises steadily as she says that the one thing that she can be sure of after spending fifteen years researching and writing reports on the impact of medical technologies on consumers is that 'most—but not all—of the demand for new medical technologies is driven by opportunistic investors seeking new products and profits—not patients seeking new diagnosis and treatments'.[39]

Whatever is driving demand, there are plenty more osteoporosis products in the pipeline and plenty more tests to help sell people the idea that they are sick enough to want to take those products. There are no less than four new osteoporosis drugs in the pipeline, and as each comes to market it will likely be accompanied by a renewed marketing effort to get as many people tested as possible.[40] And with the advent of gene technology, and the possibility of screening newborns for all their future diseases, a whole new world of testing awaits us all.[41]

The UK health advocacy group GeneWatch has already raised concern that the biotech and pharmaceutical industry may be gearing up to promote widespread genetic testing for common diseases 'because it allows them to expand the market for both genetic tests and preventive medication'. This group's worry is that mass gene screening may spark a new level of inappropriate medicalisation, as we have already seen with osteoporosis. 'Because the predictive value of most genetic tests is very low, many children could end up taking medicines that they do not need,' says the report.

Back in Alberta, Canada, Wendy Armstrong's concerns about bone density testing have only grown in the decade or so since she first got that worried call one snowy morning. She argues today that wasting money on needless tests and therapies may actually be threatening the future of publicly funded health care systems.

> There wouldn't be waiting lists if the public system and doctors spent more time and money on the things that needed to be done and quit wasting money and valuable specialists' time on tests and procedures done on the wrong person, at the wrong time, in the wrong place, for all the wrong reasons.[42]

Part of the challenge for those seeking a more rational debate about the use of drugs for osteoporosis—or any other condition—is that some of the key public agencies in health care are themselves now under the influence of the drug companies. Perhaps the best, but saddest example is the US FDA, once considered a fearless watchdog but now seen by some as making the decisions of a tamed pup.

# 9

# Taming the watchdogs

*Irritable bowel syndrome*

The sweltering days of summer were just starting to hit Washington, DC when Paul Stolley took up his job as a senior consultant at the US Food and Drug Administration, headquartered just outside the capital's border. Inside the giant grey complex of concrete and glass, the FDA's mission is to make sure medicines are safe and effective for the almost 300 million Americans it serves. Its deliberations determine which drugs get approved for sale into the massive US market, and which don't, and it influences the actions of drug regulators and health care watchdogs around the world. As a result, the decisions made behind closed doors here have a profound effect on the bottom lines of some of the world's most profitable corporations.

Dr Stolley was joining the watchdog with an impeccable record. A distinguished professor of medicine at several leading universities and a member of the National Academy of Science, he was pleased to be embarking on a new challenge. A long-time expert in drug safety, he was immediately asked by his superiors to look into a new medication that had just come on to the market. The drug was called Lotronex and it had been recently approved for women with irritable bowel syndrome (IBS), a condition not widely known, characterised by stomach pains and difficulties with constipation and diarrhoea.[1]

A few months earlier in London, *The Lancet* had published the positive results of a study of Lotronex, helping to secure its approval by the FDA. In the article a group of scientists wrote that the drug was a safe and effective treatment for people with IBS, describing their findings as 'important'.[2] In the world of medical science, a positive study in *The Lancet* is worth gold, which was good news for the drug's manufacturer GSK.[3] Company executives were banking on another billion-dollar blockbuster, because despite being poorly understood, IBS was said to be a disease affecting up to one in every five people in the western world—nearly 45 million in the US alone.[4]

Before his first summer at the agency was even over, Paul Stolley was suggesting to his FDA superiors that they consider pulling the new drug from the market because of serious concerns about its safety. Prior to his arrival, reports of severe side effects had already started turning up at the agency. As the promotion of the drug heated up and prescriptions flowed as a result, those worrying reports were now coming thick and fast, sometimes on a daily basis. Called 'adverse event reports', they are sent into the FDA by drug company officials or practising physicians, and they describe the complications people experience. In the case of Lotronex, two side effects in particular emerged as the most serious: severe constipation; and something called 'ischaemic colitis'. Both were potentially fatal.[5]

For some of those who experienced severe constipation after taking the drug, their faeces would become so impacted within their bowel that the bowel wall perforated, leading to potentially fatal infections inside the body.[6] The other side effect, ischaemic colitis, is like a heart attack happening in the bowel, and the blood simply stops flowing to it. Sometimes it fixes itself, sometimes the bowel tissue dies, and in rare cases so too does the patient.

Reading the reports arriving at the FDA, and rigorously scrutinising all the scientific data from the drug's original clinical trials, Stolley was coming to a disturbing conclusion: the drug's meaningful benefits were on average non-existent or modest at best, yet its side effects were, in rare cases, potentially deadly. By the beginning of the fall of 2000, just six months since its launch, the first reports of deaths from Lotronex were starting to arrive at the agency. Stolley's level of unease was rising sharply as it was becoming clear that for some people, this cure was proving far worse than the condition.

As a long-time academic physician, seeing patients and working in scientific research, Stolley knew that for a small proportion of people irritable bowel syndrome could be severe and debilitating, but for most people its symptoms were mild and temporary.[7] He and other safety experts inside the FDA were coming to the conclusion that some of those taking the drug were suffering life-threatening side effects far worse than the symptoms the drug was supposed to be treating. But because the FDA had officially approved the drug for sale, this potentially deadly medicine could be aggressively promoted to millions of essentially healthy people.

As Stolley would soon learn to his horror, Lotronex was just the latest in a series of heavily promoted 'blockbuster' drugs that had been approved by the FDA, but later found to cause serious harm, including in rare cases death. He would also learn that in the years before his arrival, the source of funding for the regulator had fundamentally shifted. More than 50 per cent of the FDA's work checking the safety and effectiveness of drugs was now paid for by the companies whose products were being reviewed. In many European nations the situation is similar. In Australia, also through a user-pays system, companies foot 100 per cent of the public regulator's bills.[8] Despite the dedication and commitment of staff like Stolley, critics everywhere are raising concerns about this fundamental conflict of interests at the heart of health care regulation. In Canada a former regulatory official summed up a growing sentiment about the watchdogs, saying of her ex-employer 'This dog won't hunt.'[9]

In the US, the FDA's entanglement with the pharmaceutical industry would explode into the centre of public debate during congressional hearings four years later. Long-time FDA safety expert turned whistleblower Dr David Graham would then famously tell an astonished world that 'the FDA, as currently configured, is incapable of protecting America . . .'.[10] The agency's behaviour during the debacle over Lotronex would contribute to a growing sense of alarm inside and outside the FDA, ultimately precipitating a major crisis of legitimacy for one of the world's highest profile health regulators.

Outside the FDA, back in 2000 others studying the scientific data on the irritable bowel syndrome drug Lotronex were reaching similar conclusions to Paul Stolley. Physicians at the fiercely independent US consumer group Public Citizen had used freedom of information laws to get access to internal FDA documents about the original scientific studies. This data seemed to contradict the rosy picture painted in the *Lancet* publication, and the Public Citizen team argued the article exaggerated the drug's benefits.[11] They also pointed out that five of the six authors who wrote the influential paper were drug company employees, as had been disclosed in the article. Based on their examination of the internal FDA material, the consumer group concluded that the drug was only slightly more effective than a placebo—or dummy pill—at helping treat people's symptoms. Yet for some, it was causing horrendous side effects. Like Stolley, the group pushed the FDA to immediately withdraw it from the market.

The FDA rejected calls for a ban as too drastic and instead opted for cosmetic changes to the way the drug was being marketed, introducing an educational 'medication guide', a brochure designed to inform people about risks but thought to have little meaningful impact in the marketplace. But as concern about Lotronex grew and the number of reported deaths increased, pressure for tougher action mounted. On 13 November 2000, GSK officials met with FDA staff to discuss the drug. Significantly, the scientists tracking the reports of Lotronex's side effects were not able to present their data at the meeting, apparently because of time constraints.

Three days later, Stolley and three other colleagues felt it was time to get serious, so they penned a powerful internal memo arguing that the rising toll of deaths, hospitalisations and complications had never before been seen by physicians treating irritable bowel syndrome.[12] The memo claimed that the measures being taken to inform people, and solutions being suggested by the company to manage the risks, were inadequate to stop the mounting casualties. As the scientists pointed out, there was no real way of knowing who might be at risk of a life-threatening complication from this drug. The clear implication was that anyone taking it was at risk, and that it should therefore come off the market immediately.

At a meeting two weeks later GSK officials aggressively attacked that memo, while senior FDA management sat by and listened, failing to defend their own staff's work. Stolley had by then formed the opinion that the regulator's slowness to act against Lotronex was directly related to a desire among some senior FDA officers not to offend the pharmaceutical industry, which was after all paying for half the agency's budget for its drug review work. For him that meeting sent a powerful signal to the young FDA scientists present, and it was symptomatic of a much bigger malaise. He felt it was sending the message that 'we don't argue with drug companies; we listen to their distortions and omissions of evidence and we do nothing about it'.[13] One of the senior officers at the meeting, Dr Janet Woodcock, directly rejected Stolley's view. 'The FDA wanted to determine a course forward, not to argue the details,' she said.[14]

Faced with the mounting evidence of dangerous side effects, negative media coverage and a regulator apparently unable to 'determine a course forward', the company decided to voluntarily withdraw the drug from the US market after that bitter November meeting. But like Lazarus rising from the dead, Lotronex would be re-approved eighteen months later, despite its modest benefits and potentially deadly side effects.

In January, just two months after the initial withdrawal, Stolley felt he had been frozen out of the discussions about the drug's future, until he got a call from Woodcock asking him to come and see her. He thought at first there might have been a change of heart within the FDA leadership. Instead Woodcock lectured him: Lotronex was a good drug and the FDA should work hard to bring it back on to the market. Moreover, the senior scientist was reprimanded for 'browbeating' colleagues about its risks. The message was being sent loud and clear to all those within the FDA: help get this drug back on the market. One of the most senior experts on drug safety in the agency— also alarmed at the drug's obvious dangers—was told explicitly by his superiors that he was not to work on Lotronex.[15]

Meanwhile patient groups, including at least one funded by GSK, wrote letters to the FDA demanding the drug be re-approved. At the same time company officials were in close contact with the regulator's staff, including Woodcock, causing critics to suggest the relationships were unhealthy—an interpretation both the company and the regulator firmly reject. 'The FDA had to work with the company in order to facilitate the drug's availability,' said Woodcock.[16]

As the campaign to bring the drug back intensified, the focus of attention for all the key players shifted to a forthcoming meeting of the FDA's advisory committee. These advisory committees are central to the FDA processes of drug regulation. The panels comprise a group of outside researchers who meet, usually to consider the merits of allowing a drug on to the market, what sort of warnings might be appropriate, or what sort of restrictions on prescribing might be desirable. At public hearings the advisers listen to different speakers, discuss the evidence and ultimately make recommendations back to the FDA. Usually the agency follows the committee's advice. Internal FDA emails that surfaced publicly some time later suggest that in this case GSK officials and FDA staff were working closely to try to ensure beforehand that the advisory committee was going to give the advice that the company and the senior FDA staff wanted.[17]

The advisory committee finally met to reconsider Lotronex's future in the northern spring of 2002. By then, even though the drug had been on the market for around one year and then off the market for eighteen months, there were over 200 reports of serious complications and seven reports of deaths, deemed by FDA scientists as probably linked to the drug. Given that only a tiny proportion of serious complications are ever reported to the FDA, it was possible that anywhere between 2000 and 20 000 women had been made seriously ill, and perhaps scores had died due to complications associated with a drug whose benefits were the subject of serious scientific doubt.[18]

But after listening to a public hearing that mainly featured stories from patients praising the drug, and after assessing the evidence about risks and benefits, the advisory committee went ahead and voted to re-approve Lotronex, with the caveat that there should be tough restrictions on the way it was to be prescribed. A key condition of recommending approval was that physicians would have to be trained and certified to use the drug before they could prescribe it. In their discussions committee members explicitly rejected a weaker company proposal to allow prescribing doctors to simply vouch for their own abilities, rather than have to undergo training and certification.

Six weeks later the FDA announced the re-approval of Lotronex—but amazingly, rejected the advisory committee's recommendations for the tough restrictions, and opted instead for the weaker company plan. A number of the advisory committee members were furious. One member said the company-backed proposal adopted by the FDA might have made commercial sense to the company, but not public health sense. 'The risk-benefit ratio is not worth it, unless the use can be restricted to those who really need it and who are likely to benefit from it—which is a very, very small group.'[19]

Another member also had concerns but praised the FDA staff's handling of the drug's regulation, saying that the committee's recommendations may have been too idealistic.[20] Asked why the FDA took the unusual step of rejecting the advisers' recommendations, and accepting the company proposal, Janet Woodcock explained that 'we had to address risk without placing an unnecessary burden on everyone'. The medication quietly returned to the US market just before Christmas 2002.

The real reasons why the FDA was so keen to bring this drug back are not clear, and there are very different explanations depending on the perspective of those you talk to. Janet Woodcock argues that the patient lobbying campaign that began immediately after the withdrawal clearly demonstrated the value of the drug, and that its re-approval was a victory for patients' rights. Others at senior levels within the medical establishment around the world would see the FDA's handling of Lotronex as an example of an emerging pattern of industry influence seriously undermining the public watchdog's independence.[21]

For the critics, the re-approval of Lotronex signalled a growing crisis of legitimacy at the FDA, in light of its dependence on corporate funding. Since 1992 in the US, drug companies have been required to pay fees to have their new drugs assessed. In return they have received quicker reviews and more communication with the regulator—demonstrated here by the interactions between GSK and the FDA. Because public funding has not kept pace with the agency's expanded responsibilities, a decade later we have a situation where drug companies are providing more than half of the budget for what the FDA spends reviewing drugs.[22]

Working out what to do with a drug like Lotronex is not easy. While the trial data suggests average benefits that are modest at best, testimony from patients suggests that for some people the drug may be valuable in reducing the debilitating symptoms of severe IBS. The difficulty for health authorities is to try to make the drug available to those for whom the benefits will outweigh the risks—without putting large numbers of essentially healthy people at risk of serious harm. This was the basis of the strategy suggested by the FDA advisers, but rejected by the FDA's senior officers in favour of a weaker company-backed plan.

Yet the apparent timidity of the FDA is not just due to its closeness with industry. The regulatory bodies that approve drugs in the US and elsewhere are unable or unwilling to play a bigger role in how those drugs are actually prescribed in practice by doctors, because of the tremendous political power of the medical profession and its constantly restated right to clinical freedom. As nations wrestle with exploding drug use and escalating drug costs, it may be time to look for new regulatory mechanisms to influence the way drugs are actually being prescribed in doctors' offices. Banning drugs that might be valuable to a few who are genuinely ill certainly seems an unattractive option. But approving drugs likely to harm many healthy people is surely also undesirable. Whether the established regulators like the FDA, with its recent history of close communication with drug companies, are the appropriate bodies to be forging this new role, is highly questionable. Certainly the Lotronex case is by no means the only example of this cosy relationship.

Following a lengthy investigation by the *Los Angeles Times*, journalist David Willman wrote a landmark article in 2000 that painted a devastating picture of industry influence at the FDA. He portrayed an agency rushing too quickly and too enthusiastically to approve powerful new pills. The story focused on seven drugs, including Lotronex, that eventually had to be removed from the market because they were found to be unsafe. The story was called, 'How a new policy led to seven deadly drugs'. Despite strong denials of unhealthy influence at the FDA, the piece won a Pulitzer Prize, one of the most coveted journalism awards in the US.[23]

In a stinging editorial in 2001 the editor of *The Lancet* suggested the FDA was now a place where dissenting scientific opinion was suppressed, and it had become a 'servant of industry'.[24] *The Lancet* described a 'fatal erosion of integrity' at the FDA, and accused the agency of sidelining its own scientists and conducting private back-channel communications with company staff to help bring the drug back to market. The journal, and other media outlets, published damning internal FDA emails revealing details of some of those communications. In one email about the forthcoming advisory committee meeting Janet Woodcock explained to a colleague that the company was having some 'reservations' about the planned meeting because 'the advisors may disagree with what we have negotiated and put us back at square 1'. She went on to add that she agreed with the company executive that this was a 'real liability'.[25]

In 2002 the front cover of a *British Medical Journal* issue featured a photograph of the regulator's headquarters, with the caption beneath: 'Who owns the FDA? The drug industry or the people?' The opening editorial concluded that by allowing the on-going marketing of Lotronex, a drug that poses such serious risks for people, the FDA had failed in its mission to protect public health.[26]

> Who owns the FDA? The drug industry or the people?
> *British Medical Journal*, cover story, 2002

That issue of the *British Medical Journal* also included a long article about the Lotronex debacle, and the first comprehensive interview with Paul Stolley, who had decided to speak publicly and candidly about his experiences. Cleary bruised by his treat-ment, he described the FDA as a place where dissenting voices are intimidated and ostracised and where scientific debate is repressed. He said the agency was 'confused and frightened' because it was getting money from industry and was too often afraid to offend its sponsors. He had by then left the FDA in disgust at what had happened, and joined the staff of Public Citizen. Janet Woodcock refuted his claims about industry influence, but did not comment directly on Stolley apart from saying, 'It's our responsibility to be dispassionate and not develop emotionally based positions.' As it turned out, two years after making those comments Woodcock would find herself at a special Congressional hearings on the FDA, in front of Senators from both sides of the aisle asking tough questions about alleged drug company influence.[27] Like Woodcock, GSK strongly rejects the idea there was collusion between the company and the regulator, arguing that Lotronex was re-introduced because of overwhelming patient demand.[28]

Stolley's opinions were in fact in keeping with the findings of two surveys of FDA staff. The first, run by Public Citizen from outside the agency, had found that many officers felt under pressure to approve new drugs, received inappropriate phone calls from drug companies, and too often FDA senior officials intervened on a company's behalf in drug approval.[29] The second survey was conducted within the FDA itself, by agency staff. Summarising the responses of more than 130 officers, that survey found that people reviewing drugs reported feeling pres-sure to 'favor the desires of sponsors over science and the public health'.[30] One-third reported that they did not feel comfortable expressing their differing scientific opinion. The write-up of the survey recommended encouraging more 'freedom of expression of scientific opinion'.

Whatever the concerns about industry influence and freedom of expression, one of the great strengths of the FDA is that it makes a lot of material publicly available. Some of the richest sources of information about the Lotronex story are the thousand pages of transcripts of three separate advisory committee meetings that the FDA had convened to review the safety and effectiveness of the drug. As with all committee meetings, the full transcripts are freely available on the web. Reading them offers a series of invaluable insights into the modern processes of drug regulation, the way scientific evidence can sometimes be distorted by those with vested interests, and the timidity of a tamed watchdog apparently too eager to please its sponsors.

What is particularly striking in this case is the mismatch between the hard scientific data about the drug, and the claims being made by GSK spokespeople when addressing the advisory committee meetings. At all three meetings, company staff consistently played up the drug's benefits and played down its potentially deadly side effects. FDA staff who addressed the meetings were by contrast much more sober in their assessments of benefits, and more straightforward about the risks, but their attitudes and approaches to the company's claims were almost always deferential. While GSK officers would claim the drug was 'highly' effective, FDA staff would point out that only a small number of patients would benefit from it, and that many women taking the drug would receive no benefit at all yet were putting themselves at grave risk.[31]

What also emerged from the transcripts was the way GSK officials and patient groups portrayed the condition known as irritable bowel syndrome. In a now familiar pattern, the highest estimates of how many people suffer the condition were quoted, and the condition was described in its most severe form. Company officials called IBS a 'significant disease with a large burden of illness for the individual patient' affecting up to 20 per cent of the entire population. That same figure is used in marketing materials from other companies also promoting drugs for this condition.[32] While it is clear that for some people IBS can be severe and debilitating, other estimates suggest less than 5 per cent of the population have symptoms that meet the standard classification.[33]

The FDA has suggested that only a tiny fraction of those who meet the classification for having IBS have a severe form, and that the vast majority have mild symptoms.[34] In other words, nothing like 20 per cent of people have a 'significant disease' called IBS. But, as we've seen with so many other disorders and diseases, the facts are relatively unimportant: what is important are the marketing messages that infuse multi-layered promotional campaigns involving company-sponsored medical foundations, celebrities, thought-leaders and consumer groups.

The image of a severe, widespread disease is strongly backed by one of the leading patient advocacy groups in this field, the International Foundation for Functional Gastrointestinal Disorders. Its president, Nancy Norton, spoke at all three FDA advisory meetings and as the transcripts show she never revealed that her foundation receives significant amounts of money from pharmaceutical companies, including GSK. At the time of her appearances, that industry funding was reportedly in the order of $600 000 a year.[35] Asked for an interview about this failure to disclose, Norton declined the invitation, but said in a statement that she was not specifically asked to disclose at the FDA meetings, and that these financial ties were disclosed on her foundation's website.

When the *Frasier* sitcom star Kelsey Grammer and his wife appeared on chat shows like *The Today Show*, raising the profile of the little-known syndrome, it was supposedly on behalf of Norton's foundation.[36] Yet behind the scenes and unknown to many of the viewing public GSK funded the celebrity campaign (designed to engender positive public attitudes towards GSK's controversial drug).[37] Coincidentally, the involvement of the *Frasier* star was organised with the help of Amy Doner Schachtel, the highly sought-after celebrity broker. With her company, Premier Entertainment, Schachtel puts drug companies in touch with the right sort of star.

> Companies originally wanted the biggest names, the biggest stars. Now it is finding the celebrity with the right fit—someone who has genuine connections, through suffering the condition themselves or having a family member or friend with the condition.[38]

At the same time as sitcom celebrities were educating the public about IBS in the US, the Lotronex manufacturer was working with a marketing firm planning to educate doctors and their patients about the condition in Australia. A small firm was developing a three-year 'educational program', a draft of which was leaked to the media. With aggressive language sometimes verging on the comic, the confidential document emphasised that IBS 'must be established in the minds of doctors' as a significant disease state.[39] Likewise, according to the document, patients had to be 'convinced' that IBS is a common and recognised medical disorder. Most importantly both doctors and patients were to be persuaded that Lotronex was an effective treatment for IBS, a drug that had been 'proven' to improve quality of life. In the fantasy-land of marketing dressed up as education, the drug was a 'proven' and 'effective' treatment. In the real world of medicine, the medication barely worked for many people and was considered by FDA staff, in rare cases, to be implicated in causing deaths.

While this particular educational program was not implemented in this form, the leaked document provides a fantastic insight into how drug company-funded 'education' is actually organised. The target audiences for the three-year campaign included specialists, general practitioners, pharmacists, nurses and, importantly, patients as well. Echoing the PR firm Cohn & Wolfe's strategy of 'cultivating the market', this proposal talked about the 'pre-launch' period being important to 'establish the market' for the sponsor's drug. Most valuable to this process were the senior medical specialists referred to in the document as 'Key Opinion Leaders'—or thought-leaders—who would be recruited to help 'shape' the opinions of their colleagues and other doctors. 'Advertorials' would be written for placement in magazines and journals and even a special newsletter would be created to help build the market in the lead-up to the planned product launch. The draft plan stressed that all educational materials would have to be pre-approved by the GSK marketing department.[40]

The extent of the pharmaceutical industry's influence over the health system is simply Orwellian. The doctors, the drug reps, the medical education, the ads, the patient groups, the guidelines, the celebrities, the conferences, the public awareness campaigns, the thought-leaders, and even the regulator's advisers—at every level there is money from drug companies lubricating what many believe is an unhealthy flow of influence. Industry does not crudely buy influence with individuals and organisations—rather its largesse is handed out to those considered to be most commercially helpful. The industry's sponsorship is strategic, systematic, and systemic. It is designed primarily to engender the most favourable view of the latest and most expensive products. But it is also used to maximise the size of the markets for those products, by portraying conditions like IBS as widespread, severe and, above all, treatable with drugs. And who is supposed to be fearlessly regulating this mess? The public agencies who themselves rely on the very same industry for much of their funding.

While the mass marketing of Lotronex was ultimately wound back and its recommended dose halved as part of its re-approval, other drugs subsequently approved for IBS have not faced such limitations. Switzerland's Novartis, the makers of a drug called Zelnorm, has launched a major promotional assault in recent years, marketing both its drug and the condition. Advertisements have appeared in mainstream US newspapers and prime-time TV ads, and some have featured sexy young women baring naked stomachs.[41] And just as the GSK-funded campaign featured Kelsey Grammer and his wife, Novartis ads starred TV's Wonder Woman, Lynda Carter, to help sell the message that if you experience common stomach problems you could have a 'real medical condition' called IBS, and that you should see your doctor.[42]

Abdominal discomfort or pain?
Bloating? Constipation?
It's time to talk to your doctor about IBS

Novartis ad, 2002

In the opinion of those who've taken a closer look, the Zelnorm marketing paints a misleading picture of both the condition and the drug. Before it was even approved in the US, the team from Public Citizen sent a ten-page petition to the FDA that included a rigorous analysis of the scientific studies of the drug. On the basis of its assessment it claimed the drug had 'highly questionable' benefits and serious safety concerns. Furthermore it accused the company of 'data manipulation' in order to exaggerate the benefits from the studies. 'These minor benefits for a few must be weighed against the significant dangers of the drug and the ill-defined and non-life threatening nature of IBS', said the consumer group's petition.[43]

Rejecting the call, the FDA went ahead and approved Zelnorm, but within twelve months the agency sent a letter to Novartis describing key advertisements as seriously misleading and asking the company to stop running them.[44] The FDA letter took issue with an ad in the *New York Times Magazine* featuring a couple in a swimming pool. The ad did not name the drug, but rather it described a 'Novartis treatment' for IBS, which was clearly Zelnorm. The letter accuses the company of grossly over-stating the modest benefits of the drug, widening the range of people for whom it is supposed to help, and failing to include information about side effects, a particularly important omission because the drug has 'serious safety concerns that pose a consid-erable risk to public health and safety'—and this from the very agency that approved the drug in the first place.[45]

Reading through the Public Citizen petitions about the dangers of this latest blockbuster, the FDA's letters, the full-page advertisements, and the sexy company-sponsored websites, one is struck yet again by the enormous mismatch between marketing messages and scientific truths. The gap between the two is often as wide as it is frightening. The extent to which millions of people around the world are being misled about the nature of this condition, and the value of the drugs marketed to treat it, is simply mind-boggling.

It is understandable that companies will want to maximise their markets and portray their products in the best light possible—particularly given estimates that the global market for IBS drugs might soon be worth $10 billion.[46] What is less comprehensible is the way the regulators seem to have been so well and truly tamed. The tough words of the FDA letter to the drug company might sit better in a script for a farce. Or perhaps a tragedy. There is a bark, albeit a soft one, but no bite. It is the appearance of regulation, without the substance. In this instance, as in so many others, there was no penalty even though the FDA had determined a violation of the rules on advertising.[47]

If a serious challenge to the selling of sickness is going to come from anywhere, it is not going to come any time soon from behind the grey concrete and glass exterior of the FDA or other drug regulators dependent on drug company money. But then again, those challenges are already springing up elsewhere. Perhaps one of the most creative has been born from the freshest, clearest example of the corporate-sponsored creation of disease: female sexual dysfunction.

---

*Note:* As this book goes to print the US Congressional inquiries into the FDA are soon to report, and there are calls for a new US body to regulate safety, arising from the widespread view the FDA is failing in its mission.

# Subverting the selling

*Female sexual dysfunction*

Paris was abuzz with preparations for the big race. Time trials for the Tour de France were soon to start, bringing an extra edge of excitement for international visitors to the famous capital. At the grand Palais des Congrés convention centre, with its commanding views across to the Eiffel Tower, a contest of another sort was already under way: the race to define a new disease that could create billion-dollar markets for those selling cures.

A huge international meeting on sexual dysfunctions had attracted hundreds of leading researchers, therapists and physicians from around the globe. They'd come for four days of scientific sessions, cocktail parties and exquisite French cuisine.[1] A similar gathering, held in Paris a few years earlier, had focused almost exclusively on erectile dysfunction in men. But now a new malaise had entered the medical marketplace: female sexual dysfunction or FSD, a condition claimed by its proponents to affect 43 per cent of women.[2] Yet while excitement about the size of the potential new market was running high among the drug company sponsors of the Paris meeting, scientific researchers there were still not exactly clear about how to define FSD. What's more, some researchers were rejecting the notion that there was a medical condition of that name at all, and were running a campaign to expose what they saw as drug company involvement in its creation.

On day three of the conference, hundreds of delegates packed into the congress centre's 'Blue Room' auditorium, to attend a highly unusual session. There was standing room only. They had come to hear a debate: 'Is Female Sexual Dysfunction a Marketing Construct of the Pharmaceutical Industry?' On the stage were two speakers from the 'yes' team, two speakers from the 'no' team and in between them a moderator. Somewhat ironically, the two speakers from the 'no' team, and the debate's moderator, had all worked as paid advisers to Pfizer, the company that at the time was still hoping Viagra might prove to be the blockbuster for women that it had been for men. Fittingly, Pfizer was also a key sponsor of the debate, and of the entire Paris meeting.[3]

The Paris debate reflects the much bigger global discussion about how we define women's sexual difficulties, and the role drug companies might be playing in that definition. Corporate-backed claims that almost half of all women suffer with a medical disorder called FSD have incensed many researchers and health advocates, and helped foster an alternative view that is fast gaining credibility within the health establishment. Those promoting the 43 per cent figure may have been hoping for a bonanza, but have instead sparked a backlash.

The first speaker for the 'yes' case—the proposition that drug companies are helping to construct a new condition called FSD—was psychologist Dr Leonore Tiefer, a clinical associate professor at New York University School of Medicine, and founder of the global campaign that is challenging the current medicalisation of women's sexual difficulties. Combining the wit of a stand-up comic with the rigour of a scientist, Tiefer is tackling head-on what she describes as the corporate-sponsored creation of a disease, and she and her colleagues have inspired something of a small movement.[4] For starters, she has meticulously documented the fact that for almost every key meeting where this new condition is being defined, the funding has come directly from pharmaceutical companies.

While it is not clear whether her team is winning, she's having a lot of fun playing the game. At a recent conference in Florida, while picking up an important scientific award from her peers, Tiefer delivered a paper called 'Not tonight dear, the dog ate my testosterone patch'. Her colourful campaign could well become a guide for others looking to expose and combat corporate attempts to inappropriately widen the boundaries of human illness.

Squarely on the other side of this debate about FSD is the debonair Dr Irwin Goldstein, an organiser of the Paris meetings, and a chief architect of what he sees as a whole new discipline of sexual medicine. While he was not sitting on the stage formally debating the motion that Monday lunchtime in Paris, his spirit was indeed with the 'no' team. Goldstein embraces industry sponsorship of scientific activities, but aggressively rejects claims that drug company marketing strategies are helping to construct and create a new condition. He is a key target of Tiefer's criticism, and in turn a strong critic of her views.

Goldstein started out in engineering, but switched early in his career to medicine and specialised in urology. Urology is the specialty long associated with diseases of the urinary tract, but increasingly known for dealing with men's sexual difficulties.

Based in the medical school at Boston University, he is now professor of urology and gynaecology. Within these specialties the charismatic physician has moved from a focus on male erectile dysfunction to researching, writing and speaking about female sexual dysfunction. A consultant and lecturer for almost every pharmaceutical company, Goldstein is passionate about bringing help to a whole new pool of patients because 'there is such joy in treating these people successfully'.[5]

While Goldstein disputes the drug industry's role in constructing this condition, there is little doubt how close observers of the industry's marketing see things. 'The ability to create new disease markets, as is currently happening in the area of female sexual dysfunction, will cause the overall lifestyle market to expand in a step-wise fashion over the next two decades' proclaims the executive summary of a recent *Reuters Business Insight* report from an experienced pharmaceutical market analyst.[6] The report was about what it calls 'lifestyle' drugs that are designed to improve lifestyles as much as treat serious illness. Running to over 200 pages, the report was not written for public consumption, which explains its candour about 'creating' new markets. Rather it was produced primarily for drug company marketing executives who run the industry's highly influential promotional campaigns, and for potential investors who want to back them.

The *Reuters Business Insight* report is essentially an insider's intelligence assessment. Its chapters cover several of the conditions where huge growth is expected in the sales of 'lifestyle' drugs in the coming years: depression, obesity, smoking cessation, hair loss, skin ageing, oral contraception and sexual dysfunction. The report estimates that the market for drugs to treat female sexual dysfunction, including the testosterone patch, could approach $1 billion by 2008. In the frankest of terms the report describes the selling of sickness: the analyst outlines how companies are 'expanding the patient pool' by using marketing campaigns to change public perceptions about what used to be considered normal life. 'The medicalization of many natural processes', says the report, 'is creating markets for lifestyle drugs for those who want to "optimize quality of life"'.[7]

> ... pharmaceutical companies are searching for new disorders, based on extensive analysis of unexploited market opportunities (whether recognized today or promoted as such tomorrow). The coming years will bear greater witness to the corporate sponsored creation of disease.[8]

While the business report might describe FSD as the classic example of the 'corporate sponsored creation of disease', back at the Paris debate that wasn't the way the doctors and researchers saw it. Even though there was no formal process for choosing a winner, Leonore Tiefer and her debating partner lost their debate, with the audience, via a show of hands, largely rejecting the notion that FSD was being constructed by drug company marketing.

Tiefer's team was beaten by the combined efforts of an articulate English heart specialist and a passionate Italian physician, who together had laid out the case that many women suffering with sexual difficulties were being helped by having their problems labelled and treated, medically. The heart specialist, Dr Graham Jackson, has said it is nonsense to claim FSD does not exist, or that it is a condition manufactured by the drug industry. He has pointed out that the condition has been recognised for many years, long before current drug treatments like Pfizer's Viagra were even being marketed. What's more, it is insulting to suggest scientists attending company-funded meetings are incapable of independent thought.[9]

In contrast, Tiefer's view is that the constant presence of a cashed-up industry—in clinical research, at scientific meetings, in medical education, doctors' offices and media advertisements—brings an unhealthy narrowing of the focus in the debate about sexual difficulties. She is not opposed to the development and appropriate marketing of proven medications for women in genuine need of them, or to the availability of sex aids for the public. Her concern is that the complexity of female sexual problems, which she agrees are widespread, will be swept away in the marketing hurricane promoting both the medical condition and the drugs, and the subsequent rush to diagnose, label and prescribe.

While it may well be the case that doctors attending company-sponsored meetings are capable of independent thought, it is worth laying out in full public view the extraordinary extent of pharmaceutical industry involvement in the meetings where the definitions of this new 'disease' FSD have been hammered out.

In the spring of 1997, clinicians, researchers, and drug company representatives were scheduled to meet for two days at Cape Cod, on the New England coast not far from Boston, 'to discuss the future direction of clinical trials' in this area. Importantly, the gathering was set against a backdrop of a widespread lack of agreement about the definition of female sexual dysfunction, according to those organising it. In other words, while the idea of a condition called FSD had been around for several years already, in 1997 senior figures in the field were still unclear about exactly how to define it. While this lack of agreement within the medical profession about how to diagnose and treat might have been creating obstacles for women suffering serious problems and seeking help, it was also creating obstacles for companies keen to test their products. If there was no agreement on how to define or measure female sexual dysfunction, how on earth could a company show in a clinical trial that its drug had helped fix the dysfunction? If you can't measure it, how can you market a pill to fix it?

With erection problems in men it was relatively easy to demonstrate that a drug could deliver more frequent, and/or harder erections. The complexity of female sexuality was proving a more difficult challenge. The meeting at Cape Cod would be critical to developing the definition and measurement of FSD, and potentially influence the way the scientific establishment, and the world, would think about FSD for a long time into the future.

In response to an email inquiry from Leonore Tiefer in the lead-up to that Cape Cod meeting, the co-chairperson wrote back to her. 'The meeting is completely supported by pharmaceutical companies, and approximately half of the audience will be pharmaceutical representatives.' As the email makes clear, drug company sponsorship is not simply a silent force. As in the world of political donations, money buys access. The email continued: 'The goal is to foster active and positive collaboration between the two groups. Only investigators who have experience with, or special interest in working collaboratively with the drug industry have been invited.' Nine drug companies sponsored that Cape Cod meeting. Tiefer—a leading thinker in the field with a global reputation but with no ties to drug companies—didn't attend.

Eighteen months later, what was billed as the first 'international' consensus conference on female sexual dysfunction

took place in Boston. The plan was to actually write a new definition of the condition, though this was not a public meeting,
and the deliberations took place within 'closed sessions'.
Participants were hand-picked by a group from the American
Foundation for Urologic Disease on the basis of their expertise
and their positions as thought-leaders in the field. That organisation, like many similar medical organisations, relies heavily on
money from drug companies.[10]

Working with early definitions that existed at the time,
including a definition from the psychiatrists' manual, the
*DSM*, the nineteen hand-picked participants at this Boston
meeting produced a new definition and classification of FSD,
featuring sub-disorders of desire, arousal, orgasm, and pain.
FSD, they wrote, affected between 20–50 per cent of all
women, and their new definition was to be used in 'medical and
mental health settings'. Eight drug companies sponsored this
meeting. Eighteen of the nineteen authors of the new definition had financial ties or other relationships with a total of
22 drug companies.

The following year sixteen companies supported another
FSD conference, again in Boston, where a show of hands at one
session revealed around half of the participants were connected
to the drug industry. In both 2000 and 2001, the newly formed
Female Sexual Function Forum hosted annual conferences,
supported each time by more than twenty companies, with Pfizer
as a key sponsor.

The chair of most of the company-sponsored Boston meetings was Tiefer's nemesis, Dr Irwin Goldstein. He describes
industry's role in helping build the science of this new condition as 'paramount', and dismisses suggestions that closeness
between companies and researchers is inappropriate. The

industry takes a similar position. Interviewed about their ongoing sponsorship of these important medical meetings where definitions of FSD were evolving, Pfizer's Urology Group leader, Dr Michael Sweeney, said the company only played a passive role in sponsoring a series of discussions about the disorder, simply providing unrestricted grants in response to requests from physicians.

Pfizer was not only 'passively' underwriting scientific conferences, but has also been sponsoring some of the continuing medical education where doctors learn about the latest sexual disorders. At one medical education event on male and female sexual dysfunction in New York, which was fully accredited and attended by perhaps 200 practising clinicians, Pfizer was the chief sponsor, Pfizer's Viagra was much discussed, and Pfizer-friendly speakers including Goldstein were the stars of the show. The venue for this medical education event? The Pfizer Foundation Hall for Humanism in Medicine at New York University Medical School.

At one point during this 'educational' event, in the segment about male erectile dysfunction, Goldstein told the audience that he was a 'strong believer' in taking Viagra on a daily basis to 'prevent impotence', a major change in the way the drug is currently used that would clearly expand Pfizer's market many times.[11] 'If you would like to be sexually active in five years' time, take a quarter of a pill a night,' he told the stunned audience. 'We have data to show that will facilitate and prolong nocturnal erections.'

His extraordinary recommendations of daily Viagra use caused alarm among other researchers because of potential safety problems, and even seemed to catch the folks at Pfizer offguard. In response, Pfizer's Sweeney said he had not seen convincing data to recommend the drug's daily use and that Goldstein was known as one of the most 'enthusiastic' members of his specialty. Asked about his financial ties to sponsors including Pfizer, and his positive endorsements of their products, Goldstein dismissed any inappropriate influence, explaining that he had also made some negative comments about Viagra at that same medical education meeting. 'I'm allowed to say what I want,' he snapped coldly in response to questioning, the charm quickly evaporating. 'No one tells me what to say.'[12]

Coincidentally, the *Reuters Business Insight* report on the 'lifestyle' drug market echoed Dr Goldstein's enthusiasm for using erectile dysfunction drugs more regularly. The report argues that because of the emergence of several competitors to Viagra, drug companies active in the male sexual dysfunction market would have to focus on 'shifting patients from sporadic to chronic treatment' if they were to maintain market share and protect their franchises.[13] In other words, companies would have to try to move people from taking an irregular occasional pill towards regular, long-term use of these drugs, as is the case with other heavily promoted conditions like high cholesterol, high blood pressure and osteoporosis. If all went according to plan, the report estimated the industry could build a massive $5 billion erectile dysfunction market by 2008.

When it came to female sexual dysfunction, Goldstein had told participants at the New York medical education event just before Christmas 2002 that the science was less well developed than for men. He referred to animal experiments that had been done to help discover more about the role of poor blood flow to the female genitals and other physiological problems. Based on studies in rabbits, he and other colleagues have in fact developed theories about what they describe as 'vaginal engorgement insufficiency and clitoral erectile insufficiency'. Flowing on from this research, doctors and clinics attempting to diagnose FSD are now measuring a whole set of physiological indicators including blood flow to the clitoris and vagina, vaginal pH (acidity) and the levels of different hormones, as well as doing routine physical and psychological exams.

While stressing that it was still early days in this research focused on women, and that a mind–body approach was necessary, Goldstein nevertheless gave a very strong backing to the role of drugs in treating female sexual dysfunction. Acknowledging there was not good evidence yet to support the widespread use of Viagra in women, he recommended trying androgens, a group of hormonal steroids that includes testosterone.[14] As it turns out, one of the other sponsors of the medical education meeting was Watson, a company developing a testosterone patch with the giant Proctor & Gamble that could well be one of the first pharmaceuticals approved in the US for the treatment of the condition called FSD.[15]

Sitting in the back rows of the Pfizer Foundation Hall for Humanism in Medicine, while Irwin Goldstein was still on stage below, was Leonore Tiefer, taking copious notes together with one of her academic protégés, learning the trade first hand. As she tends to do at such gatherings, during the coffee break Tiefer distributed colourful flyers that drew connections between the latest research on FSD and the marketing strategies of drug companies. Her flyer criticised the narrow focus on genitalia in discussions about women's sexuality, and pointed out the problem of side effects with treatments like testosterone.

> Women's sexual problems and satisfactions have far more to do with relationship difficulties, life stresses, and cultural expectations than with clitoral blood flow or testosterone levels.

> Don't be misled by drug-company-funded marketing masquer-
> ading as science or education.
>
> New View leaflet[16]

The flyer also referred readers to the New View campaign, which offers an alternative view of women's sexual problems. This view has been promoted by a group of academics, clinicians, researchers and activists in books, articles, conferences and the media since 2000. Unlike the corporate-backed meetings and conferences this campaign is run on a shoestring, but its impact on the public debate, particularly in terms of media coverage, has arguably been considerable.

The 'New View' acknowledges that for many women the causes of their sexual difficulties may be physical, but in most cases there are a host of other factors at play. There are similarities between this definition and the one being developed at drug company-sponsored meetings—both make clear, for example, that female sexual difficulties are multidimensional, combining biological, psychological and interpersonal elements. But there are also very important differences between the two definitions. Rather than put all these sexual difficulties under the umbrella of one medical condition, or dysfunction, the New View campaign prefers to talk more broadly about sexual 'problems'. Tiefer and her colleagues argue they have a more 'woman-centered' definition, which includes 'discontent or dissatisfaction with any emotional, physical, or relational aspect of sexual experience'.[17]

Most importantly, the 'New View' offers a definition that avoids stating what is normal sexual functioning and what isn't. While the medical profession and medicines can play a role in helping some women, proponents of this alternative view argue there are real dangers in seeing sexual difficulties primarily as medical problems to be treated by doctors. The world of medicine likes to set 'norms', but sex is not like that. 'Sex is like dancing,' says Tiefer. 'If you break an ankle while you're dancing you go to a doctor. But your doctor doesn't take a dance history and wouldn't advise you whether your dancing is normal. The medical model is about defining what's healthy and what's sick— but sex isn't like that.' She is particularly critical of the focus on testing all those physiological measures like clitoral or vaginal blood flow for every women who walks through the door of a clinic, in part because she claims there is no good science establishing what a *normal* blood flow might be.[18]

This alternative definition also outlines four separate categories of causes of sexual distress, again distinguishing it from the drug company-sponsored view. The first and most important category is described as cultural/economic/political. The other three categories are relationship-related; psychological; and medical. For Tiefer, a practising sex therapist, understanding the causes of an individual woman's sexual difficulties requires an understanding of the history of sexuality within that woman's culture and of the culture as a whole, as well as the unique history of that person in the context of their relationships and community. She strongly believes Irwin Goldstein, the medical model, and the drug company marketing strategies are wrong, and are taking the whole field in the wrong direction.[19] She fears that as drugs are approved to treat FSD, it will start to shift people's ideas about how they have to prepare themselves to be sexual. 'Your body isn't good enough. You aren't good enough. You plus products,' she says with a mix of humour, anger and sadness, 'now maybe then you're good enough.'[20]

Just like the proponents of the New View, Goldstein also argues he is motivated by a strong desire to help women who are genuinely suffering, but he angrily rejects suggestions that doctors are not best equipped to deal with sexual problems. 'Who's best equipped to deal with it? The horticulturalists? It's a form of medicine. I think physicians are most appropriate,' says Goldstein, who practises as part of a multidisciplinary team including psychologists and nurses.

Tiefer and her campaigning colleagues are not the only researchers interested in pruning back the current efforts to medicalise women's sexual problems. The former director of the Kinsey Institute at Indiana University, Dr John Bancroft, believes the actual term 'female sexual dysfunction' is misleading. A researcher specialising in sexual difficulties over many years, who has on occasions worked with drug companies, Bancroft argues that an inhibition of sexual desire is in many situations a healthy and functional response for women faced with stress, tiredness, or threatening patterns of behaviour from their partners. 'The danger of portraying sexual difficulties as a dysfunction is that it is likely to encourage doctors to prescribe drugs to change sexual function—when the attention should be paid to other aspects of the woman's life. It's also likely to make women think they have a malfunction when they do not.'

Just a few hours north of Bancroft's former workplace is Chicago, the site of the first of a national chain of sex clinics for women run by Dr Laura Berman—one half of the beautiful Berman sisters, who also host their own TV show. At the Chicago clinic's auspicious opening, Berman explained to the assembled cameras that medications and hormones would be offered along- side the sex therapy and the yoga: the approach would be to treat the 'whole woman'. A sense of entrepreneurial excitement was in the air as, after all, 43 per cent of women were said to suffer female sexual dysfunction—a figure cited more than once by clinic staff in media interviews on the day of the launch.[21]

According to Berman the clinic boasted the 'latest and greatest' in medical technology, with all kinds of fancy machinery that will measure everything from genital blood flow to testosterone levels. What is still unclear is whether the clinic has adequately determined what is *normal* in terms of blood flow, lubrication or testosterone levels. And more importantly, how often will women be inappropriatey diagnosed as being *abnormal* in order to try to sell them a medical or pharmaceutical solution? But those awkward questions didn't interrupt the clinic's launch, where the new sexual entrepreneurs boldly proclaimed their wish to make Chicago women 'the most sexually healthy in the country'.[22]

Coincidentally it was a University of Chicago sociology professor who first made the 43 per cent figure famous, when he published it in an article in *JAMA* in 1999.[23] The figure has been used constantly in marketing materials and media stories to suggest almost half of all women suffer with a medical condition, a 'dysfunction' or a disease, called FSD. In actual fact the paper in *JAMA* suggested nothing of the sort. The 43 per cent figure will likely go down in history as one of the most abused medical statistics of our time.

Sociologist Ed Laumann and colleagues arrived at that figure by re-analysing data from a big survey done years earlier. In that survey roughly 1500 women were asked to answer yes or no to whether they had experienced any of seven common problems, for a few months or more in the previous year. Those problems included things like a lack of desire for sex, anxiety about sexual performance, and difficulties with lubrication. If a woman said yes to having experienced just one of the seven problems, she was included in the group said to have sexual dysfunction.

Clearly it is absurd to suggest that a person experiencing a lack of desire for sex has a medical condition called FSD. And indeed,

Laumann and his colleagues never intended to suggest that. Their article clearly states that their findings were 'not equivalent to clinical diagnosis'. In other words they were not suggesting 43 per cent of women have a medical condition called FSD, yet this is how the figure has been used over and over again. Laumann rejects criticisms that 'dysfunction' was the wrong word to have used, but he agrees that many of the women among the 43 per cent are 'perfectly normal'. And he agrees too that a lot of their sexual difficulties or dissatisfactions 'arise out of perfectly reasonable responses of the human organism to challenge and stress'.

It may well turn out that the misuse of the 43 per cent figure could backfire on those promoting it for their own commercial or professional ends. While some reporters will simply regurgitate estimates given to them in company press releases, it seems that a healthy scepticism about inflated figures may be growing amongst the fourth estate.

When medical reporter Carla Johnson received a faxed press release claiming 43 per cent of women had a new condition called FSD she immediately smelt a rat (or should that be rabbit?). The release had been sent to her office at the *Spokesman-Review* in Spokane in Washington state by an investment firm in New York—demonstrating the close connection between medicine and the marketplace where 'diseases' are seen as investment opportunities.

The press release was advertising a new product called Alista, an experimental cream to be rubbed on the genitals that offered new hope for 'sexual healing' in women.[24] But it was not just the unbelievable 43 per cent figure that tweaked this reporter's interest. It seemed to Johnson that the press release was trying to subtly blur the boundaries between a medical condition and ordinary life. While the pharmaceutical cream was being presented in one breath as a potentially effective therapy for women with a serious medical problem, it was simultaneously being sold as something for everywoman: to 'revolutionize how women can enhance their sexual well being'.

One of the people Carla Johnson called was Leonore Tiefer on the other side of the continent in New York, who she'd heard was running some sort of activist campaign. 'Women are being sold a disease that the companies have a treatment for,' Tiefer told Johnson. The story would soon run prominently on the paper's front page.

> They're being told this is a great breakthrough for them. But if you sit women down for two minutes, how many of them would really think the type of problems they're telling their friends about could be solved by a cream you smear on your genitalia right before you have sex? They'd laugh.[25]

The *Spokesman-Review* doesn't have the biggest circulation in the world, but Johnson's front-page piece was another sign that Tiefer was succeeding in generating a debate about the role of drug companies in defining this new disorder. And as it turned out, Johnson's article also inspired others, including one in the *British Medical Journal* that would attract worldwide attention. The *BMJ* piece drew heavily on Tiefer's research, and featured interviews with Irwin Goldstein, Laura Berman, Ed Laumann, and John Bancroft. The piece provoked an immense response, both positive and negative, on the *BMJ* website, within the wider health care community and in the media in several nations. It also provoked an immediate reaction from another quarter.

Within just two weeks of the *BMJ* piece appearing, a little-known London-based PR company called HCC De Facto was quietly sending emails to women's groups around the world, confidentially seeking their help to join a campaign to 'counter' the *BMJ* article about FSD. The debate about this condition was now an international controversy. The PR firm's senior account manager said in the email that the article had questioned whether the condition in fact exists. She wrote:

> I know many support organisations have been incensed about these claims, and we think it's important to counter them and get another voice on the record. I was wondering whether you or someone from your organisation may be willing to work with us to generate articles . . . countering the point of view raised in the *BMJ*. This would involve speaking with select reporters about FSD, its causes and treatments.[26]

The author, the PR company's Michelle Lerner, when asked about her email initially denied being involved in any campaign against the *BMJ* article, but later conceded she had sent a confidential message to advocacy groups in Canada and Australia. But despite repeated questions about which drug company was behind the campaign, she refused to say. Not long after her valiant stonewalling, journalists in Canada were able to establish that Lerner and her PR outfit were in fact working for Pfizer. When the drug giant was questioned about its public relations company's secretive global attempts to 'counter' the *BMJ* article, a Pfizer spokesperson described the activities as 'customary and unremarkable'. It was simply part of a plan to 'establish appropriate platforms to increase patient awareness and recruit for study subjects'.[27] Pfizer was at the time still testing Viagra in women.

In some strange way, these clandestine yet clumsy activities seem only to make Tiefer's campaign stronger. On the streets of New York a year later, she is involved in yet another passionate discussion about the unhealthy selling of FSD, this time with an advertising executive friend of hers, as they volunteer together at one of the local homeless shelters on East 35th Street. She doesn't miss a chance to spread the word, even giving a sermon at her local mid-town church entitled 'Biotechnology and the pursuit of sexual happiness'.

Yet as the New View campaign moves forward, so too does the drug industry's selling. Pfizer may have dropped its pursuit of Viagra for FSD because the drug could do little better than a placebo—or dummy pill—at improving women's sex lives, but it is likely that it and other drug makers will remain more determined than ever to exploit what they see as the next big mega-market. Just as Tiefer's sermon was being delivered, the business pages of the press were reporting another story in the making—that a company developing a testosterone patch might spend $100 million in the first year of its advertising campaign—a campaign likely to promote the 'disease' as much as the drug.[28] While the testosterone patch was initially rejected in late 2004 by an FDA advisory panel because of potential long-term side effects, Proctor & Gamble is continuing to seek approval.[29]

The testosterone patch may well provide the perfect example of the perverse impacts of excessive and virtually uncontrolled drug company marketing. For a small group of women, whose genuine physiological problems contribute to difficulties with sexual functioning, the patch may indeed help, though the hype was well under way before the key trials were even published in peer-reviewed journals—and before any independent assessment of the drug's actual risks and benefits.[30] But without doubt, if the patch is ultimately approved, the marketing will soon move from the small group of the genuinely sick to the much bigger market of the unhappy healthy—just as we have seen with the promotion of Viagra to men.[31]

One danger here, as foreshadowed by John Bancroft, is that many women may mistakenly see their sexual difficulties as due to a highly advertised medical condition. But perhaps the bigger danger comes from the now familiar blurring of boundaries that characterises so much modern pharmaceutical marketing. If drug companies want to market their products as sexual aids to enhance the lifestyles of the healthy, they should do exactly that—though this would of course create real difficulties convincing health insurers to help pay for them. Instead the marketing strategies will use the cover of a medical condition. Yet surely, to try to rely on the fiction that half the female population is diseased, dysfunctional or suffering something called FSD is simply a sick joke. A related concern is that people in genuine need of drugs may miss out because those who fund the system refuse to subsidise them for fear of unsustainable cost escalations, as occurred in Australia when the national system declined to subsidise Viagra.[32]

The problem with this picture is by now a familiar one. Billions of dollars and euros will likely be spent attempting to treat sexual difficulties that can never be fixed with testosterone or any other drug. And they are billions that could arguably be much better spent preventing or treating the world's abundance of genuine illness, cleaning up water supplies, building bike or walking paths or funding women's shelters or adolescent's sex education, boosting employment levels in depressed neighbourhoods.[33] How to radically change the priorities in our health care spending is a question that needs a lot more attention.

Down in Orlando, Florida, Leonore Tiefer has just received a prestigious award for 'Distinguished Scientific Achievement' from her academic peers.[34] By way of acceptance, she delivered her 'Not tonight dear, the dog ate my testosterone patch' speech.

The night before she'd appeared at a small local theatre, where her colleagues had organised a fund-raiser for the coming New View conference in Canada where she plans to close the five-year campaign. Confident that scepticism towards the selling of female sexual dysfunction has risen considerably over that time, Tiefer will proudly be declaring victory.

# Epilogue

# What can we do?

Union Station in Washington, DC was somehow the perfect place to launch the world's first new major medical journal in 70 years. Just a stroll down the hill from the US Congress, the station's grand architecture and quiet palatial rooms conjure a sense of stately history, and high hopes. At the time it was built, in 1908, this train station was one of the largest in the world.[1]

The journal launched here in the fall of 2004, *PloS Medicine*, also has big aspirations, as it plans to 'challenge the status quo' by providing free web access to all of its scientific articles. What's more, unlike virtually every other leading medical journal in the world today, this journal will not accept any drug company advertisements. Nor will it publish company-funded studies that are considered to be marketing dressed up as science. The aim, say its editors, is to break 'the cycle of dependency' that has formed between medical journals and the pharmaceutical industry.[2]

Run by the San Francisco based not-for-profit Public Library of Science, the new journal's editorial board boasts some of the biggest names in global health care. By challenging the status quo, disentangling from drug company influence, and promoting more independent medical information, this journal is helping show the way forward for all of us.

Challenging and questioning the status quo is the first step for anyone concerned about the selling of sickness. Working out where the boundaries lie between health and disease is not easy, and as we've seen there are huge promotional forces at work trying to blur them. With many conditions, like high cholesterol or ADD, those boundaries just keep getting wider. These days when a doctor diagnoses a condition and gives it a medical label, that diagnosis may no longer be able to be taken at face value. Though it might seem like commonsense, there can be great value talking with family and friends about the appropriateness of a particular medical label, and debating whether the problem at hand is really a sign of disease or simply one of the ups and downs of ordinary life.

Sometimes, of course, diseases are real, painful and deadly, and treatment with the latest and most expensive drug or other medical technology or procedure is highly desirable. Yet there are many cases where a person's health problems are so mild or temporary that doing nothing is the best option. Irritable bowel syndrome, for example, will only be severe and disabling for a tiny fraction of the 20 per cent of the entire population said to be afflicted by it. The value of a healthy scepticism towards the hype about the latest disorders, and the numbers allegedly affected by them, cannot be overstated.

The obvious problem for all of us right now is finding good sources of information about human illness that are truly independent of drug company influence. Many doctors still see drug representatives; many patient groups and medical societies still accept generous grants; and most medical journals still rely heavily on the industry's advertising and its sponsored studies. Finding quality materials about the risks and benefits of drugs and other therapies is becoming easier,[3] but finding good accessible, up-to-date and independent information about disease is, as yet, near impossible.

New ways of defining diseases, and educating people about the options for dealing with them, are urgently needed. To continue to rely on drug company-funded thought-leaders to write the definitions, and drug company-funded marketing to educate us about them, is dangerous, and really rather absurd. A major renovation of how we understand sickness needs fresh ideas and radical experiments, but there are existing models that may be helpful. Around the world there are many public institutions, and some private bodies, that have found ways to rigorously review all of the available scientific studies about a particular treatment, and come up with an unbiased summary of how well it works.[4] In the United Kingdom the publicly funded National Institute for Clinical Excellence undertakes such reviews, as do many groups in the US, including the innovative private organisation ECRI.[5] Sometimes short summaries of this evidence are made available on the web to doctors and the public, like those provided by the international Cochrane Collaboration.[6]

The hallmark of systematically reviewing and summarising the evidence about treatments is that it is carried out by organisations and individuals who don't profit from selling those treatments. It is now time for similar reviews of the evidence about diseases and disorders that will produce unbiased and easy-to-read information for ordinary people. Rather than simplistic marketing messages that play on fear and use grossly inflated figures to try to scare people into drug therapy, such information would spell out the uncertainty and controversy that surrounds many disease definitions. Without such complete information about the pros and cons of accepting a medical label, informed choice is impossible.

Yet, more than being independent, the new bodies that will help to draw the line between health and disease must be more inclusive than the current panels, many of which are dominated by medical doctors. There is an old saying that when you give someone a hammer, everything looks like a nail. Sometimes it is a nail and hammering it helps get the house built. On other occasions a carpenter's skills may not be the only ones called for. Changing city planning laws to encourage more physical activity may do more to prevent disease than prescribing increasing doses of drugs. Somehow a much broader group of people, both lay and professional, must be involved in defining diseases and disorders, and producing unbiased information about the risks and benefits of various options for treating and preventing them. Health advocacy groups, university departments, and public institutions with reputations for independence, good science and healthy scepticism are obvious places to start that ball rolling.

In the meantime most people are left with little choice but to 'talk to your doctor', as the slick advertisements and the well-paid celebrities keep telling us to do. But as we've seen, many of our doctors, no matter how committed and hardworking, are still prescribing under the influence of marketing campaigns designed to sell us sickness in order to sell us pills. However, it may be that a fundamental change is coming.

With a membership of 50 000, the American Medical Student Association is literally the face of tomorrow's physician. As part of its charter the association takes no sponsorship from the pharmaceutical industry. Its 'PharmFree' campaign urges medical students to simply say no to the free lunches, the gifts, the paid speaking engagements and the lucrative consultancies. As it happens, their association's national president, Brian Palmer, was there at the historic launch of the new pharm-free medical journal at Union Station in the US capital, beaming broadly as he joked with the journal's smart young editors, all of them with wide smiles, firmly fixed on a future more about promoting health than selling sickness.

# Notes

## Abbreviations

**ACOG** American College of Obstetricians and Gynecologists; **ADAA** Anxiety Disorders Association of America; **AFR** *Australian Financial Review*; **APA** American Psychiatric Association; **BMJ** *British Medical Journal*; **BMS** Bristol-Myers Squibb; **CDER** Center for Drug Evaluation and Research; **CMAJ** *Canadian Medical Association Journal*; **CSPI** Center for Science in the Public Interest; **DEA** Drug Enforcement Administration; **FDA** Food and Drug Administration; **FFF** Freedom From Fear; **HRG** Health Research Group; **IBS** Irritable Bowel Syndrome; **IJCP** *International Journal of Clinical Practice*; **IMS** Intercontinental Marketing Services; **JAMA** *Journal of the American Medical Association*; **MM&M** Medical Marketing and Media; **NIH** National Institutes of Health; **SPC Summary** of Product Characteristics; **TGA** Therapeutic Goods Administration; **WHI** Women's Health Initiative; **WHO** World Health Organization.

## Prologue

1  W. Robertson, *Fortune*, March 1976. All figures in this book are in US$ unless otherwise noted.

2  'Worried well into worried sick' is a borrowed phrase, although there is uncertainty as to who originally coined it.

3  For US proportion of global market see http://open.imshealth.com/ webshop2/IMSinclude/i_article_20040317.asp (accessed 15 Jan. 2005).

4   *Selling Sickness*, the documentary, Paradigm Pictures, 2004.

5   http://www.nihcm.org/FinalText3.PDF p. 23 (accessed 18 Nov. 2004).

6   W. Hall, A. Mant, P. Mitchell, V. Rendle, I. Hickie and P. McManus, 'Association between antidepressant prescribing and suicide in Australia, 1991–2000: trend analysis', *BMJ*, vol. 326, 2003, pp. 1008.

7   http://www.imshealthcanada.com/htmen/3_1_40.htm (accessed 13 Jan. 2005).

8   V. Parry, 'The art of branding a condition', *MM&M*, May 2003, pp. 43–9.

9   Vince Parry's interview with Cathy Scott for *Selling Sickness*, the documentary, Paradigm Pictures, 2004.

10  V. Parry, 'The art of branding a condition', op. cit.

11  J. Coe, 'Healthcare: The lifestyle drugs outlook to 2008, unlocking new value in well-being', *Reuters Business Insight*, Datamonitor, PLC, 2003.

12  J. Coe, 'The lifestyle drugs outlook to 2008', op. cit., p. 43.

13  ibid.

14  See J. Abramson, *Overdosed America*, HarperCollins, New York, 2004; also see R. Horton, 'The dawn of McScience', *The New York Review of Books*, vol. LI, 11 March 2004, pp. 7–9; also see R. Moynihan, 'Who pays for the pizza: Redefining the relationships between doctors and drug companies. Part 1, Entanglement and Part 2, Disentanglement', *BMJ*, vol. 326, 2003, pp. 1189–96.

15  For antidepressants scandals, see chapters 2 and 7; for the alleged bribery of the Italian doctors see F. Turone, 'Italian police investigate GSK Italy for bribery', *BMJ*, vol. 326, 2003, p. 413; for the alleged bribery of US doctors see R. Moynihan, 'Bribes to prescribe', *Good Weekend, Sydney Morning Herald* 31 May 2003, cover story; and for arthritis drugs see FDA paper at http://www.fda.gov/fdac/features/2004/604_vioxx.html (accessed 15 Jan. 2005).

16  R Moynihan, 'Who pays for the pizza', op. cit.

17  See chapters 1, 5 and 10.

18  For hormone replacement therapy see chapter 3, for anti-depressants see chapter 2, for cholesterol-lowering drugs see chapter 1, for irritable bowel syndrome see chapter 9.

19  I. Illich, *Limits to Medicine*, Penguin, London, 1976.

20  ibid., p. 127.

21  L. Payer, *Disease-Mongers: How Doctors, Drug Companies, and Insurers are Making You Feel Sick*, Wiley & Sons, 1992.

22  D. Henry and J. Lexchin, 'The pharmaceutical industry as a medicines provider', *The Lancet*, vol. 360, 2002, pp. 1590–5.

## Chapter 1    Selling to everyone

1  http://open.imshealth.com/webshop2/IMSinclude/i_article_200 40317.asp (accessed 16 Nov. 2004).

2  ibid. A company called Datamonitor has a site which gives basic details about the world's leading drug companies: http://www.datamonitor. com/~50701d9bc16c47b99cd554262295c427~/companies/lists/ list/?listid=288ED715-62DE-417A-9787-A59D711272A5 (accessed 15 Jan. 2005).

3  N. Freemantle and S. Hill, 'Medicalisation, limits to medicine, or never enough money to go round', *BMJ*, vol. 324, 2002, pp. 864–5.

4  See FDA note on Baycol (cerivastatin) and deaths at http://www.fda. gov/cder/reports/rtn/2001/rtn2001-3.htm#Withdrawals (accessed 6 Jan. 2005).

5  http://www.citizen.org/pressroom/release.cfm?ID=1737 (accessed 6 Jan. 2005). Crestor's generic name is rosuvastatin. Mevacor's generic name is lovastatin.

6  http://open.imshealth.com/webshop2/IMSinclude/i_article_200403 17.asp (accessed 16 Nov. 2004). Lipitor's generic name is atorvastatin.

7  2001 guidelines at http://www.nhlbi.nih.gov/guidelines/cholesterol/ atp3xsum.pdf (accessed 16 Nov. 2004). Also see chapter on cholesterol-guidelines in J. Abramson, *Overdosed America*, HarperCollins, New York, 2004.

8  'Expert Panel on Detection, Evaluation, and Treatment of High Blood Cholesterol in Adults. Executive Summary of The Third Report of The National Cholesterol Education Program (Adult Treatment Panel III)', *JAMA*, vol. 285, 2001, pp. 2486–97.

9  ibid.

10  http://www.detnews.com/2004/health/0407/19/health-214907. htm (accessed 16 Nov. 2004). The story cites James Cleeman saying the 2004 updated guidelines will add 7 million to the 36 million already encouraged to take pills.

11  http://www.nhlbi.nih.gov/guidelines/cholesterol/atp3upd04_
disclose.htm (accessed 16 Nov. 2004).

12  D. Ricks and R. Rabin, 'Cholesterol guidelines, drug panelists' links
under fire', *Newsday*, 15 July, 2004, p. A06.

13  http://www.nhlbi.nih.gov/guidelines/cholesterol/atp3upd04_
disclose.htm (accessed 16 Nov. 2004).

14  The US government agency responsible for the cholesterol guidelines
dismissed public concerns about the extraordinary ties between eight of
the nine experts and industry, arguing that recognised experts are the
very people industry will seek to hire. See http://www.nhlbi.nih.gov/
new/press/04-07-29.htm (accessed 6 Jan. 2005). Through the NIH
press office, the chair of the 2004 panel declined requests to do an
interview for this book.

15  N. Choudhry, H. Stelfox and A. Detsky, 'Relationships between authors
of clinical practice guidelines and the pharmaceutical industry', *JAMA*,
vol. 287, no. 5, 2002, pp. 612–17.

16  See chapter 6.

17  R. Moynihan, 'Who pays for the pizza: Redefining the relationships
between doctors and drug companies: Part 1, Entanglement and Part 2,
Disentanglement', *BMJ*, vol. 326, 2003, pp. 1189–96 Part I: http://
bmj.bmjjournals.com/cgi/reprint/326/7400/1189.pdf;   Part   2:
http://bmj.bmjjournals.com/cgi/reprint/326/7400/1193.pdf
(accessed 16 Nov. 2004).

18  R. Moynihan, 'Who pays for the pizza', op. cit.

19  R. Moynihan, 'Drug company sponsorship of education could be
replaced at a fraction of its cost', *BMJ*, vol. 326, 2003, p. 1163.

20  R. Moynihan, 'Who pays for the pizza', op. cit.

21  C. Mulrow, J. Williams, M. Trivedi et al., 'Treatment of depression:
newer pharmacotherapies (evidence report/technology assessment,
number 7)', Agency for Health Care Policy and Research, March 1999, at
http://www.ncbi.nlm.nih.gov/books/bv.fcgi?rid=hstat1.chapter.84528
(accessed 16 Nov. 2004).

22  R. Moynihan, 'Who pays for the pizza', op. cit.

23  http://www.citizen.org/publications/release.cfm?ID=7320 (accessed
6 Jan. 2005).

24  B. Brewer, 'Benefit-risk assessment of Rosuvastatin 10-40 milligrams',
*American Journal of Cardiology*, vol. 92 (4B), 2003, pp. 23K–29K.

25  From evidence before the Committee on Energy and Commerce, House of Representatives, 2004 (Ref: HIF174.020). Dr Brewer declined a request for an interview for this book.

26  R. Moynihan, 'Who pays for the pizza', op. cit.

27  ibid.

28  http://www.nhlbi.nih.gov/guidelines/cholesterol/atp3upd04_disclose. htm (accessed 16 Nov. 2004).

29  http://cspinet.org/new/pdf/finalnihltr.pdf (accessed 16 Nov. 2004).

30  Letter from NIH Acting Director to CSPI, 22 October 2004 (personal communication from Merrill Goozner at CSPI).

31  J. Abramson, *Overdosed America*, HarperCollins, New York, 2004.

32  Ray Moynihan's interview with John Abramson.

33  J. Abramson, *Overdosed America*, op. cit.

34  http://www.boomercoalition.org/bc3/campaign.asp (accessed 16 Nov. 2004).

35  ibid.

36  ibid.

37  E. White, 'Behind the "Boomer Coalition", a heart message from Pfizer', *Wall Street Journal* (Eastern Edition), New York, 10 March 2004, p. B.1. The coalition site explains Pfizer is one of two founding partners: http://www.boomercoalition.org/bc3/partners.asp (accessed 16 Nov. 2004). Pfizer declined to answer questions for this book.

38  http://www.medicalconsumers.org/pages/cholesterol_skeptics.html (accessed 16 Nov. 2004).

39  'Fundraising and the growth of industry involvement', *Health and Social Campaigner's News*, published by Patient View, April 2004, Issue 6, www.patient-view.com (accessed 16 Nov. 2004).

40  The boomer site says 'Fighting CVD begins in the doctor's office. Each individual's case is different, and many symptoms of CVD, such as high blood pressure, are undetectable outside the doctor's office. Moreover, if lifestyle changes are not sufficient to lower your CVD risk, your doctor can prescribe medicine to help you along the way.' At http://www. boomercoalition.org/bc3/visit_doctor.asp (accessed 14 Sept. 2004).

41  Lisa Schwartz and Steve Woloshin interviews with Ray Moynihan, 2004. All subsequent quotes, not referenced to an article, are from these interviews.

42  K. Kerin, L.M. Schwartz, S. Woloshin, H.G. Welch 'Using C-reative

protein to guide lipid treatment decisions', *Journal of General Internal Medicine* (abstract in press).

43  J. Walsh and M. Pignone, 'Drug treatment of hyperlipidemia in women', *JAMA*, vol. 291, 2004, pp. 2243–52. This is a systematic review of all the clinical trials, a form of evidence that tends to be more reliable that the results from single trials.

44  ibid.

45  Heart Protection Study Collaborative Group, 'MRC/BHF heart protection study of cholesterol lowering with simvastatin in 20,536 high-risk individuals: a randomised placebo-controlled trial', *The Lancet*, vol. 360, 2002, pp. 7–22.

46  M. Vrecer, S. Turk, J. Drinovec and A. Mrhar, 'Use of statins in primary and secondary prevention of coronary heart disease and ischemic stroke, meta-analysis of randomized trials', *International Journal of Clinical Pharmacology & Therapeutics*, vol. 41, 2003, pp. 567–77.

47  J. Quick, H. Hogerzeil, L. Rägo, V. Reggi and K. de Joncheere, 'Ensuring ethical drug promotion, whose responsibility?', *The Lancet*, vol. 326, no. 9385, 2003, p. 747, http://www.thelancet.com/journal/vol362/iss9385/full/llan.362.9385.correspondence.26978.1 (accessed 16 Nov. 2004).

48  R. Evans, M. Barer and T. Marmor (eds), *Why Are Some People Healthy and Others Not?*, Aldine De Gruyter, Hawthorne, New York, 1994.

49  ibid.

50  The 2001 guidelines, p. 13, say everyone over twenty should be tested every five years. http://www.nhlbi.nih.gov/guidelines/cholesterol/atp3xsum.pdf (accessed 16 Nov. 2004).

51  Based on Ray Moynihan and Alan Cassels' interviews with Dr Iona Heath.

52  http://www.bma.org.uk/ap.nsf/Content/investinggp~AnnexA (accessed 8 Jan. 2005).

53  Ray Moynihan and Alan Cassels' interviews with Dr Iona Heath.

54  Ray Moynihan's interviews with Shah Ebrahim.

55  The statement: 'Forty eight of the 164 trials of statins and LDL cholesterol reported the number of participants with one or more symptoms possibly caused by the drug' comes from M. Law, N. Wald and A. Rudnicka, 'Quantifying effect of statins on low density lipoprotein cholesterol, ischaemic heart disease, and stroke: systematic review and meta-analysis', *BMJ*, vol. 326, 2003, p. 1423.

56 'Pact is reached with insurers on covering Baycol litigation', *Wall Street Journal*, 10 March 2004, p. B3. Also see FDA note on Baycol and deaths at http://www.fda.gov/cder/reports/rtn/2001/rtn2001-3.htm# Withdrawals (accessed 6 Jan. 2005). See also D. Graham, J. Staffa and D. Shatin et al., 'Incidence of hospitalized rhabdomyolysis in patients treated with lipid-lowering drugs', *JAMA*, vol. 292, 2004, pp. 2585–90.

57 Emailed communication from Bayer to Ray Moynihan, 2004.

58 http://www.citizen.org/pressroom/release.cfm?ID=1737 (accessed 6 Jan. 2005). The organisation is based in Washington DC.

59 Emailed communication from AstraZeneca to Ray Moynihan, 2004. For news of the death see http://www.guardian.co.uk/medicine/ story/0,11381,1387498,00.html (accessed 12 Jan. 2005).

60 See chapter 9. Also see J. Abraham, D. Bardelay, C. Kopp, et al., 'Making regulation responsive to commercial interests: streamlining industry watchdogs', *BMJ*, vol. 325, 2002, pp. 1164–9.

61 http://www.citizen.org/publications/release.cfm?ID=7320 (accessed 6 Jan. 2005).

62 Letter from Dr Zerhouni to Dr Wolfe, 29 July 2004.

63 Memo from Dr Brewer to Dr Zerhouni, 9 July 2004.

64 D. Willman, 'Stealth merger: drug companies and government medical research', *Los Angeles Times*, Sunday, 7 Dec. 2003.

65 From evidence before the Committee on Energy and Commerce, House of Representatives, op. cit.

66 For news of this decision see http://www.nature.com/nbt/journal/ v22/n11/pdf/nbt1104-1331.pdf (accessed 6 Jan. 2005).

67 Public Citizen is currently preparing a report for publication on FDA advisory committees and conflicts of interest. Also see the site of the Center for Science in the Public Interest www.cspinet.org (accessed 10 Jan. 2005).

68 M. Marchione, 'Cholesterol guidelines become a morality play about conflict of interest in medicine', *AP*, Sunday 17 Oct. 2004.

69 See T. Moore, *Heart Failure*, Random House, 1989. Also see Thomas Moore's site at http://www.thomasjmoore.com (accessed 6 Jan. 2005) and http://www.smartmoney.com/barrons/index.cfm?story=20040614 (accessed 6 Jan. 2005). This story starts: 'Statin drugs should probably be in the drinking water'.

## Chapter 2    Doughnuts for the doctors

1   Michael Oldani did not want to name his former employer. Paxil's generic name is paroxetine.

2   D. Katz, A. Caplan and J. Merz, 'All gifts large and small: toward an understanding of the ethics of pharmaceutical industry gift-giving', *American Journal of Bioethics*, vol. 3, 2003, pp. 39–46.

3   Paxil's generic name is paroxetine. Prozac's generic name is fluoxetine. Zoloft's generic name is sertraline.

4   W. Hall, A. Mant and P. Mitchell, et al., 'Association between anti-depressant prescribing and suicide in Australia, 1991–2000: trend analysis', *BMJ*, vol. 326, 2003, pp. 1008; IMS data shows global sales around $20 billion. http://www.ims-global.com/insight/news_story/0403/news_story_040316.htm (accessed 6 Jan. 2005).

5   http://www.imshealth.com/vgn/images/portal/cit_40000873/40054155RHMod-PressRoom-Spending%20Hits%20Wall-Sept2002.pdf (accessed 6 Jan. 2005).

6   See a good article on relations between doctors and drug companies in a special supplement of *Pharmaceutical Marketing*, Practical Guide #6, Effective Medical Education, pp. 14–22.

7   D. Healy, *Let Them Eat Prozac*, James Lorimer & Company Ltd, Toronto, 2003.

8   M. Oldani, 'Thick prescriptions: toward an interpretation of pharmaceutical sales practices', *Medical Anthropology Quarter*, vol. 18, 2004, pp. 325–56.

9   D. Katz, A. Caplan and J. Merz, 'All gifts large and small', op. cit.

10  R. Moynihan, 'Who pays for the pizza: Redefining the relationships between doctors and drug companies. Part 1, Entanglement and Part 2, Disentanglement', *BMJ*, vol. 326, 2003, pp. 1189–96.

11  J. Lexchin, 'Doctors and detailers: therapeutic education or pharmaceutical promotion?', *International Journal of Health Services*, vol. 19, 1989, pp. 663–79.

12  A. Wazana, 'Physicians and the pharmaceutical industry: is a gift ever just a gift?', *JAMA*, vol. 283, 2000, pp. 373–80. Also see D. Griffith, 'Reasons for not seeing drug representatives', *BMJ*, vol. 319, 1999, pp. 69–70, which contains this quote: 'Increased costs of prescribing are likely to be a further consequence of contact with representatives.

Selective serotonin reuptake inhibitors are just one example where promotion by drug companies has boosted sales far beyond levels that might have been expected if non-promotional literature had been heeded.'

13  J. Jureidini, C. Doecke and P. Mansfield et al., 'Efficacy and safety of antidepressants for children and adolescents', *BMJ*, vol. 328, 2004, pp. 879–83. Also see Tom Moore's pieces on antidepressants at http://www.thomasjmoore.com (accessed 6 Jan. 2005).

14  See Tom Moore's pieces at http://www.thomasjmoore.com (accessed 6 Jan. 2005). For information about all drugs mentioned in this book, see the SPC at http://emc.medicines.org.uk/ (accessed 6 Jan. 2005). The site has an easy-to-use search engine. FDA warnings on antidepressants are at http://www.fda.gov/bbs/topics/news/2004/NEW01124.html (accessed 6 Jan. 2005) and http://www.fda.gov/cder/drug/antidepressants/SSRIPHA200410.htm (accessed 6 Jan. 2005).

15  D. Healy, 'Shaping the intimate: influences on the experience of everyday nerves', *Social Studies of Science*, vol. 34, no. 2, 2004, pp. 219–45. There is also evidence showing this SSRI class was safer in overdose than older antidepressants.

16  http://www.fda.gov/bbs/topics/news/2004/NEW01124.html (accessed 6 Jan. 2005) and http://www.fda.gov/cder/drug/antidepressants/SSRIPHA200410.htm (accessed 6 Jan. 2005).

17  M. Angell, 'Is academic medicine for sale?', *New England Journal of Medicine*, vol. 342, 2000, pp. 1516–18.

18  S. Vedantam, 'Industry role in medical meeting decried; symposiums sponsored by pharmaceutical companies trouble some psychiatrists' *Washington Post*, 26 May 2002.

19  An APA spokesperson declined to comment on these charges.

20  T. Tran, S. Sengupta, S. Wolf, R. Goodman, P. Lurie, 'Violations of exhibiting rules at the 2002 American Psychiatric Association annual meeting', presentation at the 26th annual meeting of the Society of General Internal Medicine, Vancouver BC, 30 April–3 May 2003.

21  http://www.psych.org/edu/ann_mtgs/am/04/programbk/p4tues03252004.pdf (accessed 15 Oct. 2004).

22  http://www.psych.org/edu/ann_mtgs/am/04/programbk/p1sat03242004.pdf (accessed 15 Oct. 2004).

23  ibid.

24   Typically industry funding for education activities flows through 'unre-stricted educational grants'.

25   http://www.moshersoteria.com/resig.htm (accessed 6 Jan. 2005).

26   D. Healy, *Let Them Eat Prozac*, op. cit.

27   Based on David Healy's interview for the documentary *Selling Sickness*, Paradigm Pictures, 2004.

28   ibid.

29   R. Kessler, K. McGonagle and S. Zhao et al., 'Lifetime and 12-month prevalence of DSM-III-R psychiatric disorders in the United States. Results from the National Comorbidity Survey', *Archives of General Psychiatry*, vol. 51, Jan. 1994, pp. 8–19.

30   http://www.in-cites.com/papers/DrRonaldKessler.html (accessed 19 Nov. 2004)

31   Ray Moynihan's interview with William Narrow.

32   W. Narrow, D. Rae and L. Robins et al., 'Revised Prevalence estimates of mental disorders in the United States', *Archives of General Psychiatry*, vol. 59, 2002, pp. 115–23.

33   W. Narrow et al., op. cit.

34   Ray Moynihan's interview with William Narrow, now based at the American Psychiatric Association.

35   R.C. Kessler, K.B. Merikangas and P. Berglund et al., 'Mild disorders should not be eliminated from the DSM-V', *Archives of General Psychiatry*, vol. 60, 2003, pp. 1117–22. Ray Moynihan's interview with Ron Kessler.

36   Ray Moynihan's interview with Ron Kessler.

37   ibid.

38   The WHO Mental Health Survey Consortium, 'Prevalence, severity, and unmet need for the treatment of mental disorders in the World Health Organization world health mental health surveys', *JAMA*, vol. 291, 2004, pp. 2581–90.

39   ibid.

40   William Narrow used this term.

41   Support for the project from Bristol-Myers Squibb was disclosed in tiny print at the end of 'Sphere: A national depression project', a special supplement of the *Medical Journal of Australia*, vol. 175, 16 July 2001. The curriculum was independently run, see http://www.abc.net.au/science/slab/medicine/trans2.htm (accessed 6 Jan. 2005).

42   http://www.abc.net.au/science/slab/medicine/trans2.htm (accessed 6 Jan. 2005).

43  W. Hall, A. Mant and P. Mitchell et. al., 'Association between anti-depressant prescribing and suicide in Australia', op. cit. Serzone's generic name is nefazodone.

44  ibid.

45  I. Hickie, T. Davenport and D. Hadzi-Pavlovic et al., 'Development of a simple screening tool for common mental disorders in general practice', *Medical Journal of Australia*, vol. 175, 2001, Supplement, pp. S10–S17.

46  D. Clarke and D. McKenzie, 'An examination of the efficiency of the 12-item SPHERE questionnaire as a screening instrument for common mental disorders in primary care', *Australian and New Zealand Journal of Psychiatry*, vol. 37, 2003, pp. 236–9.

47  http://www.druginjurylaw.com/serzone-canada.pdf (accessed 6 Jan. 2005). For BMS explanation see http://my.webmd.com/content/article/87/99492.htm (accessed 6 Jan. 2005).

48  For information about all drugs see the SPC on http://emc.medicines.org.uk/ (accessed 6 Jan. 2005). The site has an easy-to-use search engine.

49  Importantly, the trials do not show any increase in the risk of suicide, rather suicidal behaviour and thinking. The warnings from the FDA are at http://www.fda.gov/bbs/topics/news/2004/NEW01124.html (accessed 6 Jan. 2005) and http://www.fda.gov/cder/drug/anti-depressants/SSRIPHA200410.htm (accessed 6 Jan. 2005).

50  T. Moore, 'Medical use of antidepressant drugs in children and adults, drug safety research, special report', 26 January 2004. This material was given as evidence at a February 2004 hearing of an FDA advisory panel.

51  R. Moynihan, 'FDA advisory panel calls for suicide warnings over new antidepressants', *BMJ*, vol. 328, 2004, p. 303.

52  These comments were broadcast in the documentary *Selling Sickness*, op. cit.

53  Transcripts at http://www.fda.gov/ohrms/dockets/ac/cder04.html#PsychopharmacologicDrugs (accessed 6 Jan. 2005).

54  http://www.fda.gov/cder/drug/antidepressants/SSRIPHA200410.htm (accessed 6 Jan. 2005).

55  http://www.mca.gov.uk (accessed 6 Jan. 2005).

56  http://www.fda.gov/bbs/topics/news/2004/NEW01124.html (accessed 6 Jan. 2005) and http://www.fda.gov/cder/drug/antidepressants/SSRIPHA200410.htm (accessed 6 Jan. 2005).

57  *Selling Sickness*, documentary, op. cit.

58 ibid.

59 ibid.

60 Figures on drug use at http://www.ahrp.org/risks/usSSRIuse0604.pdf (accessed 6 Jan. 2005).

61 I. Heath, 'Commentary: there must be limits to the medicalisation of human distress', *BMJ*, vol. 318, 1999, pp. 436–40.

62 D. Antonuccio, W. Danton, and G. DeNelsky et al., 'Raising questions about antidepressants', *Psychotherapy and Psychosomatics*, vol. 68, 1999, pp. 3–14. Also see D. Antonuccio, W. Danton and G. DeNelsky, 'Psychotherapy versus medication for depression: challenging the conventional wisdom with data', *Professional Psychology Research Practice*, vol. 26, 1995, pp. 574–85.

63 R. Moynihan, 'Who pays for the pizza', op. cit.

64 Alan Cassels' interview with Warren Bell.

65 ibid.

66 www.Nofreelunch.org (accessed 6 Jan. 2005).

67 R Moynihan, 'Who pays for the pizza', op. cit.

68 http://www.psych.org/edu/ann_mtgs/am/04/programbk/p5Wed042204.pdf (accessed 16 Jan. 2005).

69 M. Denarie and B. Burk, 'Evaluate return on investment of promotional events using patient-centric data', reprinted from *Product Management Today*, August 2002, pp. 23–7.

70 M. Oldani, 'Thick prescriptions: toward an interpretation of pharmaceutical sales practices', *Medical Anthropology Quarter*, vol. 18, 2004, pp. 325–56.

## Chapter 3    Working with celebrities

This chapter owes a debt to assistance from the United States National Women's Health Network, and Amy Allina and Cindy Pearson in particular.

1 Details of the award come from 'The top 25 marketers of the year', *DTC Perspectives*, vol. 1, Summer 2002, p. 20. Data about the combined form of hormone replacement therapy come from Writing Group for the Women's Health Initiative Investigators, 'Risks and benefits of estrogen plus progestin in healthy menopausal women', *JAMA*, vol. 288, pp. 321–33. Data about the effects of estrogen alone come from The

Women's Health Initiative Steering Committee, 'Effects of conjugated equine estrogen in postmenopausal women with hysterectomy', *JAMA*, vol. 291, 2004, pp. 1701–12. The chapter is mostly concerned with the combined form, where the harms are of more concern.

2 'The top 25 marketers of the year', op. cit. In response to questions from Ray Moynihan, a Wyeth spokesperson described the company's relationship with Lauren Hutton like this: 'Ms Hutton, a women's health advocate, participated in general menopause and hormone therapy advertisements and consumer outreach events supported by Wyeth to educate women about menopause and hormone therapy and encourage them to discuss menopause and symptom treatment options with their physicians. Wyeth compensated Ms Hutton for her work on behalf of Wyeth educating women about menopause and symptom treatment options. Ms Hutton participated in menopause and symptom treatment option education initiatives from 1999 through 2003. She is not currently under contract with Wyeth.'

3 Interview with Amy Doner Schachtel conducted for *Selling Sickness*, documentary, Paradigm Pictures, 2004.

4 *Parade*, Sunday 19 March 2000, cover story.

5 http://www.roymorgan.com/index.cfm?0A32A818-50BA-1DC3-650D-E1800B48F772&moduleID=100000020&morganPoll=100000183&docType=3&page=1 (accessed 6 Jan. 2005).

6 Personal communication from Wyeth to Ray Moynihan.

7 'Top 25 DTC marketers of the year' at http://www.dtcnational.com/latestnews.asp?id=127 (accessed 6 Jan. 2005).

8 Personal communication from Wyeth to Ray Moynihan.

9 Interview with Amy Doner Schachtel conducted for *Selling Sickness*, documentary, op. cit. The interview was not used in the final broadcast version.

10 'Writing Group for the Women's Health Initiative', op. cit. In absolute terms, over five years, the trial results suggested there was one extra adverse event—e.g. stroke, heart attack—for every hundred women taking HRT compared to a placebo.

11 R. Wilson, *Feminine Forever*, M. Evans and Company Inc., New York (distributed in association with J.B. Lippincott), 1966.

12 I. Palmlund, 'The social construction of menopause as risk', *Journal of Psychosomatic Obstetrics and Gynaecology*, vol. 18, 1997, pp. 87–94.

13  The line 'with estrogen therapy ...' comes from p. 51 of R. Wilson, *Feminine Forever*, op. cit. The line 'as a serious ...' and 'indifference' comes from p. 17 of that book.

14  *Taking Hormones and Women's Health: Choices, Risks and Benefits*, National Women's Health Network, Washington DC, 1995, p. 13.

15  ibid.

16  ibid., p. 9.

17  S. Bell, 'Changing ideas: the medicalization of menopause', *Social Science and Medicine*, vol. 24, 1987, pp. 535–42. Some other researchers trace the history back further.

18  http://cis.nci.nih.gov/fact/3_4.htm (accessed 6 Jan. 2005).

19  I. Palmlund, 'The social construction of menopause as risk', op. cit.

20  ibid.

21  S. Ferguson and C. Parry, 'Rewriting menopause: challenging the medical paradigm to reflect menopausal women's experiences', *Frontiers*, vol. 19, 1998, pp. 20–2.

22  ibid.

23  National Women's Health Network, *The Truth About Hormone Replacement Therapy*, Prima Publishing, Roseville, California, 2002.

24  Allina is a co-author of the book *The Truth About Hormone Replacement Therapy*, ibid.

25  National Health and Medical Research Council (Australia), booklet for health professionals, 'Hormone replacement therapy for peri- and post-menopausal women', undated. The booklet was based on consultations in 1995.

26  8th International Congress on the Menopause, 3–7 November 1996, Sydney, Australia.

27  E. Price and H. Little, 'Women need to be fully informed about risks of hormone replacement therapy' (letter), *BMJ*, vol. 312, 1996, p. 1301.

28  S. Hulley, D. Grady and T. Bush et al., 'Randomized trial of estrogen plus progestin for secondary prevention of coronary heart disease in postmenopausal women', *JAMA*, vol. 280, 1998, pp. 605–13.

29  This is a simple description. A placebo is not always used in the control group, and often more than two groups are compared.

30  S. Hulley, D. Grady and T. Bush et al., op. cit.

31  In an observational study, participants are 'observed' rather than actively assigned to two or more different groups to undergo an experiment. To

put it simply, in observational studies of HRT, a group of women taking the drugs were observed to have fewer heart attacks than a similar group of women not taking the drugs, so it was strongly assumed that the hormone replacement therapy was providing some sort of protection against heart disease. But such assumptions are often shaky with observational studies—there may have been something else different about the two groups that was causing one group to have fewer heart attacks. By way of contrast, randomised controlled trials generally produce more reliable results than observational studies because the two groups being compared are as identical as practicably possible.

32 This comes from an email exchange between Ray Moynihan and Wyeth. Ray Moynihan: Have Wyeth-funded celebrities been used to promote findings of the HERS trial or the WHI data? Can you provide as many examples of such promotion as possible? Wyeth answered: All Wyeth menopause education programs and hormone therapy advertisements, including those with celebrity spokespersons, have always provided risk and benefit information consistent with Wyeth policy and FDA regulations.

33 Letter from Philip J. de Vane, Wyeth-Ayerst, April 1998. Wyeth was at the time also concerned about other classes of drugs eating into the HRT market.

34 Hill & Knowlton press release, 14 July, 2000.

35 The *Sunday Telegraph* advertisement, 23 July 2000.

36 R Moynihan, 'New doubts over hormone drugs', AFR, 25 January 2001, p. 24.

37 'Understanding Menopause', The Australasian Menopause Society, undated.

38 Communication called 'WHI HRT Update' from the Women's Health Initiative (2000). The results being discussed here relate to that part of the WHI that was testing combined estrogen and progestin against a placebo.

39 Writing Group for the Women's Health Initiative Investigators, 'Risks and benefits of estrogen plus progestin . . .', op. cit.

40 ibid.

41 S. Fletcher and G. Colditz, 'Failure of estrogen plus progestin therapy for prevention', *JAMA*, vol. 288, 2002, pp. 366–8.

42 S. Schumaker, C. Leagault and S. Rapp et al., 'Estrogen plus progestin

and the incidence of dementia and mild cognitive impairment in post-menopausal women', *JAMA*, vol. 289, 2003, pp. 2651–62.

43  J. Hays, J. Ockene and R. Brunner et al., 'Effects of estrogen plus pro-gestin on health-related quality of life', *New England Journal of Medicine*, vol. 348, 2003, pp. 1839–54.

44  D. Grady, 'Postmenopausal hormones—therapy for symptoms only', *New England Journal of Medicine*, vol. 348, 2003, pp. 1835–7.

45  ACOG News Release, 25 Feb. 2000. Just before that ACOG recom-mendation, independent researchers published a review of all the existing studies of these drugs in *The Lancet*, which concluded they offered no benefit in terms of heart disease (E. Hemminki and K. McPherson, 'Value of drug licensing documents in studying the effect of postmenopuasal hormone therapy on cardiovascular disease', *The Lancet*, vol. 355, 2000, pp. 566–9.

46  A. Hersh, M. Stefanick and R. Stafford, 'National use of post-menopausal hormone therapy: annual trends and response to recent evidence', *JAMA*, vol. 291, 2004, pp. 47–53.

47  R. Moynihan, 'Celebrity selling', *BMJ*, vol. 324, 2002, p. 1342.

48  O. Benshoshan, 'Celebrity public relations: an alternative to DTC', *DTC Perspectives*, vol. 2, 2003.

49  ibid.

50  The section of the giant WHI study that tested estrogen only versus a placebo found no overall benefits: an increase in stroke and a decrease in hip fractures. See The Women's Health Initiative Steering Committee, 'Effects of Conjugated Equine Estrogen . . .', op. cit.

51  R. Moynihan, 'The intangible magic of celebrity marketing', *PloS Medicine*, vol. 1, 2004 at http://medicine.plosjournals.org/perlserv/?request=get-document&doi=10.1371/journal.pmed.0010042 (accessed 30 Nov. 2004).

## Chapter 4    Partnering with patients

This chapter uses the term ADD and ADHD interchangeably, for the sake of simplicity. ADHD appears when it is specifically referred to in cited materials.

1  G. LeFever, K. Dawson and A. Morrow, 'The extent of drug therapy for attention deficit-hyperactivity disorder among children in public schools', *American Journal of Public Health*, vol. 89, 1999, pp. 1359–64.

2   The figures from this and the preceding sentence come from an article by Lawrence Diller, see http://www.healthology.com/focus_article.asp?f= children&b=healthology&c=adhd_controversy (accessed 6 Jan. 2005).

3   J. Zito, D. Safer and S. dosReis et al., 'Trends in the prescribing of psychotropic medications to preschoolers', *JAMA*, vol. 283, 2000, pp. 1025–30. Drugs mentioned in this chapter include Ritalin, whose generic name is methylphenidate, Adderall with the generic name amphetamine-dextro-amphetamine, and Strattera with the generic name atomoxetine HCI.

4   'Fundraising and the growth of industry involvement', *Health and Social Campaigner's News* published by Patient View, April 2004, issue 6, www.patient-view.com (accessed 16 Nov. 2004).

5   http://www.chadd.org/pdfs/chaddincomesources2003.pdf (accessed 6 Jan. 2005).

6   Johnny Holliday's interview with Ray Moynihan for *BMJ*, 2004.

7   S. Timimi, J. Moncrieff and J. Jureidini, 'A critique of the international consensus statement on ADHD', *Clinical Child and Family Psychology Revew*, vol. 7, 2004, pp. 59–63; found at http://www.critpsynet.freeuk.com/ Acritiqueofconsensus.htm (accessed 6 Jan. 2005).

8   R. Barkley et al., 'International consensus statement on ADHD', *Clinical Child and Family Psychology Review*, vol. 5, 2002, pp. 89–111.

9   S. Timimi, J. Moncrieff and J. Jureidini, 'A Critique of the International Consensus Statement on ADHD', op. cit.

10   http://consensus.nih.gov/cons/110/110_statement.pdf (accessed 6 Jan. 2005).

11   The CHADD site says, 'There are no definitive answers as yet, however, research has demonstrated that AD/HD has a very strong neurobiological basis'.

12   Shire history at http://www.shire.com/shirepharma/Corporate Information/ history.jsp (accessed 6 Jan. 2005). Shire presentation at http://www.shire.com/shirepharma/uploads/presentations/MLConf _030204.pdf. The company declined requests for an interview for this book.

13   http://www.pbs.org/wgbh/pages/frontline/shows/medicating/ interviews/antosson.html (accessed 6 Jan. 2005).

14   Shire press release 6 May 2004 on survey at http://www.biospace. com/ news_story.cfm?StoryID=16058620&full=1 (accessed 6 Jan. 2005).

15  Shire press release, 'Regulatory approval received for ADDERALL XR™ in Canada, Basingstoke, UK', 3 February 2004.

16  http://www.chadd.org/webpage.cfm?cat_id=2&subcat_id=1 (accessed 6 Jan. 2005).

17  ibid.

18  http://www.help4adhd.org/en/about/causes (accessed 6 Jan. 2005).

19  The claim about medication is at http://www.help4adhd.org/en/treatment/medical (accessed 6 Jan. 2005).

20  http://www.chadd.org/webpage.cfm?cat_id=7&subcat_id=38 (accessed 31 May 2004).

21  DEA, 'Methylphenidate' (a background paper), October 1995, p. 4, taken from Center for Science in the Public Interest website, http://www.cspinet.org/integrity/corp_funding.html (accessed 6 Jan. 2005).

22  http://www.chadd.org/pdfs/chaddincomesources2003.pdf (accessed 6 Jan. 2005).

23  See note 12, slide 10 of presentation.

24  Shire press release on survey dated 6 May 2004 at http://www.biospace.com/news_story.cfm?StoryID=16058620&full=1 (accessed 6 Jan. 2005).

25  Ray Moynihan's visit to APA Congress, 2004.

26  See note 12, slide 11.

27  http://www.strattera.com/1_5_news/pr072203.pdf (accessed 6 Jan. 2005). For more recent developments in relation to Strattera see http://www.fda.gov/bbs/topics/ANSWERS/2004/ANS01335.html (accessed 2 March 2005).

28  The drug is a selective norepinephrine reuptake inhibitor.

29  Lilly advertisement for Strattera, US News & World Report, 26 April 2004, p. 65 (two pages after the article).

30  http://www.chadd.org/pdfs/preliminary_program_2004.pdf (accessed 2 June 2004). The conference chair stressed in her closing remarks on the site's opening conference blurb that ADHD is a lifespan disorder.

31  ibid.

32  ibid.

33  Vince Parry's interview with Cathy Scott for Selling Sickness, documentary, Paradigm Pictures, 2004.

34  ibid.

35 ibid.

36 'Living with Adult ADD', cover story, *US News & World Report*, 26 April 2004.

37 Stephen Spector, officer with CHADD.

38 'The ties that bind', seminar report, Health Action International, 1999. See www.haiweb.org (accessed 2 March 2005).

39 Teri P. Cox, 'Forging alliances, advocacy partners', supplement to *Pharmaceutical Executive*, September 2002, p. 8.

40 'The ties that bind', op. cit. One of the consequences of patient groups accepting drug company funding is that reporters tend to be supplied with patients who have had positive experiences with a sponsor's drug, rather than negative experiences.

41 Teri P. Cox, 'Forging alliances . . .', op. cit.

42 Shire explains its altruism during this interview at http://www.pbs.org/wgbh/pages/frontline/shows/medicating/interviews/antosson.html (accessed 6 Jan. 2005). The company declined an interview for this book.

43 Teri P. Cox, 'Forging alliances . . .', op. cit.

44 See J. Moncrieff, 'Is psychiatry for sale?', Institute of Psychiatry, Kings College, London, Paper no. 13, Maudsley discussion papers. See also S. Hills, 'Drugs and the medicalization of human problems', *Journal of Drug Education*, vol. 7, 1977, pp. 317–22.

45 S. Hills, ibid.

46 www.docdiller.com (accessed 6 Jan. 2005).

47 From a Diller article, found at http://www.healthology.com/focus_article.asp?f=children&b=healthology&c=adhd_controversy (accessed 6 Jan. 2005).

48 http://www.healthology.com/focus_article.asp?f=children&b=healthology&c=adhd_controversy (accessed 6 Jan. 2005).

49 Ray Moynihan's interview with Dr Diller.

50 http://www.healthology.com/focus_article.asp?f=children&b=healthology&c=adhd_controversy (accessed 6 Jan. 2005).

51 The CHADD website says: 'Today, children with AD/HD are eligible for special education services or accommodations within the regular classroom when needed, and adults with AD/HD may be eligible for accommodations in the workplace under the Americans with Disabilities Act.'

52 H. Searight and A. McLaren, 'Attention-deficit hyperactivity disorder:

the medicalisation of misbehaviour', *Journal of Clinical Psychology in Medical Settings*, vol. 5, 1998, pp. 467–95.

53   ibid.

54   A. Baumgaertel, M. Wolraich and M. Dietrich, 'Comparison of diagnostic criteria for attention deficit disorders in a German elementary school sample', *Journal of the American Academy of Child Adolescent Psychiatry*, vol. 34, 1995, pp. 629–38.

55   Ray Moynihan's interview with Judith Rapoport. One of her key articles was J. Rapoport, M. Buschbaum and T. Zahn et al., 'Dextro-amphetamine: its cognitive and behavioural effects in normal prepubertal boys', *Science*, 1978 vol. 199, pp. 560–3.

56   H. Searight and A. McLaren, 'Attention-Deficit Hyperactivity Disorder . . .', op. cit.

57   http://www.nihcm.org/spending2001.pdf (accessed 6 Jan. 2005).

58   http://www.theledger.com/apps/pbcs.dll/article?AID=/20040517/NEWS/405170381/1039 (accessed 6 Jan. 2005).

59   http://www.shire.com/shirepharma/NewsAndMedia/PressReleases/showShirePress.jsp?ref=343 (accessed 6 Jan. 2005).

60   AMA 23rd Annual Science Reporters Conference, 13–14 October 2004, Washington D.C.

61   J. Moncrieff, 'Is psychiatry for sale?' op. cit.

62   'Fidgets' comes from *Guidebook for Diagnostic and Statistical Manual of Mental Disorders*, 4th ed. (DSM-IV-TR), American Psychiatric Association, 2000. Also see H. Searight and A. McLaren, 'Attention-deficit hyperactivity disorder . . .', op. cit.

## Chapter 5   Making risks into medical conditions

1   www.ti.ubc.ca (accessed 7 Jan. 2005).

2   J. Appel, 'The verdict from ALLHAT—thiazide diuretics are the preferred initial therapy for hypertension' (editorial), *JAMA*, vol. 288, 2002, pp. 3039–42. '90 per cent' comes from A. Chobanian, G. Bakris and H. Black et al. 'The Seventh Report of the Joint National Committee on Prevention, Detection, Evaluation, and Treatment of High Blood Pressure: the JNC 7 report', *JAMA*, vol. 289, 2003, pp. 2560–72.

3   Stacey L. Bradford, 'Hearty stock', Stockwatch column in *Smart Money*, 28 March 2002. http://yahoo.smartmoney.com/stockwatch/index.

cfm?story=20020328 (accessed 4 Aug. 2004). Also see IMS Health, 'The "Boom" of the Baby Boomers', http://www.ims-global.com/insight/news_story/ 0101/news_story_010123.htm (accessed 24 Aug. 2004).

4 What follows is an approximation of the standard presentation based on Alan Cassels' attendances at many of these presentations, and repeated discussions with James McCormack and Bob Rangno.

5 This slide is based on data from the following trial: M. Heikki Frick, O. Elo and K. Haapa et al., 'Helsinki Heart Study: primary prevention trial with gemfibrozil in middle-aged men with dyslipidemia, safety of treatment, changes in risk factors, and incidence of coronary heart disease', *New England Journal of Medicine*, vol. 317, 1987, pp. 1237–45.

6 R. Moynihan, L. Bero and D. Ross-Degnan et al., 'Coverage by the news media of the benefits and risks of medications', *New England Journal of Medicine*, vol. 342, 2000, pp. 1645–50. Also see A. Cassels, M. Hughes and C. Cole et al., 'Drugs in the news: an analysis of Canadian newspaper coverage of new prescription drugs', *Canadian Medical Association Journal*, vol. 168, 2003, pp. 1133–7.

7 A. Chobanian, G. Bakris and H. Black et al., 'The Seventh Report of the Joint National Committee on Prevention . . .', op. cit.

8 See Maryanne Napoli from the Center for Medical Consumers group interview leading hypertension expert Dr Michael Alderman in August 2003 at http://www.medicalconsumers.org/pages/Prehypertension.html.

9 ibid.

10 Interviews by Alan Cassels and Ray Moynihan with Curt Furberg.

11 Alan Cassels' interview with Curt Furberg, 2004.

12 A. Chobanian, G. Bakris and H. Black et al., 'The Seventh Report of the Joint National Committee on Prevention . . .', op. cit.

13 C. Furberg and B. Psaty, 'JNC VI: timing is everything', *The Lancet*, vol. 350, 1997, p. 1413.

14 Personal communication from Bruce Psaty to Ray Moynihan.

15 University of Umea, Sweden, 2004, honorary degree.

16 Interviews by Alan Cassels and Ray Moynihan with Curt Furberg.

17 See letter at http://www.uib.no/isf/letter/ (accessed 7 Jan. 2005). Bruntlands's reply is at http://www.uib.no/isf/letter/reply.htm (accessed 7 Jan. 2005).

18  http://www.imshealthcanada.com/htmen/3_1_5.htm (accessed 7 Jan. 2005).
19  J. Graves and S. Sheps, 'Does evidence-based medicine suggest that physicians should not be measuring blood pressure in the hypertensive patient?', *American Journal of Hypertension*, vol. 17, 2004, pp. 354–60.
20  M. Kendrick, 'High blood pressure: it's a symptom, not a disease, stupid! Why almost everything written about treating blood pressure is wrong', http://www.redflagsweekly.com/kendrick/2003_jan16.php (restricted site), 16 January 2003.
21  http://www.americanheart.org/presenter.jhtml?identifier=4609 (accessed 7 Jan. 2005).
22  M. Kendrick, 21 May 2004. 'Suffer the little children', essay dated 21 May 2004, accessed at http://www.redflagsweekly.com/kendrick/2004_may21.php (and the next quote is from here too).
23  ibid.
24  See C. Mulrow, E. Chiquette and L. Angel et al., 'Dieting to reduce body weight for controlling hypertension in adults', *Cochrane Review From The Cochrane Library*, issue 4, 1998, Chichester, UK; B. Materson, D. Reda and W. Cushman et al, 'Single-drug therapy for hypertension in men: a comparison of six antihypertensive agents with placebo', *New England Journal of Medicine*, vol. 328, 1993, pp. 914–21; The Treatment of Mild Hypertension Research Group, 'The treatment of mild hypertension study: a randomized, placebo-controlled trial of a nutritional-hygienic regimen along with various drug monotherapies', *Archives of Internal Medicine*, vol. 151, 1991, pp. 1413–23; S. Whelton, A. Chin, X. Xin and J. Ha, 'Effect of aerobic exercise on blood pressure: a meta-analysis of randomized, controlled trials', *Annals of Internal Medicine*, vol. 136, 2002, pp. 493–503.
25  The ALLHAT Officers and Coordinators for the ALLHAT Collaborative Research Group 'Major outcomes in high-risk hypertensive patients randomized to angiotensin-converting enzyme inhibitor or calcium channel blocker vs diuretic', *JAMA*, vol. 288, 2002, pp. 2981–97.
26  Curt Furberg, investigator with ALLHAT, 17 December 2002, press conference remarks, 'Release of the results of the antihypertensive and lipid-lowering treatment to prevent heart attack trial: what makes ALLHAT special?', accessed online at http://www.nhlbi.nih.gov/health/allhat/furberg.htm (accessed 7 Jan. 2005).

27 The ALLHAT Officers and Coordinators for the ALLHAT Collaborative Research Group, op. cit.

28 The Therapeutics Initiative newsletter 47 is entitled, 'The answer: thiazides first line for hypertension', January–March 2003. http://www.ti.ubc.ca/pages/letter47.htm (accessed 7 Jan. 2005). Norvasc's generic name is amlodipine.

29 Curt Furberg's interview with Alan Cassels. Pfizer declined requests for an interview for this book.

30 http://www.ims-global.com/insight/news_story/0403/news_story_040316.htm (accessed 7 Jan. 2005).

31 J. Lenzer, 'Marketing: Spin doctors soft pedal data on antihypertensives', *BMJ*, vol. 326, 2003, p. 170.

32 The Pfizer email memo, 16 March 2000.
Subject: R: PPG ANNOUNCEMENT—EUROPE—ORGANIZ-ATION CHANGES.
'I saw ... here at the ACC this morning at the ALLHAT presentation. I am sure they will fill you in on the presentation of results. The good news is that they were quite brilliant in sending their key physicians to sightsee rather than hear Curt Furberg slam Pfizer once again!'

33 M. Fischer and J. Avorn, 'Economic implications of evidence-based prescribing for hypertension: can better care cost less?', *JAMA*, vol. 291, 2004, pp. 1850–6.

34 A. Fretheim, M. Aaserud and A. Oxman, 'The potential savings of using thiazides as the first choice antihypertensive drug: cost-minimisation analysis', *BMC Health Serv Res.*, vol. 3, 2003 p. 18 available at http://www.pubmedcentral.nih.gov/articlerender.fcgi?artid=201005 (accessed 7 Jan. 2005).

35 M. Nelson, J McNeil and A. Peeters et al., 'PBS/RPBS cost implications of trends and guideline recommendations in the pharmacological management of hypertension in Australia, 1994–1998', *Medical Journal of Australia*, vol. 174, 2001; pp. 565–8.

36 A. Chobanian, G. Bakris and H. Black et al. 'The Seventh Report of the Joint National Committee on Prevention ...', op. cit.

37 See page 18 of the 32 page pamphlet 'Working with religious congregations: a guide for health professionals' by the National Heart, Lung, and Blood Institute (NHLBI) at http://www.nhlbi.nih.gov/health/prof/heart/other/church.pdf. This guide builds on lessons learned from

church-based demonstration programs supported by NHLB. It provides information about how to contact and recruit congregation members, train volunteer teams within congregations, implement effective CVD prevention programs, sustain momentum for continued activity, and monitor and evaluate congregation-based programs. NIH Publication Number: 97-4058. Also see http://hin.nhlbi.nih.gov/nhbpep_kit/hpbs.htm (accessed 13 Jan. 2005).

38 Malcolm Kendrick, 'The new hypertension guidelines: now we are all to be officially ill' (essay), 21 May 2003 at http://www.thincs.org/Malcolm.htm#hypertens2 (accessed 7 Jan. 2005).

## Chapter 6    Advertising disease

The drugs discussed in this chapter have different names in some countries. For example, Paxil is Aropax in Australia and Seroxat in the UK. Paxil's generic name is paroxetine. Prozac's generic name is fluoxetine. Zoloft's generic name is sertraline. The drug name Sarafem is used interchangeably with Prozac through this chapter, as both are different brand names for the same drug, fluoxetine.

1 Mentioned in European decision at http://www.emea.eu.int/pdfs/human/referral/326303en.pdf (accessed 7 Jan. 2005).
2 PMDD is listed as a diagnosis requiring further study.
3 Paula Caplan's interview with Cathy Scott for *Selling Sickness*, documentary, Paradigm Pictures, 2004.
4 Jean Endicott's interview with Ray Moynihan.
5 B. Mintzes, 'Direct to consumer advertising is medicalising normal human experience (for)', *BMJ*, vol. 324, 2002, pp. 908–11.
6 Personal communication to Alan Cassels.
7 S. Wolfe, 'Direct-to-consumer advertising—education or emotion promotion', *New England Journal of Medicine*, vol. 346, 2002, pp. 524–6.
8 http://www.fda.gov/cder/warn/nov2000/dd9523.pdf (accessed 7 Jan. 2005).
9 Sometimes, if the misleading information is too over-the-top, the FDA will ask for corrections to be published.
10 S. Woloshin, L.M. Schwartz, J. Tremmel and G. Welch, 'Direct to consumer advertisements for prescription drugs: what are Americans being sold?', *The Lancet*, vol. 358, 2001, pp. 1141–6.

11  B. Mintzes, 'Direct to consumer advertising . . .', op. cit.

12  Barbara Mintzes interview with Cathy Scott for *Selling Sickness*, documentary, op. cit.

13  Barbara Mintzes interview with Ray Moynihan, 2004.

14  See chapter 2.

15  Barbara Mintzes interview with Cathy Scott, op. cit.

16  Jean Endicott interview with Ray Moynihan, 2004.

17  B. Mintzes, M. Barer and R. Kravitz et al., 'Influence of direct to consumer pharmaceutical advertising and patients' requests on prescribing decisions: two site cross sectional survey', *BMJ*, vol. 324, 2002, pp. 278–9.

18  S. Bonaccorso and J. Sturchio, 'Direct to consumer advertising is medicalising normal human experience', *BMJ*, vol. 324, 2002, pp. 910–11.

19  O. Schoffski, 'Diffussion of medicines in Europe' at http://www.gm.wiso.uni-erlangen.de/ (accessed 7 Jan. 2005).

20  A. Liberati and N. Magrini, 'Information from drug companies and opinion leaders', *BMJ*, vol. 326, 2003, pp. 1156–7.

21  'Providing prescription medicine information to consumers: Is there a role for direct-to-consumer promotion?', symposium report, Health Action International Europe 2002, p. 12. See www.haiweb.org/campaign/DTCA/2002_symposium_report.pdf (accessed 13 Jan. 2005).

22  Mentioned in EU decision at http://www.emea.eu.int/pdfs/human/referral/326303en.pdf (accessed 7 Jan. 2005). Also see R. Moynihan, 'Controversial disease dropped from Prozac product information', *BMJ*, vol. 328, 2004, p. 365.

23  J. Chrisler and P. Caplan, 'The strange case of Dr Jekyll and Ms Hyde: how PMS became a cultural phenomenon and a psychiatric disorder', *Annual Review of Sex Research*, vol. 13, 2002, pp. 274–306.

24  R. Spitzer, S. Severino, J. Williams and B. Parry, 'Late luteal phase dysphoric disorder and DSM-III-R', *American Journal of Psychiatry*, vol. 146, 1989, pp. 892–7.

25  Robert Spitzer interview with Ray Moynihan.

26  Spitzer wrote that the possibility of such research was a key motivation for the creation of this new mental disorder: 'Diagnostic criteria encourage research, as can be seen by the burgeoning of research on affective

illness after diagnostic criteria were developed for affective disorders [e.g. depression, social anxiety disorder]. It is for all these reasons that the members of the advisory committee, most of whom are active investigators in this area, were so enthusiastic about developing the diagnostic criteria for LLPDD that would be in DSM III-R.' From R. Spitzer, S. Severino, J. Williams and B. Parry, 'Late luteal phase dysphoric disorder . . .', op. cit.

27  ibid.

28  This paragraph based on Ray Moynihan's interviews with Sally Severino.

29  ibid.

30  Jean Endicott told Ray Moynihan that Lilly helped fund the meeting, but the company declined to answer questions about it. Also see J. Endicott, J. Amsterdam and E. Eriksson et al., 'Is Premenstrual Dysphoric Disorder a distinct clinical entity?', *Journal of Women's Health and Gender Based Medicine*, vol. 8, 1999, pp. 663–79.

31  D. Healy, *Let Them Eat Prozac*, James Lorimer & Company Ltd, Toronto, 2003.

32  Jean Endicott's interview with Ray Moynihan.

33  J. Endicott, J. Amsterdam and E. Eriksson et al., 'Is Premenstrual Dysphoric Disorder a distinct clinical entity?', op. cit.

34  V. Parry, 'The art of branding a condition', *MM&M*, May 2003, pp. 43–9.

35  ibid.

36  Vince Parry's interview with Cathy Scott for *Selling Sickness*, documentary, op. cit. The part of this interview immediately before the quote in the text is: 'How do you connect with patients? You get the profile of the patients that you've identified and you bring them into research situations. You bring them into a focus group which is maybe a dozen of these types of individuals and you expose them to different concepts, different names for instance, different colours, different packaging options, different series of messages of how you want to talk about it. And not just the name itself but the nomenclature that goes under it or the language that supports that name, the condition name. And as you go through and examine this with the patient, you find out, they'll tell you what they feel most comfortable with, a name that they identify and why they identify with it. It has a certain kind of personality that they can see themselves in. So the packaging itself, the name Sarafem has a

very nice feminine name to it. It has a soothing, reassuring quality to it, which is what they were looking for and they dyed the pill purple because that was the colour that was very appealing to women. Out of all of the colours they showed them, they thought that was something unusual and just for them.' Also, at around the time of Sarafem's launch a Lilly marketing associate told the press the company had done its homework, just as Parry has explained. 'We asked women and physicians about the treatment of PMDD, and they told us they wanted a treatment option with its own identity that would differentiate PMDD from depression ... They wanted a treatment option with its own identity.' See this quote at http://www.antidepressantsfacts.com/misleading-medicine.htm (accessed 7 Jan. 2005).

37 http://www.fda.gov/cder/warn/nov2000/dd9523.pdf (accessed 7 Jan. 2005).

38 Barbara Mintzes interview with Cathy Scott for *Selling Sickness*, documentary, op. cit.

39 Paula Caplan's interview with Cathy Scott for *Selling Sickness*, documentary, op. cit.

40 ibid. Also J. Chrisler and P. Caplan, 'The strange case of Dr Jekyll and Ms Hyde', op. cit.

41 http://www.emea.eu.int/pdfs/human/referral/326303en.pdf (accessed 7 Jan. 2005).

42 This whole paragraph comes from R. Moynihan, 'Controversial disease dropped from Prozac ...', op. cit.

43 US General Accounting Office, 'Prescription drugs: FDA oversight of direct-to-consumer advertising has limitations', Pub Number GAO- 03-177 (Washington GAO, 2002). Also see H. Waxman, 'Perspective, health affairs', 28 April 2004 at http://content.healthaffairs.org/cgi/reprint/hlthaff.w4.256v1.pdf (accessed 7 Jan. 2005).

44 http://www.paxilcr.com/pmdd/PMDD_Medication.html (accessed 26 May 2004).

45 The fine print of the official Paxil product information now warns that 'side effects may result from stopping the medication ... including dizziness, sensory disturbances (including electric shock sensations), abnormal dreams, agitation, anxiety, nausea and sweating'. http://www.paxilcr.com/pmdd/important_safety_info.html (accessed 26 May, 2004). Other side effects include infection, nausea, diarrhoea, dry

mouth, constipation, decreased appetite, dizziness, sweating, tremor, sexual side effects, injury, yawning, asthenia, insomnia, abnormal vision and sleepiness.

## Chapter 7    Shaping public perceptions

General note for this chapter: of the SSRI antidepressants, only Prozac was approved for children in the US. In Australia the regulator had early warnings against using Aropax for that group.

1   Deborah Olguin interview with Cathy Scott for *Selling Sickness*, documentary, Paradigm Pictures, 2004.

2   ibid.

3   The 'one in eight' is from the December 1998 pamphlet called 'Social Anxiety Disorder: it's more than just shyness', produced by SmithKlineBeecham. At the time the company was called SmithKline Beecham. It would become part of GSK in 2000.

4   http://www.cohnwolfe.com.

5   http://www.cohnwolfe.com/Content.aspx?NodeId=12 (accessed 7 Jan. 2005).

6   http://www.wpp.com/ (accessed 7 Jan. 2005). At the time of writing, the WPP Group included several other public relations houses that specialise in health care apart from Cohn & Wolfe, including Hill & Knowlton, Ogilvy and Burson-Marsteller.

7   This chapter owes a great debt to B. Koerner, 'Disorders made to order: pharmaceutical companies have come up with a new strategy to market their drugs—first go out and find a new mental illness, then push the pills to cure it', *Mother Jones*, vol. 27, 2002.

8   Thanks to the diligent work of several investigative journalists the world has learned what that cultivation entailed. Some of the key stories include B. Koerner, 'Disorders made to order . . .', op. cit.; M. Cottle, 'Selling shyness', *New Republic*, 2 August 1999; and S. Vedantam, 'Drug ads hyping anxiety make some uneasy', *Washington Post*, Monday, 16 July 2001, p. A01. Also, the aims and achievements of the campaign are available on the web at http://members.fortunecity.com/partnersin wellness/id23.htm (accessed 7 Jan. 2005).

9   http://members.fortunecity.com/partnersinwellness/id23.htm (accessed 7 Jan. 2005).

10 This paragraph all comes from B. Koerner, 'Disorders made to order ...', op. cit. According to Koerner's article the coalition was made up of the American Psychiatric Association (APA), the Anxiety Disorders Association of America (ADAA) and another patient advocacy group called Freedom From Fear (FFF). An FFF spokesperson appeared in *Selling Sickness*, the documentary, saying the group relied on company money, the ADAA has a corporate advisory board including drug company representatives, and the APA conference relies on industry sponsorship.

11 http://members.fortunecity.com/partnersinwellness/id23.htm (accessed 7 Jan. 2005).

12 http://www.pslgroup.com/dg/fd072.htm (accessed 7 Jan. 2005).

13 Murray Stein's interview with Cathy Scott for *Selling Sickness*, documentary, op. cit.

14 Murray Stein's personal communication with Ray Moynihan, 2004.

15 'Health Academy', *E-News 2001* (Public Relations Society of America). See http://www.healthacademy.prsa.org/images/Jan%202001%20e News.pdf (accessed 7 Jan. 2005).

16 R. Moynihan, 'Making medical journalism healthier', *The Lancet*, vol. 361, 2003, p. 2097.

17 Deborah Olguin interview with Cathy Scott for *Selling Sickness*, documentary, op. cit.

18 www.socialaudiot.org.uk (accessed 7 Jan. 2005).

19 See Charles Medawar and Anita Hardon, *Medicine Out of Control*, Asksant, Amsterdam, 2004, p. 205.

20 P. du Toit and D. Stein, 'Social anxiety disorder', in *Anxiety Disorders*, (eds) D. Nutt and J. Ballenger, Blackwell Publishers, Malden, Massachusetts, 2003, p. 107.

21 ICD-10, World Health Organization, Geneva, 1992. This is the international catalogue of mental disorders produced by the World Health Organization.

22 *Diagnostic and Statistical Manual of Mental Disorders*, 4th ed., text revision (DSM-IV-TR), American Psychiatric Association, 2000.

23 Ray Moynihan's interview with David Baldwin.

24 ICD-10, op. cit. The ICD states clearly that for someone to be diagnosed with social phobia, 'Avoidance of the phobic situation must be a prominent feature'.

25 The December 1998 pamphlet 'Social Anxiety Disorder', op. cit., suggests that SAD is about the 'fear', not about avoidance. And p. 456 of the

DSM-IV-TR, op. cit., states 'The feared social or performance situations are avoided or else are endured with intense anxiety or distress'.

26　Vince Parry's interview with Cathy Scott for *Selling Sickness*, documentary, op. cit.

27　See the important booklet B. Mintzes, 'Blurring the boundaries', produced by Health Action International, 1998.

28　Vince Parry's interview with Cathy Scott for *Selling Sickness*, documentary, op. cit.

29　R. Moynihan, I. Heath and D. Henry, 'Selling sickness: the pharmaceutical industry and disease mongering', *BMJ*, vol. 324, 2002, pp. 886–91. Aurorix's generic name is moclobemide.

30　ibid.

31　ibid. Also see R. Moynihan 'Drug firms hype disease as sales ploy, industry chief claims', *BMJ*, vol. 324, 2002. p. 867.

32　David Healy estimates less than 1 per cent. The 16 per cent is cited in P. du Toit and D. Stein, 'Social anxiety disorder', op. cit.

33　M. Liebowitz, J. Gorman, A. Fyer and D. Klein, 'Social phobia, review of a neglected anxiety disorder', *Archives of General Psychiatry*, vol. 42, 1985, pp. 729–36.

34　R. Kessler, K. McGonagle and S. Zhao et al., 'Lifetime and 12-month prevalence of DSM-III-R psychiatric disorders in the United States: results from the National Comorbidity Survey', *Archives of General Psychiatry*, vol. 51, 1994 Jan., pp. 8–19.

35　'Social Anxiety Disorder . . .', pamphlet, op. cit.

36　W. Narrow, D. Rae, L. Robins and D. Regier, 'Revised prevalence estimates of mental disorders in the United States', *Archives of General Psychiatry*, vol. 59, 2002, pp. 115–23.

37　David Healy's estimate.

38　William Narrow's interview with Ray Moynihan.

39　That's what Ricky told Oprah.

40　R. Moynihan, 'Celebrity selling 2', *BMJ*, vol. 325, 2002, p. 286.

41　http://www.ims-global.com/insight/news_story/0302/news_story_030228.htm (accessed 7 Jan. 2005).

42　R. Moynihan, 'Celebrity selling 2', op. cit.

43　ibid.

44　http://quickstart.clari.net/qs_se/webnews/wed/by/W058797.RY5t_DOH.html (accessed 7 Jan. 2005). If you want to organise an interview with Ricky Williams, you could try calling the contact person at the bottom of the press release at Cohn & Wolfe in New York, 212 798-9521. Cohn & Wolfe did not respond to requests for an interview for this book.

45  Karen Barth Menzies interview with Cathy Scott for *Selling Sickness*, documentary, op. cit.

46  David Healy's interview with Cathy Scott for *Selling Sickness*, documentary, op. cit., and Ray Moynihan's interveiws with David Healy.

47  ibid.

48  R. Moynihan, 'FDA advisory panel calls for suicide warnings over new antidepressants', *BMJ*, vol. 328, 2004, p. 303. Also see T. Laughren, 'Background comments for February 2, 2004 meeting of Psychopharmacological Drugs Advisory Committee (PDAC) and Pediatric Subcommittee of the Anti-Infective Drugs Advisory Committee (Peds AC)', Department of Health and Human Services, Food and Drug Administration, Center for Drug Evaluation and Research memo.

49  ibid.

50  T. Moore, Medical Use of Antidepressant Drugs in Children and Adults, Drug Safety Research, Special Report, 26 January 2004. This material was given as evidence at a February 2004 hearing of an FDA advisory panel.

51  R. Moynihan, 'FDA advisory panel calls for suicide warnings . . .', op. cit.

52  http://www.oag.state.ny.us/press/2004/jun/jun2b_04_attachI.pdf (accessed 7 Jan. 2005).

53  www.gsk.com (accessed 7 Jan. 2005). See news releases, 26 August 2004.

54  http://www.oag.state.ny.us/press/2004/aug/aug26a_04_attachI.pdf (accessed 7 Jan. 2005).

55  E. Silverman, 'Sales reps told not to divulge Paxil data. Drug maker memo cited risks to youth', *NJ Star Ledger*, Wednesday, 29 September 2004. The paper obtained an internal GlaxoSmithKline memo that was distributed to the company's sales representatives. The memo advises them *not* to discuss the suicide-related risk of Paxil/Seroxat with doctors. The subject of the memo: REVISED MEDICAL INFORMATION LETTER ON THE USE OF PAXIL IN PEDIATRIC PATIENTS.

56  K. Dickersin and D. Rennie, 'Registering clinical trials', *JAMA*, vol. 290, 2003, pp. 516–23.

57  September 2002, supplement to *Pharmaceutical Executive*.

58  'Social Anxiety Disorder . . .', pamphlet, op. cit.

59  W. Crozier and L. Alden (eds), *International Hand book of Social Anxiety*, Wiley, Chichester, England, 2001, p. 4.

60  R. Evans, M. Barer and T. Marmor (eds), *Why Are Some People Healthy and Others Not?*, Aldine De Gruyter, Hawthorne, New York, 1994.

## Chapter 8    Testing the markets

1  Alan Cassels' interview with Wendy Armstrong. The quote is as it was relayed to Wendy, thus it is an approximation only.

2  A. Kazanjian, C. Green and K. Bassett, 'Normal bone mass, aging bodies, marketing of fear: bone mineral density screening of well women', British Columbia Office of Health Technology Assessment, University of British Columbia, presented at the 93rd annual meeting of the American Sociological Association, held in San Francisco, 21–25 August 1998.

3  See J. Stevens and S. Olson, 'Reducing falls and resulting hip fractures among older women', National Center for Injury Prevention and Control Division of Unintentional Injury Prevention at http://www.cdc.gov/mmwr//preview/mmwrhtml/rr4902a2.htm (accessed 8 Jan. 2005). This is one of many publications on the prevention of falls.

4  http://www.drugs.com/top200sales.html (accessed 8 Jan. 2005). Fosamax's generic name is alendronate.

5  Interview by Alan Cassels for the program *Manufacturing Patients* aired by CBC IDEAS on 4 and 11 February 2003. This interview took place in the New York office of Ogilvy Public Relations in November 2002.

6  G. Freiherr, 'Strategic alliances: product promotion strategy links drugs and devices', *Medical Device & Diagnostic Industry*, November 1995. Accessed online at http://www.devicelink.com/mddi/archive/95/11/004.html (accessed 8 Aug. 2004).

7  ibid.

8  Report of a WHO study group, 'Assessment of fracture risk and its application to screening for postmenopausal osteoporosis', WHO technical report series 843, Geneva, 1994.

9  ibid.

10  These figures come from Fast Fact—National Osteoporosis Foundation website at http://www.nof.org/osteoporosis/diseasefacts.htm (accessed, 3 March 2005).

11  Based on Ray Moynihan's interviews with David Henry and material from R. Moynihan, *Too Much Medicine?*, ABC Books, Sydney, 1998.

12  Those seven markets were: the United States, Canada, the United Kingdom, France, Italy, Germany and Spain. This is from Merck's 2003 annual report. See http://www.merck.com/finance/annualreport/ar2003/driving_growth/ (accessed 27 Aug. 2004).

13  Figures from Wendy Armstrong.

14  N. Fitt, S. Mitchell and A. Cranney et al., 'Influence of bone densitometry results on the treatment of osteoporosis', *CMAJ*, vol. 164, 2001, pp. 777–81.

15  Lead Discovery article, 'Osteoporosis: R&D innovations to drive growth in osteoporosis market', 4 May 2004, at http://www.leaddiscovery.co.uk/target-discovery/abstracts/TU%20Osteoporosis%20-%20R&D%20innovations%20to%20drive%20growth%20in%20osteoporosis%20market.html (accessed 27 Aug. 2004).

16  C.J. Green, K. Bassett, V. Foerster and A. Kazanjian, 'Bone mineral density testing: does the evidence support its selective use in well women?', British Columbia Office of Health Technology Assessment report no. 97:2T, University of British Columbia, Vancouver, 1997.

17  C. De Laet, B. van Hout, H. Burger, A. Hofman and H. Pols, 'Bone density and risk of hip fracture in men and women: cross sectional analysis', *BMJ*, vol. 315, 1997, pp. 221–5.

18  T. Wilkin, 'Changing perceptions in osteoporosis', *BMJ*, vol. 318, 1999, pp. 862–5. Also see the accompanying commentary critical of this article: R. Eastell, 'Bone density can be used to assess fracture risk', *BMJ*, vol. 318, 1999, p. 865.

19  Special item in the *New England Journal of Medicine* on missed disclosures at http://content.nejm.org/cgi/content/full/342/8/586 (accessed 8 Jan. 2004). This states that in connection with a 1998 article in *New England Journal of Medicine*, Dr Eastell received grants from and served as an adviser to Eli Lilly and Procter & Gamble and served as an adviser to Novartis and SmithKline Beecham Pharmaceuticals.

20  Interview by Alan Cassels with Dr Brian Lentle.

21  C. Green, A. Kazanjian and D. Helmer, 'Informing, advising, or persuading? An assessment of bone mineral density testing information from consumer health websites', *International Journal of Technology Assessment in Health Care*, vol. 20, 2004, pp. 156–66.

22  A. Cheung and J. Feightner, 'Seeking clarification of osteoporosis guidelines', *CMAJ*, vol. 171, 2004, pp. 1022–3 at http://www.cmaj.ca/cgi/content/full/171/9/1022-b?etoc (accessed 8 Jan. 2005).

23  A. Cheung, D. Feig and M. Kapral et al., 'Prevention of osteoporosis and osteoporotic fractures in postmenopausal women: recommendation statement from the Canadian Task Force on Preventive Health Care', *CMAJ*, vol. 170, 2004, pp. 1665–7.

24  K. Bassett, 'On trying to stop the measurement of bone density to sell drugs: tribute to a friend', http://www.chspr.ubc.ca/misc/12thHP conf.pdf (accessed 13 Jan. 2005).

25  Alan Cassels' interview with Kym White.

26  See http://www.osteofound.org/member_societies/society.php?id=61 (accessed 8 Jan. 2005).

27  'On-Board PR' won an award for taking its 'Osteoporosis—Know your Enemy' campaign around rural Poland. Reported in the Golden World Awards online at http://www.ipra.org/services/gala/0154%20GWA %20v1.pdf (accessed 8 Jan. 2005).

28  Wendy Armstrong, personal communication with Alan Cassels.

29  *Health*, June 2003, pp. 88–90, published in Birmingham, Alabama, but available globally.

30  D. Black, S. Cummings and D. Karpf et al., 'Randomised trial of effect of alendronate on risk of fracture in women with existing vertebral fractures', *The Lancet*, vol. 348, 1996, pp. 1535–41.

31  R. Moynihan, L. Bero and D. Ross-Degnan et al., 'Coverage by the news media of the benefits and risks of medications', *New England Journal of Medicine*, vol. 342, 2000, pp. 1645–50.

32  Writing Group for the Women's Health Initiative Investigators, 'Risks and benefits of estrogen plus progestin in healthy menopausal women', *JAMA*, vol. 288, pp. 321–33.

33  http://emc.medicines.org.uk/ (accessed 8 Jan. 2005).

34  'Postmarket adverse drug experiences: top 10 suspect drugs 1996 (US data)', Surveillance and Data Processing Branch Division of Pharmacovigilance and Epidemiology, Office of Epidemiology and

Biostatistics Center for Drug Evaluation and Research Food and Drug Administration, 30 October 1997.

35  Personal communication, Merck spokesperson and Alan Cassels.

36  Some general references in this area include L. Gillespie, W. Gillespie and M. Robertson et al., 'Interventions for preventing falls in elderly people', The Cochrane Database of Systematic Reviews, The Cochrane Library, Issue 4, 2003, Chichester, UK, John Wiley & Sons, Ltd; A. Friedlander, H. Genant and S. Sadowsky et al., 'A two-year program of aerobics and weight training enhances bone mineral density of young women', *Journal of Bone Mineral Research*, vol. 10, 1995, pp. 574–85; G. Dalsky, K. Stocke and A. Ehsani et al. 'Weight-bearing exercise training and lumbar bone mineral content in postmenopausal women', *Annals of Internal Medicine*, vol. 108, 1988, pp. 824–8; M. Nelson, M. Fiatarone and C. Morganti et al. 'Effects of high-intensity strength training on multiple risk factors for osteoporotic fractures', *JAMA*, vol. 272, 1994, pp. 1909–14; E. Gregg, J. Cauley and D. Seeley et al., 'Physical activity and osteoporotic fracture risk in older women', *Annals of Internal Medicine*, vol. 129, 1998, pp. 81–8.

37  Alan Cassels' interview with Ken Bassett.

38  ibid.

39  Alan Cassels' interview with Wendy Armstrong.

40  http://www.bioportfolio.com/news/datamonitor_63.htm (accessed 8 Jan. 2004).

41  GeneWatch UK, 'Bar code babies: good for health', briefing no. 27, August 2004, at http://www.genewatch.org/Publications/Briefs/brief27.PDF (accessed 24 Aug. 2004).

42  Wendy Armstrong, lecture notes, 'Early assessment of health technologies: do the risks justify the benefits?'. She was representing the Consumers' Association of Canada when making this presentation to the Canadian Coordinating Office for Health Technology Assessment (CCOHTA) Symposium, October 2000, Ottawa.

## Chapter 9    Taming the watchdogs

A lot of this chapter is based on R. Moynihan, 'Alosetron: a case study in regulatory capture, or a victory for patients' rights?', *BMJ*, vol. 325, 2002, pp. 592–5.

1   Lotronex's generic name is alosetron.

2   M. Camilleri, A. Northcutt and S. Kong et al., 'Efficacy and safety of alosetron in women with irritable bowel syndrome: a randomised, placebo-controlled trial', *The Lancet*, vol. 355, 2000, pp. 1035–40.

3   The drug company GSK was just forming, through a merger, in 2000.

4   'One in five' figure comes from http://www.prdomain.com/companies/n/novartis/news_releases/200203mar/pr20020304.htm (accessed 8 Jan. 2005). The '45 million' comes from the International Foundation for Functional Gastrointestinal Disorders, press release dated 7 November 2002, from Nancy Norton.

5   Lotronex Information from a 'Dear IBS patient' letter, CDER at the Food and Drug Administration, 23 January 2002. The letter talks of 'fatal' side effects.

6   The risk material comes from K. Uhi, Z. Li, A. Mackey and P. Stolley, 'Memorandum from Food & Drug Administration, Subject: NDA 21-107: Lotronex (alosetron) safety & risk management summary', 16 November 2000 (PID number #DOOO674). Also see R. Moynihan, 'Alosetron . . .', op. cit.

7   See http://www.fda.gov/bbs/topics/NEWS/2002/NEW00814.html (accessed 8 Jan. 2005), which says less than 5 per cent of IBS is considered severe, and R. Moynihan, 'Alosetron . . .', op. cit.

8   Personal communication TGA spokesperson to Ray Moynihan, 2004. For other nations see J. Abraham, D. Bardelay, C. Koop, et al., 'Making regulation responsive to commercial interests: streamlining industry watchdogs', *BMJ*, vol. 325, 2002, pp. 1164–9.

9   Comments from Dr Michelle Brill-Edwards, who worked for Health Canada for 15 years.

10  http://www.cbsnews.com/stories/2004/12/07/health/main659529.shtml (accessed 3 March 2005). The quote continues '. . . against another Vioxx', which is a reference to the current scandal over the risks of the COX-II anti-arthritis drugs.

11  E. Barbehenn, P. Lurie and S. Wolfe, 'Alosetron for Irritable Bowel Syndrome', letter, *The Lancet*, vol. 356, 2000, p. 2009.

12  K. Uhi, Z. Li, A. Mackey and P. Stolley, 'Memorandum from Food & Drug Administration . . .', op. cit. Also see R. Moynihan, 'Alosetron . . .', op. cit.

13  R. Moynihan, 'Alosetron . . .', op. cit.

14  ibid.

15  ibid. Other quotes in this chapter from Stolley and Woodcock come from this *BMJ* article, and R. Moynihan, 'FDA advisers warn of more deaths if drug is relaunched', *BMJ*, vol. 325, 2002, p. 561.

16  R. Moynihan, 'Alosetron . . .', op. cit.

17  In one email an FDA officer reports on a conversation she had with a GSK executive about the forthcoming advisory committee meeting. 'I told him that we would work w/them on developing the agendas and questions.' This comes from D. Willman, 'FDA moving to revive deadly drug; agency director works with manufacturer to bring back Lotronex despite fatalities', *Los Angeles Times*, 30 May 2001.

18  R. Moynihan, 'Alosetron . . .', op. cit.

19  R. Moynihan, 'FDA advisers warn . . .', op. cit.

20  ibid.

21  D. Willman, 'How a new policy led to seven deadly drugs', *Los Angeles Times*, 20 December 2000, and R. Horton, 'Lotronex and the FDA: a fatal erosion of integrity', *The Lancet*, vol. 357, 2001, pp. 1544–5.

22  R. Moynihan, 'Alosetron . . .', op. cit.

23  D. Willman, 'How a new policy . . .', op. cit.

24  R. Horton, 'Lotronex and the FDA . . .', op. cit.

25  A longer extract from an email published in *The Lancet*, vol. 358, 4 August 2001, read:

> I just spoke to Tachi Yamada [a senior Glaxo employee]. He wanted to follow up on our conversation of the other day.
>
> They have talked about the Advisory Committee meeting and have some reservations: 1. that it would be a media circus, and 2. that the advisors may disagree with what we have negotiated and put us back at square 1, and 3 that it would slow things down.
>
> I told him we are used to 1 and that it is ok, we can manage it, and that it might be better to do it this way than just make an announcement. I said I agree that 2 is a real liability, and we have to consider the vulnerability vs the benefits. For 3, I said we could do it in a hurry.
>
> He asked us to consider their concerns and if we still want a meeting, to call him back. He seemed ok with a meeting, just worried.
>
> jw

26  M. Lievre, 'Alosetron for irritable bowel syndrome', *BMJ*, vol. 325, 2002, pp. 555–6.

27  http://www.antidepressantsfacts.com/2004-09-10-members-congress-blast-FDA.htm (accessed 8 Jan. 2005).

28  GSK's rapid response to the *BMJ* piece featuring Stolley at http://bmj.bmjjournals.com/cgi/eletters/325/7364/592#26347 (accessed 15 Jan. 2005).

29  http://www.citizen.org/publications/release.cfm?ID=7104 (accessed 10 Jan. 2005).

30  R. Horton, *The Lancet* (letter), vol. 358, 4 August 2001.

31  All three FDA advisory committee meetings are footnoted in R. Moynihan, 'Alosetron . . .', op. cit.

32  Novartis press release on Zelnorm, 24 July 2002.

33  R. Moynihan, 'Alosetron . . .', op. cit.

34  The range of estimates comes from the transcripts, and the 5 per cent severe comes from an FDA paper at http://www.fda.gov/bbs/topics/NEWS/2002/NEW00814.html (accessed 8 Jan. 2005).

35  J. Shapiro, 'A pill turned bitter: how a quest for a blockbuster drug went fatally wrong', *US News and World Report*, vol. 129, 2000, p. 54.

36  http://www.aboutibs.org/Publications/Zelnormtestimony2000.html (accessed 8 Jan. 2005).

37  R. Moynihan, 'Celebrity selling', *BMJ*, vol. 324, 2002, p. 1342.

38  ibid.

39  R. Moynihan, I. Heath and D. Henry, 'Selling sickness: the pharmaceutical industry and disease mongering', *BMJ*, vol. 324, 2002, pp. 886–91.

40  All of this is taken direct from the leaked 'educational' program document.

41  Zelnorm's generic name is tegaserod maleate, stomach ads are at http://www.zelnorm.com/index.jsp?checked=y—(accessed 3 March, 2005).

42  Novartis advertisement, *New York Times*, 23 December 2002, p. A15.

43  Public Citizen, 'Letter to the FDA urging that it not approve tegaserod . . .', HRG Publication, no. 1561, 22 March 2001. Novartis did not respond to questions about the Public Citizen letter.

44  http://www.fda.gov/cder/warn/2003/11577.pdf (accessed 8 Jan. 2005).

45  ibid.

46  http://uk.biz.yahoo.com/040315/241/eomg5.html (accessed 8 Jan. 2005).

47  Information provided to the latest FDA advisory meeting in 2004 on Lotronex is at http://www.fda.gov/ohrms/dockets/ac/04/briefing/2004-4040BI_20_FDA-Tab-5.pdf. In short it seems the restrictions on prescribing enacted by the FDA in 2002, may be working in terms of minimising safety dangers, but according to the available evidence from the FDA, presented for this meeting in 2004, it is still too early to say, and loopholes in system could exist.

## Chapter 10    Subverting the selling

This chapter draws substantially on material from R. Moynihan, 'The making of a disease: female sexual dysfunction', *BMJ*, vol. 326, 2003, pp. 45–7. Any quotes or facts not referenced directly in this chapter will have relied on this article as the source.

1  Second International Consultation on Erectile and Sexual Dysfunctions, Paris, 28 June–1 July 2003. The first meeting was in Paris in 1999.

2  R. Moynihan, 'The making of a disease . . .', op. cit.

3  The debate motion was 'Is female sexual dysfunction a marketing construct of the pharmaceutical industry?' The debate, sponsored through an unrestricted educational grant from Pfizer to the conference, was held on Monday 30 June 2003 at the Blue Room, Palais des Congres, Paris.

4  www.fsd-alert.org (accessed 16 Jan. 2005).

5  R. Moynihan, 'The making of a disease . . .', op. cit.

6  J. Coe, 'The lifestyle drugs outlook to 2008, unlocking new value in well-being', Datamonitor, *Reuters Business Insight, Healthcare*, PLC, 2003, p. 12.

7  ibid., 'Expanding the patient pool' is at p. 148 of this report.

8  ibid., pp. 42–3.

9  This comes from G. Jackson, 'Female sexual dysfunction: the BMJ fails to educate and fails to debate', *IJCP*, vol. 57, 2003, p. 3. Viagra's generic name is sildenafil.

10  http://www.afud.org/aboutus/sponsors.asp (accessed 12 Jan. 2005).

11  R. Moynihan, 'Urologist recommends daily Viagra to prevent impotence', *BMJ*, vol. 326, 2003, p. 9.

12  ibid.

13  J. Coe, 'The lifestyle drugs outlook to 2008 . . .', op. cit.

14  Ray Moynihan's notes of the meeting.

15  Flyer for this Saturday 7 December 2002 meeting lists Watson Pharmaceuticals as one of the sponsors.

16  Blue leaflet from 'New View' campaign at www.Fsd-alert.org (accessed 12 Jan. 2005).

17  R. Moynihan, 'The making of a disease . . .', op. cit.

18  Ray Moynihan's interviews with Leonore Tiefer.

19  Cathy Scott interview with Leonore Tiefer for *Selling Sickness*, the documentary, Paradigm Pictures, 2004. The interview did not appear in the broadcast version.

20  ibid.

21  Transcripts of interviews for *Selling Sickness*, the documentary, op. cit.

22  ibid.

23  E. Laumann, A. Paik and R. Rosen, 'Sexual dysfunction in the United States, prevalence and predictors', *JAMA*, vol. 281, 1999, pp. 537–44. Soon after, the journal had to publish a small correction to this article, revealing that two of the authors had financial ties to Pfizer. See published erratum in *JAMA*, 1999, vol. 281, p. 1174.

24  'Alista—new hope for sexual healing in women', press release from The Investor Relations Group, 9 August 2002.

25  C. Johnson, 'Female disorder disputed', *The Spokesman-Review*, 13 October 2002, p. 1.

26  R. Moynihan, 'Company launches campaign to "counter" *BMJ* claims', *BMJ*, vol. 326, 2003, p. 120.

27  Email from Pfizer to Ray Moynihan. All of this is in the letters to the *BMJ* following up the article 'The making of a disease: female sexual dysfunction' at 'Letters' *BMJ*, vol. 326, 2003, p. 658.

28  http://www.forbes.com/prnewswire/feeds/prnewswire/2004/06/29/prnewswire200406291030PR_NEWS_B_NET_PH_PHTU018.html (accessed 12 Jan. 2005).

29  R. Moynihan, 'The marketing of a disease: female sexual dysfunction', *BMJ*, vol. 330, 2005, pp. 192–4.

30  R. Moynihan, 'Fix for low sex drive puts reporters in a bad patch', *BMJ*, vol. 329, 2004, pp. 1294.

31  M. Loe, *The Rise of Viagra*, New York University Press, New York, 2004.

32  For more on Viagra and Australia see http://www.cptech.org/ip/health/firm/Pfizer.html (accessed 12 Jan. 2005).

33  For an innovative non-medical approach to improving health involving other sectors of the economy and society see the Neighbourhood Renewal project in Victoria, Australia: H. Klein, 'Health inequality, social exclusion and neighbourhood renewal: can place-based renewal improve the health of disadvantaged communities', *Australian Journal of Primary Care*, vol. 10, 2004, pp. 110–19.

34  Society for the Scientific Study of Sexuality.

## Epilogue

1  http://www.unionstationdc.com/cdinformation/history.asp (accessed 3 March 2005).

2  The PLOS Medicine Editors, 'Prescription for a healthy journal' (editorial), *PLOS Medicine*, vol. 1, 2004, e22.

3  Lots of evidence-based centres around the world produce information—see R. Moynihan, 'Evaluating health services: a reporter covers the science of research synthesis', Milbank Memorial Fund, Special Report, New York, 2004 at http://www.milbank.org/reports/2004 Moynihan/040330Moynihan.html (accessed 3 March 2005).

4  ibid.

5  http:/www.ecri.org (accessed 3 March 2005).

6  http://www.cochrane.org (accessed 3 March 2005).

# Acknowledgements

*From Alan:* Many people have been incredibly supportive in helping me see this project through. Dr Malcolm Maclure, professor at the University of Victoria's School of Health Information Science, has inspired and challenged me for over a decade with the originality of his thinking and his unbridled enthusiasm for bringing science to the rescue of health policy making. I would also like to thank Dr Joel Lexchin, who never fails to share his profound depth of knowledge on a subject he knows so well. His book, *The Real Pushers*, introduced me to the brave new world of pharmaceuticals. Ray Moynihan, whose groundbreaking analysis of pharmaceutical reporting in the US inspired me to replicate his work in Canada, has flattered me greatly by asking me to participate in this book. Many others have provided advice, support and assistance, including Jim Wright, James McCormack, Bob Rangno, Ken Bassett, Barbara Mintzes, Alicia Priest, Jeanne Lenzer, Deb Ireland, and Heather-Ann Laird, one of the best health librarians around. Kerry Patriarche is always there with patient and perennially constructive advice. And to the community of 'Biojesters' in Canada and around the world, thank you for your daily inspiration. You don't need to be mentioned by name, you know who you are.

Lastly, I would like to thank my wife, Lynda, one of the most patient editors any writer could hope for. For Morgan and Chase, whose world is still unfolding, I hope that as adults they will be puzzled by this book and it will read to them as archaic and antediluvian, evidence of a prehistoric world where irrationality ran amuck.

*Alan Cassels, Victoria, British Columbia, March 2005*


*From Ray:* The great privilege of being a journalist is getting access to some of the best talent in the business. I have been utterly spoiled. Very special thanks must go to David Henry, Andy Oxman, Taddy Dickersin, Leonore Tiefer, Steve Woloshin, Lisa Schwartz, and Lisa Bero for their time, ideas, and enthusiasm for awkward truths. For helping spark a deep curiosity about the world of health and medicine, thanks to Rowan Meadows.

There are many people at the medical journals, magazines and newspapers around the world who have supported a lot of the research and investigations that helped form the bedrock of this book. In particular, Richard Smith—the hilarious, indefatigable and inspirational maverick at the center of the medical mainstream—as well as Jane Smith, Kamran Abbasi, Annabel Ferriman, Colleen Ryan, Judith Hoare, Glenn Burge, Dan Fox and Fenella Souter.

For Pat Fiske and Cathy Scott, the dream team with whom I made the television documentary *Selling Sickness*, I have the fondest feelings. Lynn Payer's book *Disease-Mongers* is a seminal work in this field, and despite its limitations, it should be read by all self-respecting students of medicine and healthcare everywhere. Thanks for contributions to all those quoted in *Selling Sickness*, and to those who inspired the analysis, threw in ideas or criticised early drafts, including Anne Delaney, Andrew Holtz, Tom Moore, David Healy, Jo Ellins, Liz Canner, Amy Allina, Curt Furberg, Bruce Psaty, Peter Mansfield, Sid Wolfe and Peter Lurie. For Bruce Donald, a key player in making this book happen, I have thanks and admiration. Thanks too to Chris Hilton and Meredith Curnow for early enthusiasm. The team at Allen & Unwin in Sydney have been superb—many warm thanks to Rebecca Kaiser for her strong and on-going encouragement and feedback, and her efficient and fun approach, and thanks to Marie Baird, Stephanie Whitelock and others for selling and promoting this book around the world.

I can't help but feel warmly also towards the un-named sources within the world of drug marketing, who from the mid-nineties, sometimes inadvertently, introduced me to the dark world of disease-mongering, a process which I and many others have come to see as a threat to human health. Perhaps someday, some of those people will walk away from their well-paid jobs and consultancies and bring a few boxes of documents with them. The Tobacco papers have changed the way we think abut that industry. The Pharma papers will sooner or later have the same impact on this industry.

I owe a kind thank you to co-author Alan Cassels for the drafts of three chapters 2, 5 and 8, for his many ideas and feedback on the rest of the manuscript, and for his energy and humour. For any inadvertent errors or omissions, I accept full responsibility, and hope you alert the publisher in your country in order to improve subsequent editions. To my family and friends who tolerated the long rounds of fact-checking, cheers.

Most of all I want to thank Marian Wilkinson for her enthusiastic encouragement through the life of this project, for her careful criticism of early drafts, for her fearlessness, and for her energetic help cracking through some key conundrums on that Du Pont rooftop. Without her extraordinary love, support, humour and searing intelligence, this book would never have been planned, written or delivered.

*Ray Moynihan, Sydney/Washington DC, March, 2005*

# Index